Praise for *After Morgentaler*:

"*After Morgentaler* will quickly occupy benchmark status in the comparative health care and reproductive-rights policy literatures. Through case studies, Rachael Johnstone illuminates the strategies of pro- and anti-choice groups, and health-professional organizations, by situating them in Canadian institutional, legal, and political history. The result is a clear argument for why shifting to a positive-rights understanding of the Charter is needed to safeguard women's constitutionally protected access to reproductive health care."
—Melissa Haussman, professor, Department of Political Science, Carleton University

"In addition to making a strong case for reconceptualising abortion as a right of citizenship for women, this book offers a useful study of comparative provincial politics and health care more generally."
—Francesca Scala, associate professor of political science, Concordia University

AFTER MORGENTALER

AFTER MORGENTALER
The Politics of Abortion in Canada

Rachael Johnstone

UBCPress · Vancouver · Toronto

© UBC Press 2017

All rights reserved. No part of this publication may be reproduced, stored in a retrieval system, or transmitted, in any form or by any means, without prior written permission of the publisher, or, in Canada, in the case of photocopying or other reprographic copying, a licence from Access Copyright, www.accesscopyright.ca.

26 25 24 23 22 21 20 19 18 17   5 4 3 2 1

Printed in Canada on FSC-certified ancient-forest-free paper (100% post-consumer recycled) that is processed chlorine- and acid-free.

Library and Archives Canada Cataloguing in Publication

Johnstone, Rachael, author

After Morgentaler : the politics of abortion in Canada / Rachael Johnstone.
Includes bibliographical references and index.
Issued in print and electronic formats.
ISBN 978-0-7748-3438-4 (hardcover). – ISBN 978-0-7748-3439-1 (softcover)
ISBN 978-0-7748-3440-7 (PDF). – ISBN 978-0-7748-3441-4 (EPUB)
ISBN 978-1-7748-3442-1 (MOBI)

1. Abortion – Political aspects – Canada – Case studies.   I. Title.

HQ767.5.C2J65 2017   362.1988'80971   C2017-903227-5
                                                   C2017-903228-3

Canada

UBC Press gratefully acknowledges the financial support for our publishing program of the Government of Canada (through the Canada Book Fund), the Canada Council for the Arts, and the British Columbia Arts Council.

Printed and bound in Canada by Friesens
Set in Futura and Warnock by Apex CoVantage, LLC
Copy editor: Judy Phillips
Proofreader: Jesse Marchand
Cover designer: Setareh Ashrafologhalai

UBC Press
The University of British Columbia
2029 West Mall
Vancouver, BC V6T 1Z2
www.ubcpress.ca

For my parents,
Lowell and Raylene Johnstone

Contents

Acknowledgments / xi

Introduction / 3

1 The Anti-abortion, Pro-choice, and Reproductive Justice Movements / 25

2 Federal Politics and the Supreme Court / 51

3 Abortion in the Provinces / 81

4 Abortion as Health Care / 107

5 Social Movement Activism in the Provinces / 141

6 Never Going Back / 156

Appendices / 167

Notes / 179

References / 197

Index / 213

Acknowledgments

This book is the culmination of years of work, and I am so grateful to have had the guidance of Dr. Abigail Bakan since its inception. I always walk away from our discussions feeling rejuvenated, and I continue to be thankful of her constant encouragement.

Melissa Haussman also has my gratitude. Her enthusiasm and backing have been instrumental in the realization of this and related projects. I am likewise indebted to Samantha King, Margaret Little, and Grant Amyot for their invaluable feedback. Thanks also to my research fellow, Emerson Murray, who was a huge help to me in the final stages of this process. I am anticipating big things from you, Emerson.

I was fortunate enough to have the support of two fantastic editors as I completed this manuscript. Emily Andrew at UBC Press expertly guided me through the initial stages of this process, and Randy Schmidt helped me across the finish line. They helped make a daunting process clear and straightforward. This work would also not have been possible without the contributions of anonymous reviewers who helped me hone my work and get me to this final stage. I deeply appreciate all the time and effort that went into the comments that helped make this book what it is. A section of this book appears as a previously published article in *Atlantis: Critical Studies in Gender, Culture & Social Justice*, and I am grateful for the use of the material and for the reviews of the article.

One of the most difficult tasks I encountered in my research was finding individuals willing to talk about a subject that is so widely stigmatized.

This was especially true of public figures and physicians, many of whom feared harassment and violence if their identities were made public. Despite these substantive barriers, I was fortunate enough to interview twenty-eight people, including physicians and nurses, politicians and lawyers, and social activists, without whose insights and contributions I would have been unable to truly grasp the nature of access in the provinces and territories and in Canada as a whole. I am profoundly grateful to these interviewees not only for their time but also for the work they do to improve access for women on a daily basis. It is my hope that this book shines a light on their work and on all of the thankless work that goes on behind the scenes to protect access to abortion care in Canada and improve access in the future.

I have found myself living in various cities as this book came together, and it is hard to imagine having gotten to this point without spectacular friends and colleagues. Thank you Adam Slavny, Alice Leonard, Andrea Collins, Anna Drake, Beesan Sarrouh, Charan Rainford, Cheryl Hutton, Chris Samuel, Clare Bergum, David Axelsen, Erin Clow, Erin Tolley, Hwa Kim, Iain Reeve, Isabella Jope, Janice Niemann, Jeff English, Jessie Lindley, Joanne Wright, Lucia Salazar, Meg Chalmers, Megan Gaucher, Melissa Burke, Mitch Piper, Niamh O'Shea, Paul Warden, Sara Pavan, Shannon Smith, Tim Abray, Tom Parr, and Victoria Tait, for keeping me entertained and largely out of trouble. A few friends and colleagues were unable to escape the privilege of offering me feedback on my chapters, and so I owe particular thanks Erika Bennett, Margaret Bennett, and Colleen MacQuarrie for comments on early drafts. Finally, I would like to single out three people to whom I owe particularly big debts of gratitude. My father, Lowell Johnstone, to whom I will be eternally grateful for so many things, not least of which is offering me feedback on this manuscript as it developed, as well as giving me feedback on pretty much all the work I have produced since elementary school, often at the eleventh hour. My friend and regular co-author Emmett Macfarlane – thank you for the laughs, overseas chats, and your insightful comments on drafts of this book. And Aaron Ettinger – thank you for always giving me the best beta, in life and on the wall. I can always count on you to talk me over the crux.

I must also thank my parents, Lowell and Raylene, and my brother, Robert, for knowing better than to ask how the writing was going. And, in my darkest hours, reminding me that there was always law school. And I cannot forget the Chevriers, my second family, for their lifelong love and encouragement, especially Sara Dunton, for her comradery during this process.

Finally, thank you to my partner, Christopher Bennett. I love you more than I can say.

AFTER MORGENTALER

Introduction

Canada has no law governing abortion. This is the legacy of the Supreme Court ruling in *R. v. Morgentaler* (1988), the landmark case that decriminalized abortion in Canada by striking down the section of the Criminal Code that restricted legal abortions to those approved by a panel of physicians. Although the decision is often touted as affirming a woman's right to abortion, *Morgentaler* did not establish a legal right entitling women to access abortion services; rather, it struck down the existing law on the grounds that it violated women's rights to life, liberty, and security of the person guaranteed by the 1982 Charter of Rights and Freedoms, while also emphasizing the role of Parliament in legislating abortion. However, despite attempts by the federal government in the wake of the decision, no new abortion law has since been successfully passed in Canada. In the absence of a new law, abortion is now recognized as a matter of health care, an area that falls predominantly under provincial and territorial jurisdiction. Ironically, the various responses by provincial governments that were expected to facilitate access to the procedure have resulted in disparities in access that mimic those deemed unconstitutional by the Court almost thirty years ago.

Although the actions of many provincial governments suggest a reliance on nonmedical considerations in the regulation of access to abortion services, a medical rhetoric has nonetheless been widely embraced in the regulation of the procedure. This reliance on a medical discourse in virtually all official dealings with abortion policy has had mixed effects, creating inroads for improved access in some cases while also allowing for the creation of barriers in others. Politicians, for instance, have largely divested themselves of the responsibility to facilitate access by accepting a strictly medical discourse, crowning physicians as the only appropriate actors in the abortion debate, which has had the dual effect of stifling rights discourse on abortion while simultaneously silencing women's voices (Thomson-Philbrook 2014, 237). However, embracing abortion as a matter of health care has also situated the procedure within a clear regulatory framework, offering new mechanisms to challenge restrictive policies.

The path that led from abortion as a criminal matter to abortion as a routine medical procedure is complex and has been manipulated by numerous actors, with many competing motivations. This book maps the evolution of abortion access in the provinces following the *Morgentaler* decision. In so doing, it also situates larger claims about the continued value of rights claiming as a means to improve access. The involvement of both state and nonstate actors in the provision of abortion complicates its regulation. What is apparent in all cases is that the complete medicalization of abortion obscures the profound sociopolitical impacts of the procedure for women. Even as access to abortion improves in many provinces, these changes are themselves unstable, rooted as they are in a logic that prioritizes health outcomes over women's rights.

By plotting out numerous disparate policy actions undertaken across Canada in the policy void after *Morgentaler*, this book considers the continued value of rights as a tool for the substantive recognition of women's equality. Even amid a determined focus on medical rationales to regulate abortion in most official contexts, rights claims continue to inform the nature of the abortion debate in Canada – exactly whose rights, and who is responsible for recognizing them, however, remains unresolved. These rights disputes have contributed to the barriers women must negotiate in order to receive access to a safe and legal service. Although rights, both as legal mechanisms and as discursive strategy, will continue to play a pivotal role in the realization of women's reproductive equality by providing much-needed legitimacy, compelling government action, and shifting public perception, legal rights should not be seen as resolving complex social issues. Substantive solutions require a more holistic understanding of abortion and its impact on women's citizenship.

Abortion Access in Canada

Today, abortion services in Canada vary significantly from province to province, though many recent changes have helped bridge some of the starkest divides. A complex network of regulations governs abortion access both within and between provinces, and the particulars of these relationships are not always easily discernable. Information about what facilities are available in a given province, whether residents of one province can access services outside their home province, and what services are covered under their provincial health insurance is not always readily available. The reality that the regulations in some provinces are still in flux further complicates the negotiation of access.

A sizable literature has followed these changing policies and approaches to abortion politics. In the decades after the decriminalization of abortion in Canada, several influential books explored the nature of abortion politics in Canada (e.g., Brodie, Gavigan, and Jenson 1992; Haussman 2005; Tatalovich 1997), both leading up to and in the aftermath of *R. v. Morgentaler* (1988). Much of this research has been comparative, looking at the role of federalism and its influence on the nature of services (Haussman 2005; Palley 2006; Vickers 2010; White 2014), as well as the role of the courts and the federal government (Brodie, Gavigan, and Jenson 1992; Kaposy and Downie 2008; Morton 1992). More recent work has focused on the changes in social movement activity in Canada (Saurette and Gordon 2013, 2016), as well as the continued inequalities that result from extra-legal barriers to abortion access, which include travel costs (Sethna and Doull 2013), stigma and violence (Cook and Dickens 2014), and barriers erected by physicians (Kaposy 2010; Thomson-Philbrook 2014) and by governments (Brown, Ehrlich, and MacQuarrie, forthcoming). Each of these pieces offers insight into the evolution of Canadian abortion politics. Cumulatively, these works point to the impact of both state and nonstate actors in shaping levels of abortion access in Canada.

The role of state actors is perhaps the most apparent. Government action and legal decisions on abortion have discernable impacts on levels of access, though the limitations of each are not always apparent. The realities of federalism in Canada have produced jurisdictional disputes over certain aspects of health care. Health care is primarily a provincial responsibility, but is partially funded by the federal government, which may choose to pursue action against provinces that fail to adhere to the standards set out in the Canada Health Act. In addition, subject to the Charter, the federal government is able to create new restrictions on abortion access at any time by recriminalizing the procedure, in whole or in part.

To add to this complexity, court rulings at both the provincial and federal level have further clarified the rights and responsibilities of governments relating to abortion care. A close reading of these decisions, however, reveals a reluctance by the courts to recognize positive rights claims that would mandate state action. Instead, the courts have restricted their scope to the realm of negative rights claims, which protect individuals from state interference. The creation of positive rights has stayed within the purview of governments, which are often reluctant to raise the "extremely divisive" issue (Do 2014). Consequently, achieving progress on abortion rights through either legal or political venues remains difficult.

State actors, however, are not alone in their ability to influence access. Indeed, the way they treat abortion is, in many ways, the result of concerted efforts by social movement activists. Because the taboo nature of abortion has made governments reluctant to raise the matter, the activities of social movements are important catalysts to bring these debates into public forums. Indeed, activists have done more than merely bring the debate to the fore; they have influenced the very words and concepts we use to comprehend abortion.

The approaches of activist groups have changed over time, reflecting the opportunities presented by the systems in which these groups operate, as well as evolving notions about how abortion ought to be understood. Today, abortion rights activists in Canada commonly frame abortion as an equality right, entrenched in the Charter of Rights and Freedoms (ARCC 2015a; NAF 2013). The difficulties in realizing such a right, however, are not only grounded in potential legal and political resistance but in the realities of service provision.

The classification of abortion as a matter of health care was followed by several complexities in its implementation. Disputes between the federal and provincial governments about funding and jurisdiction over health care have compromised the provision of abortion services in particular. Since abortion is so often treated as controversial, many provincial governments have attempted to use their jurisdiction over the procedure to completely block access without any medical justification. Resistance to performing abortions has also been a problem at the level of providers, many of whom fear harassment or violence if they provide services. Although many physicians have worked tirelessly as advocates for abortion access and helped facilitate services for women in spite of these concerns, other physicians have claimed the right to refuse to perform procedures to which they conscientiously object. Despite their training being subsidized by public funds, the professional regulation of physicians is undertaken by largely nongovernmental bodies, as is their medical school training, which has a poor track record of including abortion in its curricula. As such, even when access to abortion is sanctioned and funded by government, access on the ground has the potential to differ dramatically from provider to provider.

Understanding access, then, is not as straightforward as counting the number of available facilities or recognizing restrictive provincial policies. Accounts from women seeking access to abortion suggest that the way individuals experience these attempts varies both within and between provinces, depending as much on the gatekeepers they encounter as on the regulations governing the procedure (Arts4Choice 2015; Shaw 2006; Sovereign Uterus 2015). The procedure itself also takes various forms, dependent on the services available and the length of gestation. Generally, references to abortion in Canada refer to a range of surgical procedures, but with the recent approval of a new abortion pill by Health Canada, medical abortions (drug induced, nonsurgical) are poised to become a more common alternative. Consequently, mapping access is no easy task. Recognition of the interplay between the political, legal, social, and medical dimensions of abortion today, especially the ways in which the different groups view their rights, is therefore crucial.

Methodology

The ways in which individual actors, social movements, and institutions have helped shape abortion access in Canada is not generalizable across the country. Such significant differences in access are in no small part owing to the dynamics of Canadian federalism (Vickers 2010; White 2014). Although the Supreme Court legalized abortion in 1988, and subsequent federal governments abstained from introducing new restrictions on the procedure, the implementation of abortion services occurs at the provincial level. Linda White (2014) explains that

> because a federal system of government provides for two loci of authority and thus two levels of government acting on behalf of the people, and neither level of government is able to authoritatively coerce the other, legislative compliance with the wishes of the people as interpreted by the Supreme Court becomes difficult to ensure, even if one level of government is agreeable. (158)

When cooperation cannot be achieved in this system, as has often been the case with the regulation of abortion services, serious problems arise. When assessing these issues, there is a need, as White (2014, 158) suggests, to examine the more subtle ways in which the state avoids implementation that moves beyond analysis of formal legal or regulative responses postjudicial review to uncover a broader range of regulative practices by state and nonstate agents. Studies of implementation also need to pay attention to the complexities and challenges posed by divided jurisdiction in ensuring implementation of equality principles in law and policy.

The goal of this book is to provide precisely such an analysis. To do so, I outline provincial regulations and relevant court cases, and investigate and analyze the motivations behind, as well as significance and impacts of, legislative and judicial actions that influence access to abortion.

One important feature of my analysis is that I integrate a strong emphasis on the role of nonstate actors in the creation of access. Social movement activists help shape access by doing more than advocating for legal and policy changes. Social movements have actively structured the language we use to think about abortion in Canada, language that appears in legislatures and courtrooms, as well as in homes across the country, language that shapes not only how the public understand abortion but also how women seeking abortion services understand their decisions.

In addition to social movement activists, the medical profession plays a fundamental role in shaping Canadians' access to abortions. Although health care falls under provincial jurisdiction, medical professionals – whose practices are regulated independent of the government – are responsible for the administration of services. What training, if any, physicians receive in medical school and residency is at the discretion of independent bodies and often fails to include abortion. Even if physicians are taught the necessary material, the specifics of their practices are left largely to them, with provincial colleges stepping in only to discipline in specific cases. Although health care is often talked about as a right, the way it is practised, and who is qualified to provide it, continues to fall largely outside government control, though it does not escape state influence.

To fully understand these intersections, it was necessary to employ multiple methods. This was particularly important given the still taboo nature of abortion in much of Canada, coupled with an aging literature addressing its continued political and social salience in the country. Although secondary-source research provided a crucial starting point, relatively little academic research on abortion politics has been conducted since the 1990s. As such, the use of a range of primary sources, including *Hansard* transcripts, acts and regulations, court cases, and media coverage, allowed me to explore the means by which different groups and institutions have shaped access via traditional state-based mechanisms and by influencing public perception of abortion and abortion services.

Public perception, however, is difficult to assess when it comes to uncomfortable subjects. When the profound role of abortion in women's equality is considered, the stakes of its treatment become all the more contentious, and the sentiments expressed by advocates are likely to be carefully considered and strategic, and may not reflect their actual views. Moreover, the kinds of questions asked in polls can easily skew perception. For instance, asking whether abortion should be legal under all, certain, or no circumstances can yield dramatically different results than asking people whether they would like to see abortion regulated by the state, or asking if they identify as pro-choice or anti-abortion. Despite their potential deficiencies, these types of questions are often used to make larger claims about social attitudes. Although inferences can be drawn using polling data and primary sources, these data and sources are not definitive. Still, I felt it was important to try to capture some of the nuances of how different actors perceive abortion politics in Canada. Whether or not, for example, physicians providing abortion care tend to see abortion as safe and accessible likely reflects the manner in which it has been regulated in medicine more broadly. In this way, the views offered by relevant actors offer important hints about the evolution of abortion politics, especially the implications of existing regulations in their fields.

To offer additional context, I conducted twenty-eight in-depth interviews with a diverse sample of voices in the abortion debate, at both the federal and provincial levels, including politicians, lawyers, social activists, and physicians. I began by identifying key figures through secondary sources and contacting them via email. This process was not always easy, as many actors involved in the abortion debate are accustomed to stigma and wary of being identified to the public or having their views misrepresented. As such, once I was fortunate to secure a few interviews, I employed a snowball sampling technique, concluding each interview by asking for the names of other people the interviewee felt could offer insight relevant to my research. In so doing, I amassed a longer list of potential interviewees. Many interviewees were kind enough to allow me to reference them when making contact with people they had suggested I speak with, which seemed to encourage those individuals to accept my interview requests. This was particularly important when it came to interviewing abortion providers, as they are often faced with threats of violence and are careful to safeguard their identities.

The perspective of actors who have been deeply entrenched in these issues helps to provide a clear picture of key events as they took place on the ground and to identify areas of immediate and future concern. In many instances, these accounts provide insight into the motivations for, and consequences of, activity in the provinces that may lack formal documentation. Using interviews to shed light on government policy, legal decisions, demonstrations, and the activities of the medical profession, both historically and today, I am able to provide a more nuanced and complete picture of abortion access in Canada than through using secondary source material alone. In so doing, the motivations and tactics of the relevant actors become clear, affording me the opportunity to make what I hope are compelling claims about the continued value of framing abortion as an equality right. Importantly, as a result of the continued stigma surrounding abortion in many parts of Canada, many of my interviewees elected to remain anonymous.

I completed two rounds of interviews, one in 2011 and another in 2015. This time frame is especially pertinent given the many changes to abortion policy in Canada that have taken shape since 2015 – Mifegymiso, a new medical abortion pill, was approved by Health Canada; New Brunswick liberalized its abortion law; Prince Edward Island promised to provide access to services on the Island; and the newly elected federal Liberal government under Prime Minister Justin Trudeau has been vocal about its pro-choice platform. Some of these shifts were noted in my final round of interviews, whereas others had not yet taken place. I have nonetheless endeavoured to engage with each of these changes in turn, ending my study with the announcement by the government of Prince Edward Island that abortion services are now available in the province. It is my hope that the framework I have provided will help inform the discussion surrounding abortion politics in Canada as the details and implications of these shifts continue to unfold.

Only when the unique challenges of Canadian federalism are considered alongside the powers of both state and nonstate actors in shaping services can a relatively complete understanding of abortion access in Canada be achieved. The variation in access between the provinces, however, renders generalizations about abortion access in Canada difficult. Thus, in order to provide the detail necessary to capture what access really looks like in Canada today, I employ case studies of three provinces: New Brunswick, Ontario, and Quebec. These cases provide depth to assessments of the roles different institutions and actors have played in shaping access in Canada as a whole, while highlighting the strategies employed and the values embraced by the institutions and individuals who created and maintain them. These provinces were selected not only because they each possess notably different levels of access to abortion services but also because the pathways they took to influence access were distinct, making them useful to showcase the ways in which relevant actors have used institutional and social opportunity structures. I use these case studies to show what access can and does look like in Canada as a result of its current classification as a health care issue. In so doing, I am able to make a case for the need to classify abortion access as a right.

Ultimately, these provincial case studies provide the empirical foundation for this book's exploration of the actors and institutions that influence abortion access in Canada. Cumulatively, these cases reveal the fragility of abortion access and demonstrate the inherent problems in restricting abortion access to the realm of health care. Although I was not able to conduct interviews in every province, my findings uncover the need to recognize abortion as an equality right for all Canadian women.

A Right to Abortion

In many respects, the *Morgentaler* decision was a victory for rights claiming. Morgentaler's earlier attempts to dispute the constitutionality of restrictions on abortion access failed on jurisdictional grounds; it was the enactment of the Charter of Rights and Freedoms that finally afforded him the necessary tools to have the law struck down. Indeed, since *R. v. Morgentaler* (1988), extensive litigation has demonstrated the value of Charter guarantees in shaping abortion access across the country. Morgentaler's Supreme Court victory clearly established the power of Charter rights as a tool to challenge government policy, and social activists took note. Both pro-choice and anti-abortion social movements in Canada have embraced a rights-based rhetoric to advance their respective agendas through the courts, the government, and public opinion. This approach demonstrates the power of individual rights protections to not only shape legislation but also to influence the manner by which individuals understand their rights. Supreme Court Chief Justice Beverley McLachlin (2001) explains that the Charter has done more than provide new means to influence policy; it has fundamentally "changed the way Canadians think and act about their rights":

> The Charter has made Canadians realize on a profoundly personal level what perhaps they had formally recognized only in a detached, intellectual sense: that their rights belong to them, that these rights are a precious part of their personal inheritance, and that they must exercise them and vigilantly protect them if they are to keep them healthy and strong. (67)

Since the enactment of the Charter, Canadians have put greater store in the courts and, more broadly, in the significance of rights recognition, a confidence echoed in social movement activism (ARCC 2015a; McLachlin 2001; NAF 2013).

Taking advantage of rights claiming, pro-choice and anti-abortion social movements have overwhelmingly shaped perceptions of abortion since 1988. More recently, reproductive justice activists have also played a part in shaping views on abortion politics. Because of its relative infancy in Canada, reproductive justice, an approach that seeks to link reproductive rights with more expansive social justice activism, is by no means yet a full-fledged social movement, though pro-choice activists have gradually begun to reflect its principles. The diverse views endorsed by these (often conflicting) social movements have worked their way into the reasoning that politicians, physicians, and judges have adopted in their attempts to regulate the procedure, in turn shaping the nature of debates and interpreting outcomes for public consumption. Importantly, in the Canadian context, all these groups, whether working in support of abortion or in opposition to it, have embraced a language of rights. This is understandable, as the concept of rights holds significant legitimacy in Canada. By providing a powerful, well-respected platform for the often controversial topic of abortion, individual rights recognitions have contributed to substantial improvements in access across the country, as well as creating support for anti-abortion advocacy. However, a deeper consideration of the history of abortion access in Canada provides a cautionary tale about the risks inherent in an overreliance on rights claims.

The specific rights violations that were considered by the Court in *Morgentaler* did not necessarily cohere with the understanding of abortion advanced by feminist groups at the time. Although it was a momentous decision that paved the way for further reforms, including many improvements to access in the provinces that have ensued as a result of provincial rights litigation, supported by Charter guarantees, these changes typically came about without undermining the official medical discourse on abortion or offering any positive rights guarantees to safeguard women's equality. As tools for litigation, this strategic use of rights has contributed to distrust of the concept of rights for larger emancipatory projects. Although framing issues in term of rights is sometimes useful to achieve a means to an end, there is concern that doing so risks distorting the core messages of movements.

Despite the success of Charter rights recognitions in decriminalizing abortion in Canada, there are compelling criticisms of the rights paradigm on these grounds:

> On the one hand, scholars hail the empowering effects that rights review has on citizens, particularly for historically disadvantaged groups and individuals. On the other hand, some view as problematic the capacity for rights claiming to harm political discourse by rendering it absolutist, divisive, and uncompromising. (Macfarlane 2013, 3)

Understood in this way, rights have impacted not only the nature of social movement organization but the very character of democratic debate. As later chapters demonstrate, this is a serious concern. Despite the important role courts play in interpreting the Charter, rights claims are not comprehensively defined by the courts but are inherently political.

Governments, both provincial and federal, are the only bodies that possess the democratic legitimacy to recognize rights claims, in addition to having the means and ability to create the infrastructure to protect and promote these rights. Although courts do have an important role to play in hearing rights claims, they have generally been wary of infringing on the role of government in their interpretations of such claims, particularly through the recognition of positive rights, which would require state action (Macfarlane 2014). This wariness is appropriate but has unfortunate implications when governments distance themselves from debating rights claiming, preferring to leave potentially divisive decisions to the courts. If courts are normalized as the appropriate venue for rights claiming but generally do not wish to pronounce on positive rights claims, and governments avoid these claims altogether, then no body is seemingly available to hear these claims. This is one reason some groups are skeptical of the value of rights in securing access. Even those that do support these claims recognize that the nature of the rulings may not be ideal. Others may support litigation because they feel that, even when imperfect, the outcomes for their cause in court have been favourable. Of course, the belief that these decisions were, in fact, made in clear support of their cause often neglects the context in which these decisions were made.

When considering the value of rights in shaping abortion access, it is important to acknowledge that the mere recognition of individual rights in the Charter did not guarantee the outcome of the *Morgentaler* decision or related cases, such as *Tremblay v. Daigle* (1989), which ruled that a fetus has no legal status in Canada. The lack of federal law on abortion was the product of several factors, including social mobilization and fortuitous timing. In essence, although rights recognitions in provincial and federal courts have generally produced favourable outcomes for women's reproductive rights to date, they have not done so without substantial social backing. Indeed, although rights played a pivotal role in striking down the existing law, current levels of access were shaped in a policy vacuum, with few provinces taking a clear stance on the issue. To be effective, rights also require public understanding and support. Advancing claims to abortion rights, then, not only means demonstrating that women's equality necessitates access to abortion services in court and in the public eye but also requires that the public hold governments accountable for validating these claims.

Keeping in mind the perceived limitations of this framework, I contend that rights still offer an important tool to advance emancipatory claims. That said, it is problematic to interpret legal rights as resolving complex social issues. Substantive solutions require a more holistic understanding of abortion and its impact on women's lives, of which rights recognitions are one component. The enforcement of constitutional rights guarantees are especially powerful for issues that have a history of being treated as controversial. Even if members of the public are unable to agree on their own views of such a subject, the acceptance of individual rights as a primary social good in Canada makes claims articulated in this language persuasive. In time, formal recognition of rights has also been shown to shift public opinion (Matthews 2005).

Despite laudable guarantees of women's equality in the Charter, it seems that the political reality lags behind. Rights protections exist in the constitution, but whether specific issues are recognized as implicating rights, and what actions, if any, this recognition requires, involves legal or, preferably, political action. No Supreme Court case has yet considered whether abortion constitutes an equality right,[1] and neither has any federal government yet recognized abortion as an equality right through formal statutes.

Even though abortion rights have yet to be recognized by either the Court or in the House of Commons, the rights protections afforded to citizens through the Charter suggest a path forward toward such recognition. The ultimate goal is a society in which women are not only "perceived as full members of society, but believe themselves to be" (Erdman 2007, 1155). After all, the abortion debate raises fundamental questions about women's equality, bringing them into public and political discourse in the hopes that links between reproductive autonomy – that is, the ability of women to make decisions about their reproductive lives independent of external forces – and the belief that women should be equal members of society, a belief that already informs the Canadian constitution, will be recognized.[2]

Citizenship

It is no coincidence that the first countrywide action undertaken by the Canadian women's movement concerned access to abortion (Rebick 2005, 35).[3] The fight for access to safe, legal abortion services implicates all women, regardless of their reproductive choices. In their seminal work, written shortly after the *Morgentaler* verdict came down, Janine Brodie, Shelley Gavigan, and Jane Jenson (1992, 14) caution against reductive treatments of abortion, saying, "Now more than ever the politics of abortion contest the social meanings attached to gender and representation as well as women's access to social equality and self-determination. We ignore this crucial dimension of the abortion debate only at great costs to ourselves and our daughters."

Indeed, the treatment of abortion as a hot-button or stigmatized topic serves an important purpose for the anti-abortion movement. By artificially separating abortion from more expansive discussions of women's equality and their roles as citizens, it seems possible to reduce the abortion debate to one concerning morality, or the nature of services – a matter of health, best dealt with between a woman and her doctor. But abortion is precisely such a controversial and deeply held issue because it implicates the nature of women's membership in their communities. Although the *Morgentaler* decision did not engage with substantive issues of women's equality, Justice Bertha Wilson's judgment demonstrates an awareness of the sociopolitical context in which women exercise the choice to have an abortion:

> This decision is one that will have profound psychological, economic, and social consequences for the pregnant woman. The circumstances giving rise to it can be complex and varied, and there may be, and usually are, powerful considerations militating in opposite directions. It is a decision that deeply reflects the way the woman thinks about herself and her relationship to others and to society at large. It is not just a medical decision; it is a profound social and ethical one as well. Her response to it will be the response of the whole person. (171)

This book starts with the premise that abortion is not a stand-alone topic but a procedure inextricably tied to the status of women citizens. Whether a state provides access to abortion services, and how those services are framed, is a direct reflection of the status of women in that state. Although abortion is only one issue on a spectrum of reproductive rights, and substantive equality for women extends far beyond access to abortion care, long-held stigma against the procedure means that recognition of its significance to women's equality would be an essential symbolic victory.[4] But what, exactly, does it mean to think of abortion as a right of citizenship?

The force of citizenship comes predominantly from its inclusive narrative. As citizens, all members of a given society are bestowed a status that gives them equal membership, and all the rights and obligations that status entails (Marshall 2006, 34). Of course, not all models of citizenship are created equal. Since different societies will work to develop their own ideals, there are no comprehensive guidelines outlining what the rights and obligations of citizens in a given state ought to comprise (ibid., 18). Nonetheless, the universality of this status, at least within a given society's borders, remains a defining characteristic of citizenship theory. Ruth Lister (2010, 195) captures this idea when she asserts that citizenship "represents an abstract, universal concept," the reality of which varies depending on the context in which it is articulated. Even today, in relation to a rich literature on citizenship theory and a substantial body of applied examples, the weight of the concept continues to be tied to its promise of universality.

It is, however, on these very grounds that citizenship has become a contested concept. There is continued disagreement over the nature and extent of the rights and obligations in theory and its limitations in practice, in which the rights and obligations of citizenship have never been accessible to everyone. Nonetheless, a growing body of feminist scholarship suggests that, properly conceived, citizenship can provide a helpful tool to promote women's equality rights (Abraham and Ngan-ling Chow 2011, 9).[5] Indeed, the contention that citizenship is a concept that can be reimagined in profound ways led John Hoffman (2004, 138) to characterize it as a "momentum concept," that is, a concept that we can continuously rework in order to realize "more and more of [its] egalitarian and anti-hierarchical potential."

In order to reimagine citizenship in this way, it is useful to first engage with some of the most serious shortcomings of the concept. Feminist critiques of citizenship are linked by the shared perception that the concept is limited, often relying on objectionable membership criteria and proscribing what aspects of life fall under the umbrella of citizenship in troubling ways. Looking at each of these critiques in more depth helps identify which elements of citizenship must be rethought in order for the concept to remain applicable.

The first line of argument concerns who is recognized as a citizen, and what this membership includes. Over time, "inclusive citizenship" has come to signify recognition as much as it does access to formal rights (Lister 2007, 51). Implicit in the realization of full citizenship is therefore the ability to pursue these rights without fear of discrimination or retaliation (Nossiff 2007, 62).[6] As both a legal and social status, the concept of citizenship fundamentally implicates a delicate balance between inclusion and exclusion (Abraham and Ngan-ling Chow 2011; Ackelsberg 2005; Lister 2007, 2010). Historically, women have been overwhelmingly excluded from this category. Throughout most of human history and in all regions of the globe, women of all classes, races, ethnicities, and religions were, and in some instances continue to be, denied state citizenship of even the lowest rank. So exclusively male has this status been for nearly all of human history that it is a singular development of women's movements in the twentieth century to have ended this exclusion in many places (Friedman 2005, 4). Moreover, even when women are recognized as citizens, they are not necessarily recognized as having the same standing as men.

In its real-world iterations, citizenship has been criticized for its adherence to a masculine norm (ibid., 93) that creates barriers that make it difficult for women to exercise the rights associated with this status (ibid., 4).[7] Because only men have traditionally had access to the category of citizenship, this apparently universal category has often failed to address concerns faced only by women. After all, if personal agency and autonomy are necessary for full citizenship, as Rosemary Nossiff (2007, 62) contends, "few issues affect women's rights to self-determination more directly than access to abortion," yet reproductive rights are often excluded from citizenship frameworks. Looking to the impetus for restrictive abortion laws, she further contends that the assumptions about women on which these laws are necessarily based inhibit the ability of women to participate as full citizens by not only removing their autonomy and a host of basic rights but also by challenging their standing in sociopolitical matters. Indeed, the United Nation's Platform for Action shares this perspective, stating that "the ability of women to control their own fertility forms an important basis for the enjoyment of other rights" (United Nations 1995).

The continued force of these norms is especially evident in restrictive abortion laws, which are often based on religious beliefs that life begins at conception and that abortion is therefore tantamount to murder. These beliefs are shaped by traditional attitudes about women in their roles as wives and mothers, which reveal two interrelated assumptions. The first is that women are incompetent to make decisions and are unaccountable for their actions. The second is that, once a woman is pregnant, her citizenship can be abridged and her right to privacy and equality shared with her physician, the state, and the fetus she is supporting. She is a patient and future mother first, and an individual with constitutional rights second (Nossiff 2007 61–62). Lister (2003, 126) supports this idea when she argues that "without such rights [to contraception, abortion, and reproductive health] women cannot take control of their bodies or their lives; their agency, and hence their citizenship, is profoundly compromised."

These problems reveal two key issues with citizenship. The first is that a workable definition of citizenship must move beyond the assumption of a universal male citizen to take into account the unique relationship of women to the state. Reproductive politics is an obvious example of such a relationship, though the limitations relating to deep-seated assumptions about the value of women must also be addressed if equality is to be realized. The second concerns the shortcomings of a legal definition of citizenship. Even though, as this book contends, rights continue to have a significant role to play in securing women's equality, despite the power of citizenship to legitimize certain rights claims, "it neither consists of a prerequisite for the acquisition of social rights nor does it constitute a sufficient guarantee for the protection of social, cultural, political and economic rights of all citizens" (Abraham and Ngan-ling Chow 2011, 1). Legal rights alone go only so far. One of the main challenges from feminist scholars to the widespread inclusion of women as citizens stems from frustration that, even after securing formal rights, women continue to be poorly represented in the top positions of both business and government (Jaggar 2005, 93). As such, in order for citizenship to be a relevant framework, it must extend beyond legal in order definitions to include a more substantive interpretation of community membership.

The second critique of citizenship concerns its reach within individuals' lives and clearly ties back to the problems of exclusivity discussed above. Substantive definitions of citizenship often limit the importance of engagement by citizens to the public or political domains, which have traditionally excluded women. Martha Ackelsberg (2005) explains that,

> while the public realm is presented as one where free and equal citizens engage together in striving for some common good, that arena depends on a private/domestic realm that is characterized by relationships of *in*equality and dependence, and is focused on meeting life's necessities. (69, emphasis in original)

The implications of this divide are weighty, impacting not only what issues are considered public or political, but also influencing who is able to participate, and to what effect, in politics broadly conceived (Ackelsberg 2005, 70). Abortion and other reproductive health concerns are a clear casualty of this divide. Reproduction, and the responsibilities central to it, though essential to human survival, are also markedly undervalued and considered distinct from public concerns (Luxton 2006, 32). Sue Ferguson (1999, 6) maintains that "reproductive activities, in which women have historically played a central role, have been neglected as sites for political struggle." Bryan Turner (2008) further reinforces this contention, but complicates the relationship of reproduction to politics:

> Because reproduction is regarded by the law as an activity that takes place privately in the domestic sphere, the contributions of women to civil society and the reproduction of the nation have often been ignored, insofar as women are ascribed to the private sphere. By contrast, because reproduction is crucial to the survival of the nation and hence the state, women's reproductive choices are typically controlled by men through the regulatory institutions of the state and religion. (47–48)

The precarious placement of reproduction between public and private spheres has been a central focus of feminist activism for decades.[8] Even with this long-standing attention, however, the perception of this divide remains strong. Its continued rhetorical power goes a long way to explain why, despite a long history in the feminist movement, calls for reproductive autonomy are not a core issue in the study of citizenship (Roseneil et al. 2013, 901).

By way of challenges to the notion of a defined public-private divide (Abraham and Ngan-ling Chow 2011; Lister 2007), expanding the terrain and methods on and via which citizenship is practised and internalized (Jaggar 2005; Kershaw 2005; Lister 2007), and going beyond purely legal conceptions of citizenship to recognize that it is a process rather than a static framework (Abraham and Ngan-ling Chow 2011; Bakan and Stasiulis 2005; Turner 2008), citizenship can serve as a compelling lens with which to understand abortion politics. Recognizing abortion as inextricably tied to women's equality, and their equal citizenship, not only situates the denial of abortion access in broader denial of women's equality but ties these issues to women's experiences as members of a political community, opening the door for broader considerations of how reproduction implicates women's equal citizenship. The concept of citizenship, then, is a useful frame through which to understand abortion because it puts the procedure in the larger context of women's participation in Canadian society.

Perhaps unsurprisingly, framing abortion access as a right, particularly a right necessary for equal citizenship, has been met with resistance in Canada. As an overtly gendered right without any clear analogous grounds, abortion poses difficulties for traditional conceptualizations of citizenship. Indeed, abortion is, arguably, the only human right to date that did not originate as a right granted solely to men (Asal, Brown, and Figueroa 2008, 280). In political discourse today, abortion is commonly positioned as a hot-button topic or women's issue, rather than as a procedure necessary to allow women to control their own health and, further, to protect their economic, social, and political lives.

Although not all women can or will become pregnant, all women are nonetheless characterized by gendered stereotypes relating to their reproductive capacity in both official and private discourse, which have traditionally placed them, as well as their struggles relating to reproduction, outside the political sphere – although, as Turner (2008) explains, this has not stopped governments from legislating women's reproductive rights and obligations. When women's rights claims are located outside politics, women's standing to legitimately advocate for themselves in politics, and even within their communities, is likewise diminished. In essence, to deny the significance of abortion to women's equal citizenship is to effectively deny women a place at the table.

Abortion politics are the focus of this book, but I want to be clear that a positive right to abortion access cannot alone guarantee women's equality. Such recognition would be a major and deeply symbolic step in a larger project of equality, but it is important to situate abortion, as a deeply contested and emblematic issue, in a broader social context. During the second wave of feminism, Western feminists focused on issues of body politics, of which abortion rights activism was a major component. Although this focus on women's bodily rights is still important, current research does not operate in the same marginalizing discourses for which the second wave was criticized; it has moved to a more intersectional approach, which recognizes that substantive equality is elusive for many demographics.[9] To this end, I adopt a view of citizenship as a dynamic concept, experienced by individuals in unique ways depending on myriad factors, including gender, race, class, and location.

Citizenship is best thought of as existing "on a spectrum, involving a pool of rights that are variously offered, denied, or challenged, as well as a set of obligations that are unequally demanded" (Bakan and Stasiulis 2005, 2).

Recognizing the "complex and multifaceted relationships of individuals to territories, nation-states, labour markets, communities and households" problematizes simplistic legal categories and extends understandings of citizenship beyond the public sphere (ibid., 11). The way women experience attempts to terminate unwanted pregnancies is, after all, the result of interactions between state and nonstate actors, mitigated by their own position and status in society. Such an approach also challenges critiques of the false universalism of citizenship. Recognizing the different ways individuals experience or are denied their citizenship, we are able to utilize citizenship as a theoretical tool to assess women's marginalization and subordination, and as an instrument to challenge these inequalities, all the while shining "a searching light on difference" (Lister 1997, 195).

Although I do not attempt to suggest that creating a positive right to abortion access will impact all women in the same way, I do contend that such a move would create some benefit for all women. Moreover, recognition of these rights in context provides a platform for future challenges, in no small part by validating women's reproductive lives as central to their experiences as citizens.

Chapter Organization

In the chapters that follow, I pursue three questions: What forms of access have appeared in the provinces since *R. v. Morgentaler* (1988)? What roles have state and nonstate actors played in the creation of this access, or barriers to it? And what role has and should Charter rights play in the future regulation of abortion in Canada? I explore these questions using a thicker definition of access than the simple existence of nearby facilities that are able to perform the procedure. Although accessible facilities are still necessary for women to exercise their rights to terminate unwanted pregnancies, the nature of these facilities also matters, as does the personnel working there, the woman's ability to enter the facility, and her overall sense of safety. The realization of substantive access requires that we question not only which women do and do not have access but also how we can remove existing barriers. Must women negotiate with demonstrators when entering medical facilities? Will they face harassment or a loss of anonymity if they seek abortion services? How will the staff at the facility, including the physician, interact with them? Moreover, will women be able to speak openly about their experiences in their communities without fear of stigma or violence?

This view of access requires a comprehensive approach to abortion, which recognizes the procedure not as a single moment in a woman's life but as a decision rooted in a larger social structure, with real implications for her familial, social, economic, and political life. Questions about the implications of abortion for women's lives informs social movement activism surrounding the issue – championed by pro-choice, reproductive justice, and anti-abortion activists – which, in turn, inform social rhetoric that is reflected in the treatment of abortion by the medical profession, politicians, and the courts. In order to situate the parameters of the debate, Chapter 1 explores the motivations and evolution of these social movements in Canada.

Social movement activity surrounding abortion in Canada has long been presented as two-sided: between the pro-choice movement and anti-abortion movement. This view represents a dramatic oversimplification of the complex issues at stake in the debate. Although the pro-choice movement wishes to ensure the continued legality of abortion and improved access, and the anti-abortion movement continues to push for a return toward restricting or prohibiting access entirely, important nuances influence the nature of these claims in different contexts. Moreover, even groups operating under the same movement banner do not necessarily adopt identical viewpoints and strategies. The relationship between these groups is further complicated by the emergence of the reproductive justice movement in Canada. Through a careful unpacking of all three movements, I explore the role rights play in their strategic activities. In so doing, I show that the divisions between the pro-choice and reproductive justice movements in the Canadian context, particularly their views of rights, are not as exaggerated as the literature (which generally focuses on the United States) suggests. I therefore suggest a more contextualized understanding of abortion that might help to bridge these two movements, treating them as allied. This more holistic treatment of abortion grounds my arguments about the nature and relevance of access going forward.

Chapters 2 through 5 consider the roles of both state and nonstate actors in the regulation of abortion access in Canada – including the federal government and the Supreme Court, provincial governments and provincial courts, the medical community, and social movement activists – each of which has played a central role in the regulation of abortion, be it through legislation, clinical guidelines, the training of providers, or ethical and moral debate.

Chapter 2 looks at the regulation of abortion at the federal level. Before 1988, the availability of abortion was dictated by the Criminal Code and was thus under federal jurisdiction, and attempts to challenge the existing abortion law ran up against a jurisdictional wall until the implementation of the Charter of Rights and Freedoms. On the Charter's enactment, the Supreme Court was given increased discretionary power in its application, because it was designed to be interpreted as a living tree; that is, to adapt to changes in the social landscape. The landmark decisions that came after, such as *R. v. Morgentaler* (1988), would change the perceived role of the courts in the public eye and, in many cases, elevate its perceived legitimacy. Litigation came to be understood as an important tool for social change, often above engagement with the federal or provincial governments. This shift afforded more power to social activists, but it may have done so at the cost of engagement with formal political institutions. Through an exploration of the federal regulation of abortion over the last quarter century, alongside relevant Supreme Court rulings, this chapter questions the role that the federal government and the Supreme Court took in shaping the current landscape of abortion access in Canada, and what role they should be expected to play in future. Although this chapter demonstrates that rights played a crucial role in the decriminalization of abortion, it also attempts to show that the path toward decriminalization was by no means guaranteed.

Chapter 3 turns to the regulation of abortion by provincial governments after 1988, when abortion was reclassified as a health care issue. In each case, I explore the responses of provincial governments to this new jurisdiction, including their interactions with the courts. I also investigate the motivations for different approaches to the regulation of abortion access, observing the rhetoric of various social movements echoed in each institution. This discovery demonstrates the value of rhetoric and social perception in the regulation of abortion, and the need to influence these attitudes to realize change. In addition, it showcases how a language of rights, or the avoidance of such a language, is reflected in the nature of access to services.

According to Canada's constitution, health care falls under the jurisdiction of the provinces, though the medical community dictates many aspects of the way services are provided. The nature of physician training and licensing, as well as what is deemed to be ethical and professional conduct, are set out by provincial colleges of physicians and surgeons. Surveying the ways in which the medical community has regulated abortion after its decriminalization, Chapter 4 explores the implications of the classification of abortion as a health care issue in the provinces. Exploring how abortions are, and can be, provided, it offers a nuanced picture of what abortion provision does, as well as could, look like in Canada. Indeed, the emergence of improved medical abortion in the Canadian market in January 2017 marks the first major shift away from a focus almost exclusively on surgical abortions. Given the important role nonstate actors, like those in the medical profession, have played in shaping access, it is necessary to understand the way the medical community itself is regulated, both internally and by external forces, in order to better grasp what access provision looks like across the country, and to suggest potential avenues to influence it. Ultimately, this chapter reveals the drawbacks of treating abortion as a purely medical issue, highlighting the need to create a solid foundation to improve access in Canada – a foundation I believe can be aided through rights recognitions and realized through social change.

The role of social movements comes to a head in a broader discussion of the nature of provincial social climates in Chapter 5. Here, I argue that a province's social climate is influential both in the regulatory decisions of institutions and in the experiences of individuals seeking abortion access. Ultimately, the realization of substantive abortion access is not only a political and legal question, it also relies on social acceptance of the procedure as necessary to women's equality.

In the final chapter, I turn to one last case study, with the aim of drawing together the actors impacting the landscape of access in Canada's most staunchly anti-abortion province: Prince Edward Island. Although largely stagnant during the time most of this book was written, the province has recently undergone major changes to the way it regulates access to abortion care, from an effective prohibition to accessible care in one of its urban centres. By looking to the rationale for changes in the province, this chapter affirms the role of rights in realizing women's equality, while reflecting on the potential of the Trudeau government to affect change federally going forward. Importantly, although rights recognition will certainly help provide abortion with much-needed legitimacy in the political sphere, and further challenge its treatment as taboo, they should not be thought of as an end point in the quest for equality. Rather, in advancing an argument for the recognition of reproductive rights as essential to women's equal citizenship, I recognize specific rights protections as important stepping-stones toward broader recognition of the role of reproduction in women's lives.

1

The Anti-abortion, Pro-choice, and Reproductive Justice Movements

Social movement activism has played a pivotal role in shaping the landscape of abortion access in Canada. In order to justify their actions or, as is often the case, their inaction, scores of politicians, judges, and physicians have adopted the arguments and language used by these social movements, which today include anti-abortion, pro-choice, and reproductive justice activists. Any study of abortion politics in Canada that hopes to accurately represent the various forms of access across the provinces must therefore be grounded in an understanding of the history, motivations, and strategies of these movements. As this chapter demonstrates, the evolution of each movement is clearly tied to both changing social dynamics and political opportunity structures, and their evolution, in turn, impacts the realities of access in the provinces.

The nature of pro-choice and anti-abortion activism in Canada has been the focus of a noteworthy body of literature in Canadian politics, much of which draws parallels with movements in the United States. The relative newness of the reproductive justice movement, however, has meant that work on the movement in a Canadian context is not as developed as that addressing its United States counterparts.[1] Nonetheless, all three movements have some representation in Canada. Evidence of their strategies, motivations, and interrelationships is obtainable through their websites, social media presence, and other activities, which include demonstrations and interactions with the media. Cumulatively, these sources provide a clear picture of abortion-related activism in Canada today, as well as the forces that shape it.

A brief history of each movement reveals the influence of major events in Canadian and international politics that have helped shape their respective approaches and mandates. For example, the entrenchment of the Canadian Charter of Rights and Freedoms was a turning point for pro-choice and anti-abortion organizations. The Charter's focus on individual rights created new tools to challenge existing restrictions on abortion. Indeed, Miriam Smith (2005, 347) contends that such restructuring has transformed the very relationship of social movements to the state. In the decades following the enactment of the Charter, she explains, judicial empowerment "has encouraged and reinforced a certain type of social movement politics, one that is dedicated to liberal rights-claiming using litigation as its greatest strategic asset." Arguing that legislatures and parties have declined in importance while the courts have become an important venue for policy change, she shows how social movements have been able to exploit these new opportunities. Certainly, there is ample evidence of these influences on the Canadian pro-choice and anti-abortion movements.

In the case of the pro-choice movement, its success in *R. v. Morgentaler* (1988) and the jurisprudence that emerged from the ruling contributed to the movement's long-standing focus on improving access and securing women's rights to equality through legal recognition. The pro-choice movement is by no means limited to litigation in its work, though this approach has been hugely successful in advancing the movement's claims. The anti-abortion movement, in contrast, has not had the same experiences. Failing to capitalize on the Charter, at least in terms of legal victories, considerably hampered the movement. Even though the anti-abortion movement has attempted to increase its legitimacy through claims for "fetal rights," the legal campaign was a nonstarter. Over time, an inability to capitalize on these rights has contributed to a notable change in the rhetoric of the anti-abortion movement, from a language of protecting "the unborn" from selfish pregnant women to assertions that abortion must be stopped because it is dangerous to women (Saurette and Gordon 2013). This shift in focus from rights to social and medical concerns about the well-being of women seeks to capitalize on the values that underlie the Charter, such as women's equality, as well as the successes of the women's movement. Like previous iterations of the movement, however, it relies on an idealized view of the world as well as women's experiences to advance its claims – claims that rely on the treatment of abortion as separate from women's citizenship. These are precisely the views that fall apart when abortion is framed holistically, as the latest activist group on the scene aims to do.

The reproductive justice movement was first organized in the United States, where it was formed in response to the perceived limitations of a reproductive rights and health framework advanced by the United Nations. Like the pro-choice movement, reproductive justice advocates support the legality of abortion, but the scope of their goals is more expansive, encompassing not only a right not to have children but also a right to have children and to parent existing children (L. Ross 2006, 14). The movement's core strength is its holistic treatment of reproduction, which it sees as linked to myriad other social justice issues, all of which need to be addressed to achieve substantive equality.

In many respects, the reproductive justice and pro-choice movements seem to be natural allies, but there are numerous concerns that have divided the movements, particularly in the United States. Indeed, reproductive justice was very much created in response to the perceived failures of the pro-choice framework. One big difference between the two groups is the wariness that some reproductive justice advocates express toward the use of individual rights protections to advance their cause, rights that they often see as limited to the domain of negative rights. Although the movement is supportive of reproductive rights recognitions in general, it would consider mere freedom from state interference with reproduction to be insufficient – what good are rights that an individual lacks the means to exercise? In addition, if the legality of abortion is treated as a kind of end point, these protections risk obscuring the relationships between specific issues, like abortion, and the larger social structures in which they are embedded.

Importantly, the above concerns are rooted in manifestations of both movements in the United States and are not necessarily demonstrative of their relationship in Canada. Although Canada does not yet have a reproductive justice movement to speak of, the ideals of the movement have permeated the missions of many pro-choice groups, and a few dedicated reproductive justice groups have begun to emerge across the country. Indeed, it is very possible that reproductive justice may have been slower to develop in Canada because the country's pro-choice movement does not share the same values or focus as its United States counterparts.[2]

This chapter attempts to show that the pro-choice movement and emerging reproductive justice advocates in Canada actually share substantial theoretical grounding and strategic interests. Both groups benefit from a more contextualized view of abortion to advance their claims, and I suggest that either one could use individual rights claims to its desired ends. Building on these points of similarity, these two movements should be understood as allies in their desire to improve the reproductive lives of citizens. In making this claim, I point to the value of individual rights in advancing a contextualized understanding of women's equality claims in Canada while acknowledging the shortcomings of litigation in working toward this end.

However, just as structural shifts have influenced the strategies of these movements, which have historically focused on rights-based litigation in Canada, it would be a mistake to assume that institutional changes alone can account for social movement activities. In many cases, the outcomes of these shifts are dramatically influenced by nonstructural factors, such as the timing of the legal decisions. Moreover, nonstructural factors also play an important role in the actions, strategies, and successes of movements, which will become increasingly apparent through the case studies in later chapters that show how the fortunes of these groups have unfolded. The significance of elements like emotion, understanding, and even luck demonstrate the limits of structural explanations of social movement genesis. Recognizing the power of such factors in shaping the nature of movements also reveals the importance of thinking about rights in a similar way.

If we limit our understanding of rights to formal protections validated through court decisions, these institutions and the often narrow rights protections they provide seem like a risky means to advance women's equality claims. A more holistic understanding of rights, however, sees even individual rights claims as tools that are deeply socially embedded. Even without formal rights protections, a language of rights shapes public perception and, in turn, the ways of thinking about specific issues to which both state and nonstate actors are exposed. Although formal rights protections may compel institutional change, a widespread sense of entitlement to a particular right can also be a potent force. One movement that has certainly embraced the value of shifting social perception through nonlegal means is the anti-abortion movement.[3]

The Anti-abortion Movement

The anti-abortion movement in Canada began to organize in response to the liberalization of the 1969 law, gaining momentum in the decades following the decriminalization of abortion. According to Chris MacKenzie (2005, 105), "Initially mobilizing under Alliance for Life, Canada's first national pro-life organization, the movement has solidified and diversified itself both nationally and provincially into educational, political, and counseling branches." Traditionally, anti-abortion activists have operated under the larger umbrella of the "pro-family" movement, which sees "the traditional family as under attack and falling into an ever-deepening crisis because of an overly intrusive state and an ever-expanding secular value system" (ibid., 5). Although abortion remains a central focus of these larger movements, they position it as one issue among many – including euthanasia, same-sex marriage, and reproductive technologies – that are symptoms of this larger social problem.

Historically, those in the anti-abortion movement have been clear about their belief that a return to a more traditional, nuclear family model and a shift away from sex-positive education and acceptance was the desired effect of restrictions on abortion. Today, these attitudes are still evident in the mission statements of prominent Canadian anti-abortion groups, including REAL Women of Canada (2015), which advocates "the values of traditional family and marriage" and the Campaign Life Coalition (2015), which aims to "defend the sanctity of human life against threats" especially those posed by abortion and "threats to the family" (such as same-sex marriage). Despite this continuity, the movement has responded to changing social conditions and political opportunity structures by employing various strategies, many of which now work to obscure the larger goals of the project.

A large-scale study of the anti-abortion movement in Canada by Paul Saurette and Kelly Gordon (2013, 158) reveals that the "traditional portraits" of the discourse employed by North American anti-abortion groups – which suggest that "(a) it is primarily aimed at driving legislative change; (b) it is highly critical of women in its tone; (c) it frequently appeals to religion; and (d) it uses fetal-centric arguments to defend its position" – belie the complex strategies they now employ. Alternatively, their study argues that the new anti-abortion discourse in Canada:

> increasingly (a) focuses beyond legislative change for its objectives; (b) is adopting a "pro-woman" tone; (c) avoids public appeals to religion to ground its position; and (d) employs new explicit arguments (the abortion-harms-women argument) and revises older ones (the older fetal-centric argument) in ways that market the anti-abortion position as more modern, individualistic and pro-woman than ever before. (158)

These shifts in framing, particularly the pro-woman language, is also noted by Sonya Bourgeois (2014, 23) in her study of Canadian anti-abortion advocacy materials and backbencher bills in the House.[4] She identifies four themes in the narratives adopted, three of which – abortion is traumatic;

women are first and foremost mothers; and women do not really need abortion – focus on the role of women in abortion politics. She also notes the continued assertion that "the fetus has rights" appearing in anti-abortion material. The significance of these framings within the anti-abortion movement in Canada are made plain through an exploration of the earlier strategies adopted by the movement.

The traditional rhetorical strategies that Saurette and Gordon identify are rooted in the activities of the anti-abortion movement leading up to, and immediately following, *R. v. Morgentaler* (1988). The enactment of the Charter of Rights and Freedoms, which established the individual rights guarantees exploited in the *Morgentaler* decision to decriminalize abortion, also created potential inroads for the anti-abortion movement to have its plight heard. Indeed, both the pro-choice and anti-abortion movements attempted to use the protections in section 7 for life, liberty, and security of the person toward dramatically different ends. While Morgentaler was fighting legal battles in Ontario, Joe Borowski, a former Saskatchewan politician, was fighting for public standing to challenge the same section of the Criminal Code that Morgentaler was working to overturn – except that Borowski wanted to see stricter regulations in place. Specifically, he asserted that the fetus has a "right to life" that he wished to see recognized under the Charter.[5] The Supreme Court never heard Borowski's case, the details of which are discussed at length in Chapter 2, because another case, *Tremblay v. Daigle*, rendered his claims moot in finding that a fetus had no legal status in Canada.

Despite this early loss, the anti-abortion movement continued efforts to recast its position as a rights issue by claiming the *unborn child's* right to life. This language appears in numerous backbencher bills and is still regularly employed by the anti-abortion movement. Although, in formal terms, the fetal rights framework was a nonstarter, the rhetorical value of rights was seen to add clout to the anti-abortion cause and rapidly became a staple of the movement's strategy. Rights-based claims had been successful for the pro-choice movement and seemed to carry the promise of legitimizing its cause as well. In its framing of the issue in the context of public debates on abortion, the anti-abortion movement focused on the fetus as either the most or sole deserving subject. In so doing, the anti-abortion groups attempted to erase women from discussions of pregnancy.

Historically, many campaigns have attempted to reduce conceptualizations of pregnant women to "pregnant bodies" rather than as full human beings with individual needs and aspirations (Brodie 1992, 86). This strategy is still evident in the way the movement uses visuals, which often feature a fetus in-utero, with the woman's body either obscured or cut off. Alternatively, some visuals depict the fetus after miscarriage or abortion, with the woman's body completely out of sight.[6] This division between a woman and a fetus is a phenomenon exacerbated in large part because of improvements in imaging technologies (Stabile 1998, 172). Carol Stabile (1998, 172) suggests that this "project of disarticulation" can be understood either as "anti-essentialist (insofar as it denies the material specificity of women's bodies) or as a process of humanizing technology, which then figures as the sign of paternalistic intervention." The feared outcome of these images for feminists is the same: the removal of women from deliberations over reproduction altogether (Stetson 1996, 222). Dorothy Stetson (1996, 222) warns that the push for fetal rights recognitions aims to recast the abortion debate in gender-neutral terms so that the recognition of women as individuals disappears.

Unfortunately for the anti-abortion movement, demonizing women or removing them altogether from discussions on pregnancy have proven to be unpopular discursive strategies, which remain a sticking point in the movement's attempt to sway public opinion. Leslie Cannold (2002, 172) explains that anti-choice activists have learned that "women greatly resent this fetal-centred focus and perceive anti-choice activists as uncaring and judgmental." As such, in order to promote its movement, a new discursive strategy was necessary. The shift toward messaging that is ostensibly woman-friendly has been well documented in Canada in recent years (e.g., Saurette and Gordon 2013; Bourgeois 2014).

Although the anti-abortion movement's belief that the state should regulate women's bodies is unchanging, the movement has attempted to rebrand itself as more woman-centric, even feminist in character. Seeing the success of a women's rights framework, many groups within the anti-abortion movement have attempted to reposition the fight to recriminalize abortion as one of women's rights, alleging that abortion must be banned to protect women – pregnant women and female fetuses alike – from harm (Saurette and Gordon 2013).[7] This apparent harm can take several forms, including health risks to the pregnant woman, rooted in false assertions that abortion causes breast cancer and symptoms akin to post-traumatic stress disorder, and claims that the consequences of abortion bear striking similarities to other forms of physical or emotional violence, such as sexual assault (ibid., 176). In essence, women have been recast as the victims of the pro-choice movement, because what woman would willingly and knowingly choose to cause themselves harm? The new rhetorical tools of the anti-abortion movement seem to suggest that we should never see the rights of pregnant women and *the unborn* as potentially conflicting, because no woman really wants or needs abortion; moreover, no woman has the ability to rationally chose abortion. As Leslie Cannold (2002, 172) puts it, "Women-centred discourse describes women facing an unplanned pregnancy as 'confused and despairing' and thus lacking the rationality and autonomy required to make and implement the decision they know to be right and truly wish to make: to continue the pregnancy and become mothers."

Justifications that the anti-abortion movement has offered in order to explain why women cannot really choose abortion vary from assertions that women are never able to make rational decisions because they lack complete information about their decision and its consequences to assertions that the hormones associated with pregnancy render women "constitutionally irrational" (ibid., 173). This portrayal of pregnant women not only removes the potential for pregnant women to exert any agency in decisions about their bodies and lives but also seeks to repair the damaging portrayal of women in fetal-centric arguments by absolving them of any blame for having an abortion. In this way, the movement may avoid or downplay its demonization of women who have had or may wish to have an abortion. Perhaps most importantly, "unlike fetal-centred activists, [woman-centred activists] do not explicitly oppose the legality or availability of abortion. Instead, they depict themselves as having an agenda-less desire, grounded in their concern to protect vulnerable women's rights from being trampled by abortion service-providers" (ibid., 172).

Although the eventual recriminalization of abortion, in whole or in part, or a reduction in services may be a by-product of the anti-abortion movement, members deny that this is the focus of their efforts. By asserting a desire not to remove services or create laws, they position themselves as less threatening, encouraging women to "choose" to continue an unwanted pregnancy (despite the apparent inability of pregnant women to make rational choices about their bodies while pregnant).

Notably, fetal rights claims have not disappeared from the movement; they have simply changed form. Unlike previous claims that a fetus has a right to life for religious reasons, rooted in the belief that a fetus has a soul from the moment of conception, the movement now attempts to utilize scientific language to advance claims of personhood to avoid accusations of bias. This approach is evident in recent backbencher bills such as Stephen Woodworth's 2012 motion – Motion 312 – to revisit the definition of a human being in the Criminal Code (more on this in Chapter 2). These rights claims are reinforced through attempts to draw parallels between the denials of rights of the fetus and those of other progressive social justice movements throughout history (Saurette and Gordon 2013, 177).

The new anti-abortion movement in Canada has thus rebranded itself and shifted its focus from legislative and legal action to "broad cultural and value change" (ibid., 178). This focus does not mean that anti-abortion activities in the House and provincial legislatures are no longer an issue – they are – or that the anti-abortion movement will not attempt to advance claims through the courts – it does; it simply signifies a new approach to securing social change. Indeed, despite the new rhetorical tools of the anti-abortion movement, the prevalence of backbencher bills that target abortion services and their legality suggests that the movement wishes to maintain a political presence. This presence is valuable in shaping public perception of abortion, if only by suggesting that certain elites still support an anti-abortion agenda, so it is likely to continue. That said, those in the anti-abortion movement seem aware that the only real possibility of creating new, substantive restrictions on abortion is to change public perception in a manner in keeping with widely held values, such as safety and equality, that have been successfully used to advance a pro-choice agenda. This approach necessitates a conception of rights that extends beyond legal categories to encompass perceptions of how rights are understood and internalized.

A focus on rhetoric and social shifts may seem apolitical, but it would be a mistake to interpret this strategy as no longer threatening women's rights. The power of this strategy is its ability to appear apolitical and nonthreatening while pushing at the edges of women's rights claims. At the same time that a woman-centric anti-abortion movement claims that abortion harms women's rights, a fetal-centric focus continues to utilize the language of fetal rights to challenge women's rights claims. When we begin to unpack the significance of rights as both a rhetorical and institutional tool, the continued need to understand how rights impact abortion politics in Canada is obvious, not just from the perspective of anti-abortion groups but for pro-choice and reproductive justice advocates as well. Moreover, by adopting a more contextualized understanding of abortion, which sees the procedures as a right of citizenship necessary for women's equality, the idealized and often contradictory nature of the anti-abortion movement's approach becomes all the more obvious.

The Pro-choice Movement

Although medical and legal associations exerted pressure to challenge restrictions on abortion access as early as the 1930s, what would eventually become known as the pro-choice movement only began to organize some thirty years later. By the early 1960s, several women's and social justice groups had begun to mobilize against criminal restrictions on abortion (Pro-Choice Action Network 1999). These groups gained momentum by the end of that decade, thanks in no small part to the revival of the Canadian women's movement in the late 1960s. This period, later categorized as second-wave feminism, was defined by a concerted effort to secure bodily autonomy for women, of which abortion was a central but by no means sole concern (Pierson 1993, 99). The rights to give birth, to avoid sterilization, and to control one's own sexuality were all part of this larger project (ibid., 105).

The first national action of the women's movement was the formation of the 1970 Abortion Caravan, bringing abortion to the forefront of calls for women's autonomy. This caravan consisted of a group of women from the Vancouver Women's Caucus, who drove from Vancouver to Ottawa to protest the 1969 abortion law, which legalized abortion, but only for women who received the approval of therapeutic abortion committees (Rebick 2005, 35). The caravan grew as its journey progressed, gaining not only participants but also press coverage along the way. On arriving in Ottawa, and learning that no government representatives would speak with them, around 30 women from the caravan, in a nod to the demonstrations of British suffragists a century earlier, protested by chaining themselves to their seats in the House of Commons' public gallery (ibid., 36).

The caravan was hugely successful in garnering attention and support, and seemed to act as the catalyst for the creation of abortion rights groups. According to Ruth Pierson (1993), shortly after the caravan arrived in Ottawa, several national associations were created:

> A large organization, originally called the Canadian Association for Repeal of the Abortion Law, was formed in 1974 to support Dr. Morgentaler's challenge of the 1969 abortion law. Later changing its name to Canadian Abortion Rights Action League/Association Canadienne pour le Droit a l'Avortement, with provincial and local chapters across Canada, CARAL/ACDA has spearheaded the campaign for decriminalized abortion. According to its constitution, CARAL/ACDA's purpose has been to "ensure that no woman in Canada is denied access to safe, legal abortion" and to gain

recognition of "the right to safe, legal abortion as a fundamental human right." (100, 102)

Organizations such as Canadians for Choice (incorporated in 2002) and the Abortion Rights Coalition of Canada (founded in 2005) formed later, with mandates to help protect and improve abortion access in Canada.

In the early days of abortion rights activism, a language of rights was regularly employed, much as it is today, but the language of choice, with which the movement is now synonymous, originated in the early 1980s. Judy Rebick (2005, 157) explains that this shift in language followed multiple raids on the Morgentaler clinics in Winnipeg and Toronto: "Women mobilized to support Morgentaler and demand reproductive rights. The popular slogan changed from 'Free abortion on demand' to 'A woman's right to choose.'" This language was also emerging in the United States in what Rickie Solinger (2013) characterizes as the post-rights era of *choice:*

> The language of choice centred reproductive experiences in the domain of women's bodies, and validated women's needs to respond to their reproductive capacities within the context of their whole lives. Also, abortion rights activists were determined to develop a respectable, nonconfrontational movement after *Roe v. Wade*. Many proponents wanted to adopt the term *choice* because they realized that some people in the United States were weary of – or hostile to – *rights* claims after the civil rights movement. Many people believed that choice, a term that evoked women as individuals, not as an activist mass – even as women shoppers selecting among options in the marketplace – would offer a kind of "rights lite," a less threatening package than unadulterated *reproductive rights*. (156, emphasis in original)

Choice, in the context of the United States, hinged substantially on a right to privacy, a right that has meant abortion is commonly believed to be a very individual matter (Solinger 2013, 1). The belief that women ought to exercise rights as individuals to choose abortion is part of the history of the term in Canada also, but the realities of socialized medicine meant that the nature of what had become known as the pro-choice movement took on a much more expansive character.

Although reproductive rights activists initially mobilized in response to a nearly complete ban on abortion access, their activities increased only after the liberalization of Canada's abortion law in 1969. This may seem counterintuitive, but the liberalization of the existing law gave advocates hope for increased change. In addition, the problematic nature of the therapeutic abortion committees (TACs) created by the new law underscored more fundamental concerns with the federal regulation of abortion.[8] Activists continued to not only raise consciousness of the shortcomings of the existing law but also to assist women, often illegally, to find safe abortion services. Indeed, one of the doctor's providing these services, Dr. Henry Morgentaler, later became the champion of the pro-choice movement.

Years before his landmark Supreme Court victory, Morgentaler was a regular fixture in Canadian courtrooms, after repeated arrests for the performance of illegal abortions in Quebec and Ontario. In those cases, which included a trip to the Supreme Court in 1973, Morgentaler relied on a defence of medical necessity to justify his actions. Although this defence was unsuccessful in eliminating the 1969 law, his activism was given a public stage, and support for his activities grew. His notoriety increased in no small part because of the refusal of juries, on hearing the testimony of women he helped, to convict him.

Morgentaler's approach to the decriminalization of abortion changed with the entrenchment of the Canadian Charter of Rights and Freedoms in 1982, which created individual rights protections for Canadian citizens. The Charter would prove to be an important tool for Morgentaler, who, only six years later, would use its guarantees to safeguard "life, liberty and security of the person" to strike down section 251 of the Criminal Code, decriminalizing abortion in Canada. Although litigation was by no means unheard of as a tool for the pro-choice movement to press for change before the Charter, the patriation of the constitution created new opportunities that they carefully exploited.

The 1988 *Morgentaler* decision was a watershed moment for pro-choice activists, many of whom saw it as the final battle for reproductive rights. The decision turned on individual rights to life, liberty, and security of the person, which bore significant similarities to the guarantees to privacy that liberalized abortion laws in the United States.[9] However, despite the decriminalization of abortion in Canada resting on the treatment of abortion as a private, individual matter, Shelley Gavigan stresses that this "has *not* been the characterization of Canadian pro-choice and feminist activists, who have consistently framed abortion as an issue of equality and access" (1992, 127, emphasis in original).

From the beginning, the logic behind the rhetoric of the pro-choice movement was that the choice to have an abortion was a woman's alone, not a lawmaker's, not a medical professional's, not her partner's. This language has, however, been critiqued for its apparent limitations. Depending on how choice is defined, it may simply mean legality, or freedom from state interference, in seeking access. As Rickie Solinger (2013, 2) explains, "Many believe that a woman's decision to get pregnant, or not, and to have a baby, or not, remains a private manner, an orientation reflected in the commonly used term 'choice.'" Understood in this way, choice is inadequate because the end result is not the creation of a means to access for all, but access only for those fortunate enough to have the means and support.

This interpretation has not, however, characterized the Canadian pro-choice movement, whose focus moved quickly from legality to access following the decriminalization of abortion in 1988. In more than twenty-five years without criminal restrictions on abortion in Canada, the Canadian pro-choice movement would have disappeared altogether – except, perhaps, to safeguard the status quo – if legality were its sole focus. Moreover, the pro-choice movement avoided stopping at legal recognition; it mobilized to ensure that governments would abstain from creating new laws, and to influence the kinds of access that emerged in the wake of the decision.

Following the *Morgentaler* decision, litigation became an important tool to challenge government restrictions on access. Most of these challenges were successful, yet in many instances, the verdicts were limited and failed to compel meaningful action on the part of governments. Since Canadian courts have been wary to validate positive rights claims, the inadequacies of these rulings have been a point of contention with the reproductive justice movement, which sees negative rights protections as an extension of a limited belief in the concept of choice.

In the United States, choice is commonly advocated on an individual basis, without recognition of the contexts in which individuals make choices, or the reality that systemic inequality often renders genuine choice impossible (FQPN 2014b, 7). The continued legality of abortion services is still a preoccupation of the pro-choice movement in Canada, though the new focus is access, the realities of which require an intersectional understanding of the origins of specific barriers. Funding, facilities, harassment, travel, and culturally sensitive and dignified services are all causes that the Canadian pro-choice movement has championed since abortion was decriminalized. By no means echoing the singular focus of the movement in the United States, the Canadian pro-choice movement has adopted a more substantive understanding of choice, one which recognizes the social, political, and economic challenges of individuals attempting to access abortion services.

The federal structure of Canadian government further complicates these barriers to access. When abortion was decriminalized, it was reclassified as a matter of health care, a responsibility under provincial jurisdiction. Each province responded to these new powers in unique ways, creating a patchwork of services across the country. As a result, even without criminal restrictions, not all women have been able to access services equally across Canada. In response, the pro-choice movement has continued to work diligently to maintain and, in some cases, improve access by working with abortion clinics (National Abortion Federation), lobbying governments (Abortion Rights Coalition of Canada), and consciousness raising (Action Canada for Sexual Health and Rights; Fédération du Québec pour le planning des naissances), though constant fear of losing ground has contributed to a cautionary approach by some groups more willing to push for recognition of existing policy than to demand improvements. Melissa Haussman's (2005) characterization of the Canadian pro-choice movement reflects these concerns:

> The major focus for the Canadian pro-choice movement [since the *Morgentaler* decision] has been to ensure that funding for abortion access in hospitals and free-standing clinics (as well as the development of other methods like RU-486) – and the discourse surrounding these issues – is largely based on the terms of "funding" and "medically necessary services" as set forth in the revised criminal code. (99)

There are many reasons the movement has often restricted discussion of abortion to the medical realm. Significant gains in access were made when the procedure shifted to the provinces as a health care issue, not to mention the widespread respect and support for health services in Canada. Moreover, by highlighting a lack of funding as a problem, abortion is connected to a range of other medical services that are seen to lack funding. Unfortunately, this language can be problematic, as it denies a more holistic understanding of abortion and obscures the intersections of oppressions that different women face in their attempts to access even a funded, widely available service. It is these shortcomings that the emerging reproductive justice movement aims to address.

Reproductive Justice
The reproductive justice movement has its roots in the United States, where it was created by feminists of colour in the wake of the 1994 International

Conference on Population and Development (ICPD) (Luna and Luker 2013, 328). The ICPD, held in Cairo, was a milestone event for reproductive rights activism, marking the first official recognition that women's reproductive rights are human rights (Chrisler 2013, 1) and a shift away from policy focused on population control to that concerned with reproductive health and rights (Briggs et. al. 2013, 109). At the conference, the World Health Organization debuted its definition of reproductive rights as

> the basic right of all couples and individuals to decide freely and responsibly the number, spacing, and timing of their children and to have the information and means to do so, and the right to attain the highest standard of sexual and reproductive health. It also includes their right to make decisions concerning reproduction free of discrimination, coercion, and violence, as expressed in human rights documents. (United Nations 1995, 60)

Despite its laudable goals, this definition was deeply aspirational and failed to reflect many of the substantive barriers to reproductive rights women faced internationally. Although the ICPD has since been celebrated as advancing a significant and intersectional statement on reproductive rights, it was not without limitations (Briggs et al. 2013, 110). Perceiving these shortcomings, members of the United States Women of Color group in attendance began to question the utility of the reproductive rights framework. Joan Chrisler (2014) explains that,

> as they listened to discussions of the need to slow population growth and debates about the extent to which women's reproductive rights could and should be guaranteed, they realized that rights that cannot be exercised do women little good. Women need more than rights; they need resources, accessibility of services, equality in other areas, and respect for their decisions in order to meet the aspirations set forth in WHO's definition. (205–6)

Later that same year, Loretta Ross and her colleagues formed SisterSong Women of Color Reproductive Justice Collective and embarked on their work for reproductive justice. Ross (2006), the national coordinator of SisterSong from 2005 through 2012 and one of the women in attendance at the ICPD, defines reproductive justice as:

> The complete physical, mental, spiritual, political, social and economic well-being of women and girls, based on the full achievement and protection of

women's human rights. It offers a new perspective on reproductive issue advocacy, pointing out that for Indigenous women and women of color it is important to fight equally for (1) the right to have a child; (2) the right not to have a child; and (3) the right to parent the children we have, as well as to control our birthing options, such as midwifery. We also fight for the necessary enabling conditions to realize these rights. (14)

In contrast to the traditionally white, middle-class focus of the pro-choice movement, the reproductive justice framework is deeply intersectional, recognizing individuals as inextricably tied to communities (Luna and Luker 2013, 329). By linking reproductive rights and health to a wider range of issues, from climate change to poverty to violence (Price 2010, 43), the reproductive justice movement highlights the need to address reproductive health ("service delivery"), rights ("legal issues"), and justice ("movement building") to combat reproductive oppression. Although these frameworks operate in unique ways, all are necessary to secure substantive change (L. Ross 2006, 14). Importantly, in an effort to ensure that the reproductive justice movement retains its intersectional focus, those undertaking this work are meant to "put the most excluded/marginalized communities into positions of leadership; build their capacity for social, political, and economic empowerment; integrate grassroots issues and multi-racial, multi-generational and multi-class constituencies into the national policy arena; [and] build networks with allied organizations" (FQPN 2014b, 13).

These requirements point to the centrality of ensuring that marginalized groups are kept at the core of the movement. This is not to say, however, that other individuals are unable to participate and become allies by adopting a reproductive justice framework. Indeed, such alliances are required for the movement's success (L. Ross 2006, 16), and this imperative merely highlights a need to guard the movement from appropriation by dominant groups.

The formation of the reproductive justice movement, as evidenced by Loretta Ross's language above, is often seen as a response to the perceived limitations of the pro-choice movement, particularly in its emphasis on the language of choice. Many felt that, at least in the context of the United States, such language only implies the right to choose abortion (Luna and Luker 2013, 329). The quest for choice is often understood as a push for recognition of a negative right – freedom from state interference in decisions regarding reproduction – rather than of a positive right, which would require state support for reproductive choices. The reproductive justice movement is more commonly associated with the latter view of rights, whereas the pro-choice movement is seen to adopt the former.[10]

The continued wariness to recognize positive rights protections that courts in the United States and Canada have expressed has contributed to concerns in the movement that individual rights protections may have limited use in advancing its cause. Despite express comfort with human rights recognitions in their quest to challenge reproductive oppression, some reproductive justice advocates remain circumspect of the use of individual rights to achieve their ends. Lisa Schwartzman (2002, 465) explains that certain advocates "avoid appeals to liberal rights, arguing that such rights often work to reinforce structural hierarchies, including male dominance and racial oppression." Wendy Brown (1995, 86), an adamant critic of rights frameworks, asserts that rights "necessarily operate in and as an ahistorical, acultural, acontextual idiom" and thus present themselves as universal. This alleged universality may be beneficial at certain moments but can also be used as "a means of obstructing or coopting more radical political demands" (Schwartzman 2002, 465).[11] Rosalind Petchesky (2008) further argues that

> rights are by definition claims staked within a given order of things. They are demands for access for oneself, or for "no admittance" to others; but they do not challenge the social structure, the social relations of production and reproduction. The claim for "abortion rights" seeks access to a necessary service but by itself fails to address the social relations and sexual divisions around which responsibility for pregnancy and children is assigned. In real-life struggles, this weakness exacts a price, for it lets men and society neatly off the hook. (108)

The fear of the "nominal universalism of rights" rests in its potential to obscure systemic inequality (Luna and Luker 2013, 343). Thus, the use of an individual rights framework is not always seen as compatible with radical social projects, as it demands claims be focused, limited, and argued within strict parameters. Rights, particularly when advanced through litigation, require compromise, which often means that the interests and issues of already marginalized communities are the first to go.

This fear is not without grounding in Canada. *R. v. Morgentaler* (1988) decriminalized abortion because the existing law was seen as violating security of the person, but a more nuanced argument hinging on its implications for equality has yet to enter the courts. The language under which abortion was decriminalized impacts not only strategies for maintaining and improving access but how we think about these services. Recognition of a negative right to access is an improvement from previous restrictions, yet this conceptualization fails to consider the ability of women to act on this right. Abortion is widely positioned as a personal decision, but what about the social dynamics that influence women's choices? What about the women whose choices are constrained? Although the realities of Canada after the *Morgentaler* decision differ from that of the United States after *Roe v. Wade*, individual rights recognitions are still often seen as validating the narrow language of choice of which reproductive justice advocates are critical.

In some cases, however, if both negative and positive rights could be achieved, individual rights may cease to pose the same problems. For instance, Zakiya Luna and Kristin Luker (2013, 328) characterize the movement as demanding "a negative right of freedom from undue government interference and a positive right to government action in creating conditions of social justice and human flourishing for all." Kimala Price likewise stresses that the reproductive justice movement supports legal abortion, and pursuing legality where the procedure is still criminalized, they simply do not limit themselves to this framework (Price 2010, 56). Thus, although many reproductive justice activists in the United States remain wary of the courts, having witnessed their limited ability to protect individuals from marginalized groups on many issues, some still employ a legal route to equality toward specific ends (ibid. 330). It is at this nexus that we can begin to think about the relationships between the pro-choice and reproductive justice movements in Canada.

Allied Movements?

In recent years, many groups in Canada have embraced the principles of reproductive justice. Although lacking any clear national organization in Canada, many local groups identifying as reproductive justice advocates have begun to emerge across the country, including the Native Youth Sexual Health Network, the Support Network for Indigenous Women and Women of Colour, Reproductive Justice New Brunswick, and the Reproductive Justice League (Concordia). The use of this framework in Canada has not been without challenges. Although some pro-choice groups have endeavoured to adopt reproductive justice frameworks or goals into their mission statements, many groups in Canada have been reluctant to adopt the phrase itself.[12]

Heeding Loretta Ross's warning, many within the activist community, and in particular pro-choice groups, have taken caution to avoid appropriating the reproductive justice framework without adhering to its principles in their goals, approach, and organization. Few groups have actually adopted this label as a result of these concerns.[13] When questioned, however, representatives of some of the major pro-choice organizations in Canada shared that they have a profound respect for the goals of reproductive justice. Most have also attempted to incorporate some of its core ideas into their own mandates, though a desire to continue with their existing work and, more commonly, a lack of resources were cited as reasons these groups have foregone using the phrase itself. Sandeep Prasad, executive director of Action Canada for Sexual Health and Rights, says that his organization "would like to describe ourselves as using a reproductive justice framework or, at least, actively considering the implications of such a framework in terms of how we operate," but consciously avoided using this language.[14] He explains:

> Reproductive justice is a term that has a very particular history to it, so we have really been quite concerned about the appropriation of that term to describe what is simply abortion rights advocacy without any real intersectional perspective to it. I think, for that reason, that we don't describe ourselves as a reproductive justice organization in terms of actually using the "capital R, capital J Reproductive Justice." I think we, certainly in our alliances, are seeking to be allies of diverse movements, diverse social justice movements. We seek to embody that and continue to learn more about it and to improve our work in that way.

In a similar vein, a representative of the Fédération du Québec pour le planning des naissances (FQPN) explained: "We're definitely trying to work with the reproductive justice approach, but we realize that we'll never be that, there is no way, because we are a federation, and we are not representative of the diversity of the population, and we are not a social movement."[15] In the case of the FQPN, like many other such organizations in Canada, size and means were weighty considerations. Activist organizations are typically quite small and not always well funded, which makes adopting a truly intersectional approach difficult, even when the approach itself is thought of as best. Highlighting this challenge, the FQPN representative acknowledged that everyone in the activist movement is excited about the possibility of approaching these issues more inclusively, but often do not consider the practical implications: "They still want us to do the same as we are doing plus new things, and we're two people working there two days a week." Nonetheless, the FQPN has attempted to broaden its mandate. It continues to focus on abortion, but the organization has been increasingly focused on creating access for vulnerable populations. Recently, it has worked on creating access for migrant students by partnering with other organizations, including Médecins du Monde Canada.[16]

Reproductive Justice New Brunswick (RJNB) seems to be an exception to this trend, having adopted both the approach and terminology of the movement. The group itself is new, formed in the wake of the closure of the Fredericton Morgentaler Clinic in 2014. RJNB member Jessi Taylor explained the group's origin:

> There were a lot of people who really wanted to do something and were desperate. What had already been a sorry situation became that much more deadly. The Fredericton Youth Feminists, who are a big group of mostly high school youth, came together and were instrumental in the formation of RJNB, as well as a number of local activists who have been working in various capacities for access to reproductive health services for decades, and some who are newer, like myself.[17]

According to Taylor, at the time, the group felt that a reproductive justice framework "was a lot more holistic and identified a lot more of our needs." Citing the history of the movement, she said that the group "wanted to create an organization that would start identifying and working with those concepts from the get-go, rather than coming to them later."

RJNB has attempted to live up to its name, having partnered with various organizations and groups, including First Nations communities and unions, to address a range of issues. Despite these positive aspects, Taylor acknowledged that the group had adopted the reproductive justice framework before they had a solid understanding of the history and implications of the concept. However, whereas other organizations have "stopped using those words until they can actually legitimately reflect what it is they're trying to do and who it is they're trying to be," an approach RJNB supports, it has not chosen to take the same step yet: "Part of it is that we're so small that if we keep changing our name, people don't understand who we are, what to call us, but mostly it just gives us more pressure to live up and work towards those goals." She added: "We're small, we're always learning, and because most of us are white and fairly privileged, it's not perfect, but we've made it a priority that we're always striving for something more."[18]

Even when the phrase "reproductive justice" is not explicitly used, a growing respect for and adoption of a reproductive justice approach is evident across

Canada. Indeed, the lines between these groups in Canada have already begun to blur, in large part because the pro-choice movement in Canada, unlike the movement in the United States, has long focused on issues beyond legalization, stressing the need for equality of access. In the United States, where pro-choice advocates continue to fight against criminal restrictions on the procedure, to suggest that choice is synonymous with legality may be a more accurate depiction of the movement's core goals. Certainly, as a result of the Hyde Amendment, which restricts federal funding for abortion services, coupled with the country's largely privatized health care system, legality itself fails to provide many protections for women who seek abortion services. This reality differs dramatically from that in Canada, where socialized medicine is perceived as a right (Parliament of Canada, Standing Senate Committee on Social Affairs, Science and Technology 2002; Maioni 2010, 226). Moreover, the complete decriminalization of abortion in Canada, unlike the gestational limits created in the United States, created a policy gap that allowed social movements space to advocate for improved access. Much of this advocacy happened through litigation, which came with its own risks but has had largely positive outcomes for pro-choice advocates.

As such, to assume that the pro-choice movements in both countries continue to share the same goals and strategies would be misleading. Although the pro-choice movement in Canada often restricts itself to a focus on abortion, it has taken up the task of realizing access to services, a task that belies critiques of the pro-choice movement as concerned only with the legality of abortion. With the majority of work on reproductive justice activism emerging from the United States, these characterizations of the relationship between pro-choice and reproductive justice movements are unsurprising, but it is important not to assume that these critiques always reflect the relationships between these movements in Canada.

In the United States, Loretta Ross (2006, 15) envisions reproductive justice as a "theoretical bridge" between the pro-choice movement and those "grappling with how to work together across fissures of race and class, especially white women working with women of color," suggesting that this framework will help pro-choice advocates recognize the shortcomings of the language of choice. The way choice is understood in Canada, however, is more expansive. Pro-choice organizations in Canada advocate for a more substantive understanding of choice, which holds that all women not only require safe and funded access to abortion services but also must be able to make reproductive decisions free from harassment, threats, and stigma. For instance, the Abortion Rights Coalition of Canada's mission is to "ensure women's reproductive freedom by protecting and advancing access to abortion and quality reproductive health care" (ARCC 2015b), and the Ontario Coalition for Abortion Clinics was founded "on the idea that women have the right to control their bodies. This means the right to choose if and when to have children, and it means the right to safe, free abortions" (OCAC 2015). In the same vein, the National Abortion Federation Canada "works to ensure that abortion is safe, legal, and accessible," while Action Canada for Population and Development works to "enhance the quality of life of women, men and young people by promoting progressive policies in the field of human rights and international development with a primary focus on reproductive and sexual rights and health" (ACPD, n.d.).

Choice, interpreted in this way, requires both a negative right to abortion and a positive right to access. Access also takes on more noteworthy dimension in Canada because of its public health care program. Canadians have widely interpreted the legality of abortion, which is now classified formally as a health care issue, to mean a right to access services under their provincial health care plans. If abortion is a health care procedure, and medically necessary health care is a guaranteed service for Canadian citizens, it follows that Canadians ought to expect abortion services to be accessible.[19]

Despite the commonalities between the groups in Canada, the reproductive justice movement remains concerned that pro-choice groups will "not fully integrate the intersectional, human rights–based approach SisterSong promotes, but merely substitute the phrase 'reproductive justice' where previously they said 'pro-choice'" (L. Ross 2006, 18). Jessica Danforth (n.d., 4) has voiced similar concerns.[20] Citing examples from both Canada and the United States, she notes that "several organizations seem to insert RJ now as the progressive 'badge' of attempting to be equitable, even if they still operate within a hugely oppressive stronghold of refusing to accept the fact that, for many people, there are no choices to begin with."[21] Appropriation, even by well-intentioned groups, may potentially undercut the values and goals of the reproductive justice movement in substantive ways and must be guarded against.

If the groups are to work together as allies, an important first step in the prevention of this appropriation in Canada is to recognize the contributions that both the pro-choice and reproductive justice movement have made. In so doing, they may be able to avoid a reactive rebranding of the pro-choice movement in the name of reproductive justice – resistance to which is already evident in the Canadian pro-choice movement. Reproductive rights and health are two core issues in reproductive justice that pro-choice advocates directly address, and even though the pro-choice movement is more limited in its focus, both groups work to challenge forces that create and maintain reproductive oppression. Both groups, then, are participants in a larger project of challenging women's equality. They have the potential to be strong allies.

To this end, Zakiya Luna (2011, 240) advocates that both movements recognize their past "missteps" and commit to consistently reevaluating their movement's goals and approaches, ultimately "strategizing within and across movement sectors to develop coalitions, and actively linking lived personal experience to a range of political realities," thereby "strengthen[ing] their own efforts without increasing intramovement tensions." These steps are already evident in national pro-choice organizations, many of which are working to reimagine their missions and goals, in keeping with the lessons of reproductive justice activists. Of course, these shifts need not mean that organizations whose primary focus is abortion health, rights, or access should completely refocus or disband. Rather, informed by the reproductive justice movement, pro-choice groups can self-evaluate and ally themselves with the movement and work toward more expansive advances. Equality rights will continue to play an essential role in the advancement of this joint cause.

Rights provide a commonly accepted language of legitimacy in the current political culture in Canada, particularly since the enactment of the Charter of Rights and Freedoms. Indeed, Scott Matthews (2005) uses the example of same-sex marriage in Canada to argue that rights recognitions have the power to shift public perception of controversial topics. His findings were twofold: "First, by framing the issue as one of equal rights, the courts and legislatures induced many Canadians to weigh equality-related considerations more heavily in the formation of opinions on same-sex marriage. Second, legal recognition of same-sex relationships directly persuaded many Canadians that such recognition was legitimate" (843).

There are, however, clear limitations to rights raised by the reproductive justice movement, along with genuine concern that their use could constrain the possibilities for change, or at least the parameters in which it takes place. My intention is not to dismiss these concerns. In fact, in order to use a rights framework effectively, I believe that social movements must be aware of these limitations so that legal or political victories are incremental improvements, rather than ends in themselves.

Thus, although reproductive justice advocates in the United States may see the approach and goals of the pro-choice movement as inherently inadequate and problematic, the pro-choice and reproductive justice movements in Canada are less oppositional in their approach to reproductive rights and health. Indeed, they have already taken on roles as allied movements. In so doing, pro-choice activists in Canada have begun to build far-reaching networks, allying with other social justice groups to situate abortion in a larger project of equality. Although, in Canada, such alliances are by no means new to pro-choice activists, who have long seen abortion as an equality right, the influence of reproductive justice has pushed the boundaries further. Assumptions about the significance of the environment, Indigenous rights, racism, and income inequality are but a few of the issues that can situate the relevance of abortion in a larger social context. This approach has done more than help revitalize abortion rights activism in Canada. An understanding of abortion in context, supported by pro-choice and reproductive justice groups with clear links to the realities of reproduction in a social justice framework, also has the advantage of unravelling the arguments of the anti-abortion movement in important ways.

The anti-abortion movement's ideals are, in many respects, in direct conflict with their strategies. The creation of legislation criminalizing abortion across the world, for instance, has had very clear consequences. When abortion is illegal, women do not suddenly stop needing or wanting to terminate unwanted pregnancies; these procedures just become more dangerous, and the women who attempt to access them, vulnerable (Guttmacher Institute 2015). This is because abortion services do not occur in isolation, and the legalization of abortion or restrictions that surround it often occur in a climate that respects equality and self-determination. Thus, birth control is also more readily available, as is comprehensive sex education, which reduces the overall number of unwanted pregnancies. If the goal of the anti-abortion movement is to prevent abortions, attempting to criminalize the procedure or block access is ineffective, producing undesirable outcomes. Working toward the creation of substantive reproductive freedoms would be a more intuitive route toward the movement's ends, though it will never remove the need for abortion services.

If the anti-abortion movement contends that a reduction in the frequency of abortion is not the goal, and that only a complete ban will do, the means to achieve this end is unclear. It is a goal routed in an idealistic world in which women never find themselves facing unwanted pregnancies. Indeed, emerging strategies of the anti-abortion movement suggest a move away from overt recriminalization and toward shifting women's views of abortion and ensuring that they simply never choose the procedure. Choice, of course, requires options, so this language is misused in this context. Even so, the movement's strategies do not suggest a desire to work toward this end. If banning abortion proves impossible, why not look toward other means of social change so that women have more options to have children? Why not fight for pay equity or a national daycare program, to give women substantive choices? When contextualized, the strategic choices of the anti-abortion movement reveal deeply troubling beliefs about women and their roles in society that underpin calls for a return to traditional family values.

A Canadian Movement

It is important to draw a distinction here between the relationships of the pro-choice and reproductive justice movements in Canada and their US counterparts. The realities of socialized medicine and legal abortion in Canada, in contrast to largely private health care and criminal restrictions on abortion in the United States, have meant that activist groups in these countries have developed in unique ways. The continued legal restrictions on abortion in the United States have led the pro-choice movement in this country to continue to focus its efforts on the legality of abortion, while the decriminalization of abortion in Canada has led to a greater focus on the nature of access across the country. This focus means greater similarities in both strategic focus and goals with the reproductive justice movement in Canada.

Ultimately, an understanding of abortion firmly rooted in women's lived experiences is the only foundation through which to achieve long-standing change in keeping with ideals of equality. The pro-choice and reproductive justice activists in Canada have embraced such an understanding, and each adopt an intersectional approach to the realization of improved abortion services. Unlike *Roe v. Wade*, the landmark case that liberalized abortion laws in the United States, *R. v. Morgentaler* (1988) decriminalized abortion entirely. Although pro-choice groups remain vigilant about the possibility of new restrictions on the procedure, they have moved their focus away from the legality of the procedure toward questions of access. In so doing, pro-choice groups have identified and sought to challenge barriers that impact women as a result of intersecting oppressions (such as their class, race, age, and location). The focus remains on ensuring that women have access to abortion services, as opposed to the expansive goals of the reproductive justice movement, though, as allies, the movements have the potential to work together toward a common end. Indeed, in Canada, this alliance is already evident.

Some in the reproductive justice movement remain wary of individual rights protections, yet the pro-choice movement continues to use these rights claims to advance its cause. I have argued that individual rights should not be understood as undermining more substantive goals of equality. In advancing this claim, I stress the importance of a contextualized understanding of abortion as part of a larger project of women's equality. If rights are understood as tools rather than resolutions, they can be useful in reshaping public opinion. To use rights effectively, however, it is necessary to understand the institutions that regulate them.

After the entrenchment of the Charter, the relationships between the courts and politicians changed. Although legal decisions have been responsible for major changes to the treatment of abortion in the wake of the *Morgentaler* decision, they have overwhelmingly avoided interpreting rights as having a positive character, treating such recognitions as within the purview of governments. At the same time, governments, particularly the federal government, have increasingly offloaded potentially controversial rights debates to the courts. I do not want to suggest that litigation has ceased to be useful for the protection of individual rights, but I do wish to acknowledge the limitations of legal reasoning to create a positive right to abortion in Canada. It is clear that, going forward, governments need to be held accountable for protecting the rights they helped create.

2

Federal Politics and the Supreme Court

Abortion has a long history of federal regulation in Canada. It no longer falls under federal jurisdiction, but it remains a contentious topic of debate in the House of Commons, where the creation of a new law could recriminalize abortion, in whole or in part, at any time, though such a move would be politically dubious. Although no government has attempted to recriminalize abortion since the Mulroney government's failed attempt in the wake of the *Morgentaler* decision, questions about abortion resurface in federal politics every year. Sitting governments, however, have generally responded with avoidance, treating abortion as a controversial and potentially divisive subject rather than as a matter of paramount importance to the status of women as citizens.

The ability of governments to avoid this debate stemmed in no small part from the enactment of the Charter, which changed the relationship between the federal legislature and the House. Emmett Macfarlane (2013, 11) explains: "The arrival of the *Charter* is often described in revolutionary terms, not only in having transformed the judicial and legal system but also in having a significant impact on Canadian political culture." The ensuing "judicialization" of politics has meant that the courts have become a central actor in politics, influencing policies in ways previously thought to be solely the responsibility of legislatures. Whether such a shift is desirable or democratic has been the subject of extensive debate in Canada, with many asserting that the impact of the Charter has been the elevation of legal deliberations, to the detriment of parliamentary dialogue (Hirschl 2004; Morton 1992; Morton and Knopff 2000). Others contend that such a shift has merely created new avenues of political participation for individuals and groups (McLachlin 2001; M. Smith 2002).[1] An exploration of the treatment of abortion by federal institutions following the *Morgentaler* decision, regardless of its impact, reveals an increasing reliance on the courts.

Ever since the Senate narrowly defeated the Mulroney government's proposed abortion legislation in 1991, subsequent governments have been reluctant to discuss abortion. Former Prime Minister Stephen Harper, for instance, went so far as to declare that his government would abstain from any attempts to reopen the abortion debate. By asserting a desire to avoid discussing abortion and outsourcing debates on the matter to the courts, the House has positioned itself as an inappropriate venue through which to discuss women's reproductive rights. Although this may seem like a deeply troubling approach, abortion rights advocates have not been overly critical of it. Their wariness is understandable. When it comes to the issue of abortion being raised in the House, the track record of past governments, as well as those individual MPs, is worrisome, with many MPs committed to an anti-abortion agenda. As such, the decisions of multiple federal governments to avoid discussing abortion are often seen as safeguarding the status quo by tacitly recognizing a negative right to abortion.

The problem with this approach is that it has the troubling side effect of effectively absolving the House of its responsibility to actively participate in safeguarding women's constitutional rights. As a result, citizens are increasingly expected to believe that silence or inaction on abortion is the best they can hope for from their government. The treatment of abortion in federal politics, then, implies that reproductive issues are not weighty political problems but rights questions that have been somehow divorced from the democratic process. The impact of the conspicuous absence of these considerations in the House goes beyond this one case; it also influences public perception of the role of the government more broadly. When abortion is regularly classified as out of bounds for politicians, more appropriately left to the courts to consider, the reality that MPs and governments alike are also bound to uphold the same individual rights guarantees in the Charter quickly gets lost.

Despite these drawbacks, encouraging debates on abortion in Parliament still seems like a risky endeavour.[2] As a result, protecting the access that exists today seems like the only safe option for many. This approach, however, effectively leaves women's reproductive rights in limbo: If the courts lack the inclination or support to create positive rights, then substantial changes to the law are unlikely to happen without political action. And if politicians fail to see themselves as responsible for promoting Charter rights without having their hands forced by the courts, more substantive access is unlikely to result.

Notably, the view that litigation is the most effective means to ensure that women's rights to abortion are recognized often ignores the context in which key rulings were made, while also obscuring the shortcomings of this approach. To be sure, Charter jurisprudence plays an important role in shaping rights rhetoric, influencing public perceptions of rights and, in turn, impacting the responses of politicians to these judgments (Macfarlane 2013, 3). This work is significant, but it creates a risk of selectively interpreting the specific rulings of the court, rendering them more palatable for the public by stressing some elements while overlooking others. Moreover, this view often ignores the drawbacks of framing issues in legal terms, which often require that the claims of social movement actors are adapted or bounded, to ensure their claims have traction in court. The *Morgentaler* decision, and subsequent decisions that helped shape its reach, are clear examples.

R. v. Morgentaler (1988) dramatically altered the landscape of abortion access across the country and is often portrayed as the final battle for women's reproductive rights in Canada. A close reading of the decision, though, reveals that the ruling actually validated some degree of state intervention in pregnancy at the same time that it invalidated the existing abortion law. Indeed, this decision and those that followed in its wake, including *Tremblay v. Daigle*, in which the Court ruled that a fetus has no legal rights, each approached concepts pivotal to abortion rights activism, such as choice and autonomy, in diverse and sometimes disquieting ways. I do not seek to diminish the magnitude of the *Morgentaler* decision in helping to create abortion access, but an exploration of the reasoning and language adopted in this and related rulings contextualizes these decisions, revealing the pivotal role of politicians and social activists in shaping the way we understand these decisions today. Court rulings can be influential, but they are also imperfect. Indeed, were it not for the influence of social activists on members of Parliament and the Senate, the reach of the *Morgentaler* decision would be read much differently than it is today.

By examining how the regulation of abortion by Canadian federal institutions has evolved, this chapter aims to draw attention to the role of the Supreme Court and the federal government in conceptualizing the procedure. Even though the courts are increasingly framed as the appropriate venue through which to challenge, debate, and affirm rights claims, I suggest that confining the sphere of rights discussions to the courts is not only risky but also prevents the realization of a more holistic conception of women's reproductive rights and freedoms. The courts continue to provide a valuable means to have rights claims heard, but they should not be seen as the sole, or even primary, arbiters of rights. Instead, politicians must be accountable to uphold the rights laid down in the Charter. Moreover, we must recognize that the power of rights is more than their ability to force institutions to provide services; their rhetorical strength has the capacity to shift public perceptions of who is an equal citizen, worthy of recognition. An approach to reproductive rights grounded in the broader objectives of reproductive justice demands formal protections such as access, yet the belief that women are equal, and should expect to be treated as such, is equally weighty.

Abortion Politics before 1988

Looking back at the origins of Canada's abortion law, it is obvious that the justifications for restricting access to abortion have changed dramatically over time. Canada's abortion law, like the majority of laws adopted at the time of Confederation, mimicked existing British law, conceived well over a century before. Britain first adopted formal restrictions to abortion in 1803 with Lord Ellenborough's Act, which prohibited certain kinds of abortion after the "quickening," the stage in pregnancy, normally at the beginning of the second trimester, when pregnant women first detect fetal movement (Keown 1988, 15). The law was designed to protect women from what were seen as unsafe medical practices (often associated with midwives) and to safeguard the domain of the medical profession (Gleeson 2011, 217).

In the years that followed, the British act was broadened to include abortion at all stages and by multiple methods, though those performed before the quickening were only seen as felonies and not as destroying a human life (Keown 1988, 18–19). The maximum penalty facing a woman procuring an abortion, or a provider willing to perform one, was life in prison. The goal of these modifications to the existing act, according to John Keown (1988), was primarily to simplify the law, making it more easily enforceable, though these precautions did not have the desired effect. The public did not perceive abortion as a crime, and public sympathy for women seeking abortions made sentencing difficult. The belief that abortion was immoral was not prevalent at the time, when the deaths of young children, as well as death in childbirth, were commonplace.

In 1869, Canada inherited a more recent iteration of Lord Ellenborough's Act when it mimicked Britain's 1861 Offences Against the Person Act, which prohibited abortion without exception (Haussman 2002, 63).[3] This act would remain largely unchanged for a century. Notably, restrictions on other aspects of reproduction were also included later with the creation of Canada's first criminal code in 1892; for example, the sale and promotion of contraception was banned. The relationships between these issues, and their impact on women's lives, warrant our attention. The reality that abortion is often treated as separate from birth control, despite the centrality of both to women's reproductive lives, demonstrates the rhetorical dangers of positioning abortion as a stand-alone issue. Indeed, the impetus for the eventual decriminalization of abortion cannot be understood without first considering the work of activists who legalized birth control.

Dorothy Palmer's work is one such example of the role of contraceptive activism in determining the future of abortion access in Canada. In 1936, Palmer was charged for canvassing her Ontario community of Eastview (now Vanier, a neighbourhood of Ottawa) in order to share information on birth control, despite the laws at the time against disseminating information on contraceptives. Although she was acquitted in 1937 for her intent to serve the public good, this case is notable not primarily for its outcome but for the manner in which contraception was framed in its wake (McLaren and McLaren 1997, 93). In order to endear the public to the notion of birth control, which had thus far been a cause associated with more "radical groups, it was often framed as a tactic to combat economic and racial concerns (ibid., 123).[4] In the period immediately following the Great Depression, the middle classes were encouraged to see birth control as a means to reduce the state's welfare burden if used by lower-class families (a disproportionate number of whom were racial minorities).[5] The new birth control campaigners presented family planning as a way to maintain the status quo rather than encourage what might be seen as immoral behaviour (ibid., 93).[6] In this way, campaigns for contraception became more palatable through assurances that they would leave existing social structures, including traditional gender roles, untouched.

The same desire to protect existing power structures also influenced the evolution of Canada's abortion law. Seventy years after the original law was implemented, an influential British case, *R. v. Bourne* (1939), found that a woman's mental state was grounds to deem abortion a medical necessity. The precedent set in this case suggested that abortion could be permissible if a woman's health, including her mental health, was compromised (Jenson

1992, 24). This ruling afforded physicians some discretion to provide abortions if they judged it necessary to preserve the life or health of the pregnant woman, and created inroads for Canadian doctors in the provision of abortion care. Jane Jenson (1992, 24) explains that, "taking the lead from developments in British law, many Canadian doctors considered the Criminal Code's injunction against 'procuring a miscarriage' inapplicable to abortions performed to save the life of a woman. Such exceptions depended, of course, on their peers and the courts accepting their professional judgment about what was necessary for their patients." However, even with this precedent in place, doctors remained wary of the ambiguity surrounding the meaning of *health* and were alarmed by the potential for legal action. Fearing life imprisonment, many doctors chose not to offer abortion services (Jenson 1992, 25).

In 1969, the Trudeau administration, motivated largely by a desire to protect physicians, made major changes to the Criminal Code (Haussman 2002, 66). The Code was amended to permit abortions only if they were "performed in an accredited or approved hospital and approved by a three-physician therapeutic abortion committee (TAC) from that hospital as necessary to protect the woman's life or health" (Brown and Sullivan 2005, 287).[7] The rationale was the protection from prosecution of medical professionals for instances in which they deemed abortions necessary. Interestingly, physicians rejected the full legalization of "abortion on demand," where a woman would have a right to control her pregnancy (Haussman 2002, 66). Once again, although regulations on reproduction were modified in a manner that would pave the way for women's reproductive rights, the intent was to modify them while maintaining "concepts of hierarchy and scientific and male privilege" (ibid., 67).

Under the new law, TACs operated at the discretion of hospitals, of which only one in five across Canada chose to establish them. Many of those that were in operation were highly discriminatory against certain groups of women (Rebick 2005, 157). For instance, some committees "required the consent of a husband from whom the woman was separated or divorced and the consent of the father where the woman had never been married" (Gavigan 1992, 134). Others, however, chose to simply rubber-stamp the woman's decision. Dr. Carolyn Bennett, a former family physician and now the federal minister of indigenous and northern affairs, spoke about her early career experiences with TACs in an interview, noting that most of the places she worked deferred to a woman's choice to terminate an unwanted pregnancy. "It was just a joke," she said, "in that the family doctor would clean up the pile of applications for termination and they were just passed around the radiology room in the dark and the three radiologists just signed them all."[8]

Ultimately, however, the 1969 amendment to the Criminal Code would be relatively short-lived.[9] A series of legal challenges against the amendment were brought about by the actions of Dr. Henry Morgentaler, a name now synonymous with the fight for women's rights to abortion access. One of these cases would culminate in the 1988 Supreme Court decision that decriminalized abortion in Canada. The decision rested on the violation of women's Charter rights to security of the person owing to the unequal operation of the abortion law. However, comprehension of the magnitude of this case, and its implications for the language of rights that is now fundamental to abortion politics, necessitates a deeper understanding of Morgentaler's path to victory.

Dr. Henry Morgentaler and the Morgentaler Decision

Dr. Henry Morgentaler, a Polish immigrant and survivor of the Auschwitz concentration camp, moved to Montreal in 1950 on a medical scholarship to McGill University. After obtaining his degree, he opened a small family medicine practice in the city. It was there that Morgentaler first encountered women seeking abortion services, women he was legally required to turn away. Without any safe options available, some of the women attempted to self-abort or commit suicide.[10] As a medical professional, Morgentaler felt that turning women away violated his sworn oath to do no harm.[11] He closed down his family practice and set up an abortion clinic.

In 1968, the year his clinic first opened, the conditions under which a legal abortion could be performed were still regulated by the Criminal Code. Nonetheless, his clinic began to provide abortion services in "complete illegality" (FQPN and CFC 2010, 16). Two years later, following the 1969 amendment to the Criminal Code, Morgentaler's clinic was raided and he was arrested, but the charges of "conspiracy to commit abortion" and "procuring abortion" were later dropped because of the "improper use of a search warrant" (Dickens 1976, 230, 232; NAF 2010). Despite the raids, Morgentaler made no attempts to conceal his actions – rather, he broadcasted them: publicly announcing in 1973 that he had performed five thousand abortions (Pelrine 1975, 104). It was clear that the government of Quebec was not sure how to handle Morgentaler's decision to publicly defy the law, initially opting to keep his actions from public attention. They were, however, only able to ignore his activism for so long. Police reentered the Morgentaler Clinic later that same year and arrested Dr. Morgentaler. The resulting court case, now well known in Quebec, led to a surprising non-guilty verdict that both shed light on the changing social climate in the province and foreshadowed Morgentaler's lifelong pursuit of women's rights to abortion access.

The "French Canadian, [and] predominantly Roman Catholic jury" that heard the case consisted of eleven men and only one woman (Pelrine 1975, 93–94, 110). At the time, the social shifts from the Quiet Revolution were still settling in Quebec, and the influence that personal religious beliefs might have on the jury was uncertain. In the end, however, the role of class interests in the jury's decision seemed to prevail. The testimonies from women who had gone to the Morgentaler Clinic to terminate their pregnancies – women often desperate to control their reproduction in the face of poverty – swayed the jury, just as the women seeking abortions had swayed Morgentaler years earlier. Indeed, "class interests were never absent and often quite transparent" in debates on women's rights to bodily autonomy in Quebec during that period (McLaren and McLaren 1997, 141).

The crown promptly appealed the verdict, and the Court of Appeal of Quebec overturned the decision, citing jury error (Arthur 1999). Morgentaler was sentenced to eighteen months in prison. He appealed the decision to the Supreme Court. His appeal, in 1975, was grounded in the dual assertion that the Criminal Code was, in this instance, rendered "inoperative by virtue of the Canadian Bill of Rights," and that he was therefore entitled to use the defence of necessity to defend his actions despite the lower court's dismissal of this claim.[12] Morgentaler further asserted that the "Court of Appeal could not substitute a conviction for an acquittal in a jury trial."[13]

Morgentaler's claim that the Bill of Rights rendered section 251 of the Criminal Code moot was based on guarantees of women's rights to privacy and security of the person under the Canadian Bill of Rights. He argued that section 251 infringed on these rights because its vagueness allowed for unequal treatment before the law. In essence, "since there is a right to abortion under certain conditions without risking criminal penalty, there is a right to a fair hearing thereon in accordance with the principles of fundamental justice established by section 2(e) of the *Bill of Rights*" (Dickens 1976, 237). After all, the government did not require that hospitals form TACs; even when they were assembled, they were neither subject to review nor required to justify their decisions. Further, women were not provided with council before or during their appearance in front of these committees. This arrangement, he argued, denied women equal treatment and due process to access a safe procedure. Morgentaler felt that these restrictions constituted "cruel and unusually treatment" for both women and physicians (ibid.).

In the end, Morgentaler's appeal was rejected, with three of the eight judges dissenting. The dissenting opinion was that the acquittal be restored on the grounds that section 251 would not necessarily trump either section 45 of the Criminal Code, which lays out the nature of criminal accountability for surgical procedures, or the Bourne defence, a precedent from the United Kingdom commonly called the "defence of necessity," which allowed for the performance of an abortion to protect the life and health of a pregnant woman (Tatalovich 1997, 74). The dissenting opinion further stated that the jury was provided with ample evidence to consider on the matter and that the trial judge appropriately left the decision with them (ibid., 238). The majority, however, ruled that section 45 cannot be applied such that it removes criminal liability under section 251, and they did not feel the evidence of necessity presented demonstrated a level of urgency necessary to justify a contravention of the Criminal Code (ibid.).

In the midst of Morgentaler's hearing, public outrage at the court's unusual decision to overturn the verdict of a jury prompted then federal minister of justice Otto Lang to propose a legislative amendment (Dickens 1976, 241). The amendment, commonly known as the Morgentaler Amendment, prevents appeal courts from nullifying a jury verdict. The amendment was ratified, and Morgentaler was released from his incarceration eight months early, but not before he reentered court on new charges.

In 1975, while still in prison, Morgentaler was charged with performing an illegal abortion. He once again employed the defence of necessity, drawing attention to the difficult and occasionally impossible nature of receiving TAC approval. Although the jury was instructed that the defence of necessity could not be used, it nonetheless returned with a verdict of not guilty. The prosecution appealed the ruling, but the Court of Appeal upheld the lower court's verdict, this time finding evidence for the use of necessity as a defence (ibid.). This decision on behalf of the appeal court led then Quebec minister of justice Ronald Basford to set aside Morgentaler's 1973 conviction and order a retrial. Yet again the jury voted to acquit Morgentaler. The next year, 1976, shortly after his release from jail, Morgentaler was charged once again and had to return to court. A jury – again – found him not guilty.

Following Morgentaler's third acquittal, the Parti Québécois took power in Quebec and vowed not to pursue further legal action against him, de facto legalizing abortion in Quebec. The procedure was also funded at this point, with the exception of clinic fees. (Quebec's refusal to fund clinic abortions is discussed in detail in Chapter 3.) These moves by the Quebec legislature strengthened pro-choice activism in the province and seemed to bolster more expansive legal activity by Morgentaler. At the same time, the federal government was making moves to evaluate its new abortion law.

In 1976, in the wake of the Quebec Morgentaler trials and under pressure from "consistent organizing and lobbying by feminists," the federal minister of justice created a Committee on the Operation of the Abortion Law (Rebick 2005, 157). The goal of the committee was to report on whether "the procedure provided in the Criminal Code for obtaining therapeutic abortions [was] operating equitably across Canada" (Badgley 1977, 17). The committee submitted the report, known as the Badgley Report, after its chair, Dr. Robin Badgley, the following year. Its conclusions vindicated Morgentaler's portrayal of TACs in court, demonstrating that "the procedures set out for the operation of the Abortion Law [were] not working equitably across Canada" (ibid., 17). Specifically, it found that unclear standards and social inequity created extreme disparities and delays in access, forcing many women to go to the United States to terminate their pregnancies. According to one feminist legal scholar, the report made apparent what feminists had been aware of since the law was implemented, namely that "in some parts of Canada the liberalized abortion law was a dead letter."[14]

Meanwhile, despite his loss in the Supreme Court, Morgentaler had made a great deal of progress in Quebec and decided to expand his practice to meet demand outside the province. In 1983, Morgentaler opened an abortion clinic in Toronto with doctors Leslie Smoling and Robert Scott, and another clinic in Winnipeg, also with the help of Dr. Scott. According to Ellen Kruger, founder of the Manitoba branch of the Canadian Abortion Rights Action League (CARAL), "Henry came here [to Winnipeg] because we had an NDP government" (quoted in Rebick 2005, 164). Despite the more favourable political climate, the clinic was raided three times – once in 1983 and twice in 1985 (Rebick 2005, 165). The pro-choice movement expected then attorney general Roland Penner to intervene, but he claimed that he "could not interfere with the role of the police" (ibid., 165). Penner refused to involve himself despite the disturbing manner in which the raids were carried out. Kruger recounted witnessing a raid, recalling "the horror of them parading seven women out and arresting them, women who had just had abortions, three of them still in recovery. It was horrible, horrible" (ibid.).

The Toronto clinic was also raided in 1983, and Morgentaler, Scott, and Smoling were charged. The doctors employed the same defence that Morgentaler had used in Quebec, challenging the constitutional validity of section 251 of the Criminal Code (NAF 2010). As in Quebec, the jury refused to convict the doctors, and they were acquitted.[15] The Ontario attorney general promptly appealed the verdict. In 1985, the Ontario Court of Appeal set aside the acquittal and ordered a retrial. The doctors appealed the decision to the Supreme Court of Canada.[16] The Court agreed to hear their appeal, making this Morgentaler's second appearance in the Supreme Court to fight the constitutionality of section 251 of the Criminal Code. This time, however, would be different, because new tools were at his disposal.

The Charter of Rights and Freedoms, introduced in 1982, guaranteed extensive individual rights to Canadian citizens, dramatically changing the tools available to the women's movement to secure change. Of course, these changes were hard won, as the original Charter was not designed with women's equality in mind. Feminist groups mobilized to ensure that the wording of the Charter would be favourable to women's interests. They successfully had the wording of section 129 changed from "non-discrimination" to "equality rights" in order to "emphasize that equality means something more than non-discrimination" (Morton 1992, 111). They were less successful in altering the wording of sections 7 and 12. Section 7 guarantees that "everyone has the right to life, liberty and security of the person and the right not to be deprived thereof except in accordance with the principles of fundamental justice," while section 12 guarantees that "everyone has the right not to be subjected to any cruel and unusual treatment or punishment." Despite lobbying to have "everyone" changed to "every person" to ensure that fetal rights could not be read in above women's rights, these sections were not changed. CARAL opposed the final draft of the Charter because it potentially threatened women's rights to access abortion (ibid., 112). Despite these shortcomings, never before had individual interests had such force in Canadian policies. The significance of this framework was as yet unknown in Canada, but activists, including Morgentaler, had the advantage of drawing from the experience of the United States to develop a persuasive case.

The landmark Supreme Court decision in *Roe v. Wade*, which legalized abortion under certain parameters in the United States, was argued using the Fourteenth Amendment, which guarantees individuals the right to privacy. Although a woman's privacy was guaranteed in her first trimester, in the second and third trimesters, "the state would demonstrate an increasing 'compelling interest' in regulating abortion procedures, based on the mother's health in the second trimester and that of the fetus in the third" (Haussman 2005, 47). Using a similar defence, Morgentaler, Smoling, and Scott argued that the requirement that a woman must seek permission from a therapeutic abortion committee before having access to a legal abortion violated her security of the person. The Court agreed, ruling that the constitutionally guaranteed right to personal liberty and security of the person included women, but it stopped short of acknowledging women's full bodily autonomy. Macfarlane (2013, 145) explains that "the four justices in the plurality wrote decisions that rest, on the surface at least, on procedural grounds, avoiding the substantive issue of whether women have the right to an abortion."

The ruling was split five to two, with four separate judgments. The Court's decision did hint at considerations of abortion as necessary for women's equality but fell short of validating these claims. Chief Justice Brian Dickson and Justice Antonio Lamer famously wrote, "Forcing a woman, by threat of criminal sanction, to carry a foetus to term unless she meets certain criteria unrelated to her own priorities and aspirations, is a profound interference with a woman's body and thus a violation of security of the person."[17] Justice Bertha Wilson further stated that treating women as a means to an end, serves to deprive them of their "essential humanity."[18]

The case struck down the existing regulations on abortion in Canada, yet it also reinforced a troubling hierarchy. The ruling validated the interest of the state in the fetus and "invited Parliament to limit women's access to abortion (and indeed other medical procedures) in the later stages of pregnancy" (Gavigan 1992, 126–27). In response, Shelley Gavigan, a prominent legal scholar at Osgoode Hall Law School, warned that the *Morgentaler* decision was "fragile, incomplete and contradictory" (1992, 126).

For many, the success of Morgentaler, Smoling, and Scott signified the final victory for the pro-choice movement, guaranteeing Canadian women the inalienable right to control their reproduction.[19] A careful reading of the decision, however, suggests that this is not the case. The Court did not validate any positive rights to abortion in its ruling. Moreover, the ruling in *R. v.*

Morgentaler (1988) invited Parliament to respond with new legislation, and the Mulroney government obliged. Ultimately, the way events unfolded in the years that followed the decision would solidify its significance and alter public perception of its reach.

The Mulroney Government

At the time of the *Morgentaler* decision, Brian Mulroney's Progressive Conservative government held a substantial majority in the House of Commons. In response to the Court's invitation to create a new law to regulate abortion, the Mulroney government moved swiftly to create new criminal restrictions on the procedure. Indeed, the prime minister announced that "the federal government would not leave this dimension of Canadian life unregulated" on the same day the decision was given (Brodie 1992, 64). Almost thirty years after the fact, it remains the only federal government in Canada to have attempted to draft such a law.

Janine Brodie (1992, 67) explains that, as Mulroney began the process of creating a new bill to regulate abortion, it became clear that his caucus was divided, and so he announced that "a new abortion law, like the capital punishment issue before it, would be put to a free vote in the House of Commons." This decision meant that the MPs would be allowed to vote according to their conscience, a move Brodie calls "a tacit admission on the part of the government that abortion was a moral issue to be decided by individual conscience" (ibid.).

To deal with the contentious issue "as painlessly and quietly as possible," (Gray 1988, 327) the government suggested the adoption of a new procedure:

> A complex motion which would have the MPs vote on the abortion issue in three stages. The final stage would be to debate a motion that would suspend the normal rules of debate and create special rules for this subject. If the motion was adopted, MPs would then vote on a three-option abortion resolution. The options were to take a moderately pro-choice route, which the government preferred, to be entirely pro-choice, or to be moderately antiabortion. After the vote was tallied, the government would draft legislation expressing the most popular of the three options. (ibid., 328)

The proposed legislation, which would have been at the heart of this debate, favoured a gestational approach like that adopted by the United States, "in which access to abortion would be relatively free during early pregnancy and more restrictive later" (Brodie 1992, 68). It also contained two conflicting amendments, one prioritizing fetal rights, and the other women's rights.

This new strategy was met with immediate resistance from the House, which felt it risked compromising Canadian democracy by altering the nature of parliamentary process to address this one issue. In response, MPs stood fast against the motion, refusing to grant the government the unanimous consent necessary to implement the exceptional procedure (ibid.). Declassified federal cabinet documents reveal that this opposition came at a time when Mulroney believed "the debate was too wrenching and divisive to be allowed to continue much longer" (Tromp 2013). The government quickly moved on to a new approach.

The next attempt at introducing legislation occurred late in the summer of 1988 when the government, rather than introduce new legislation, opted to take the pulse of the House by once again introducing its restricted abortion bill, but without amendments, to allow MPs to voice their concerns and introduce amendments (Brodie 1992, 69). The speeches that followed demonstrated strong divisions along both party and gendered lines. Conservative MPs, all of whom were male, delivered the majority of anti-abortion speeches. Although women made up only a small percentage of the representatives in the House (holding 22 of 295 seats), Brodie notes that "some 30% of the women sitting in the House gave speeches and all but one were uncompromisingly pro-choice" (69). Indeed, after an extensive debate in which five amendments to the government's resolution were tabled in the House, this gendered divide reasserted itself. The most egregiously anti-abortion of the proposed amendments was the Mitges amendment, "which would have prohibited abortion except when two doctors agreed that continuing the pregnancy would endanger the life of the mother" (86). In an unprecedented move, the women in the House, all of whom were present, voted as a block to strike down the amendment, which would have passed without this action.

In the end, there was no agreement in the House. The pro-choice MPs were unsatisfied with serious restrictions on the procedure, whereas the anti-choice MPs felt the restrictions did not go far enough; the bill and all five amendments were voted down (Brodie 1992, 87). Despite this failure, the Mulroney government had not made its last attempt at creating a new abortion law. Indeed, the summer of 1989 included two crucial legal decisions, namely *Tremblay v. Daigle* and *Borowski v. Canada*, which put increasing pressure on them to pass a new law (ibid., 96).

Testing the Limits of the *Morgentaler* Decision

As the federal government struggled to find a solution to the "intolerable" legal void left in the wake of Morgentaler (Tromp 2013), the limitations of the decision were being tested in court. The most pressing issues that the decision left largely unresolved were the extent of men's rights over their potential future offspring and the status of fetal rights. The first, and most well-known, case to address these issues in the Supreme Court was *Tremblay v. Daigle*.

Following the *Morgentaler* decision, men in four provinces (British Columbia, Manitoba, Ontario, and Quebec) attempted to secure injunctions against their pregnant former partners to prevent them from accessing legal abortion services.[20] Of the four, only two injunctions were granted and only one went to court. The case of Quebec citizens Jean-Guy Tremblay and his former girlfriend, Chantal Daigle, was widely followed and changed the course of abortion politics in Canada.

In 1989, Tremblay was granted an interlocutory injunction to prevent his former girlfriend, Daigle, from accessing a legal abortion. He sought the injunction on the basis that "under Quebec law a foetus has a right to life and a potential father has a right of veto over a woman's decision to have an abortion" (Greschner 1990, 656). These claims were based on his own interpretations of the law, which he felt guaranteed a fetus the right to life and, by extension, provided a potential future father rights to prevent the woman carrying his child from seeking legal abortion services (these rights were not explicitly stated in either the Quebec or Canadian charter). Importantly, since injunctions are intended only to ensure "substantive rights and neither the right to life of the foetus nor the potential father's rights could be found in Quebec legislation," the granting of the injunction itself was not explicitly legal (ibid., 656–57).

To the horror of the feminist movement, the Quebec lower court ruled in Tremblay's favour, finding that "a foetus is a 'human being' under the Quebec *Charter of Human Rights and Freedoms* and therefore enjoys a 'right to life' under s. 1," and that this right should prevail over those guaranteed to the woman under the charter.[21] The court's judgment rested, in part, on Daigle's actions before becoming pregnant. It was revealed in her testimony that, shortly before becoming pregnant, she had stopped taking birth control pills at Tremblay's insistence (Kaposy and Downie 2008, 298–99). The court did not take into account the implications of the physical and emotional abuse Daigle suffered at the hands of her partner on her ability to exercise reasonable judgment.[22] The court interpreted the fact that she had stopped taking birth control as reflective of Daigle's desire to become pregnant, a desire it saw as negating her right to bodily autonomy.

Daigle appealed her case all the way to the Supreme Court, but although the Court agreed to hear the case, the time elapsed since the beginning of the injunction continued to push her unwanted pregnancy along, increasing the risk of harm in termination. Daigle decided to travel to the United States to access an abortion before the trial was over. Although her actions effectively rendered the Court's decision in her particular case moot, the Supreme Court decided to rule on the case "in order to resolve the important legal issue raised so that the situation of women in the position in which Ms. Daigle found herself could be clarified."[23]

Daigle's defence was rooted in the "irreparable psychological and moral harm" she felt that continuing her pregnancy would have. She maintained that Tremblay's sole motivation in pursuing the case was to "maintain his hold" over her.[24] She wished never to see him again and had no desire to raise a child in a violent environment.[25] The Supreme Court accepted her argument and ruled in her favour, overturning the rulings of the lower courts. The Court found that the Quebec charter "does not display any clear intention on the part of its framers to consider the status of a foetus" and that, "if the legislature had wished to accord a foetus the right to life, it is unlikely that it would have left the protection of this right in such an uncertain state."[26] It was this landmark case that found that the fetus has no legal status in Canada.

Although the precedent set in the case has since been interpreted as a validation of women's autonomy, a consideration of its impact on the social climate is necessary. Gavigan (1992, 136) describes the general sense of defeat that stemmed from this case, and previous litigation relating to abortion, particularly "the clear empathy expressed in many of the cases for the men, especially the husbands, especially by the male judiciary." Activists also took heed of the fact that the Supreme Court judgment did not "proclaim her [Daigle's] freedom," choosing instead to base their decision on "the failure of the legislative assembly to grant the specific rights asserted by Tremblay" (ibid., 636). The flaw in Daigle's victory, in legal terms, was that it failed to recognize her rights, focusing instead on procedural concerns. Moreover, the dismissal of her own reasoning, specifically her desire to be disassociated from her abusive former partner, and the power relationships at play in the decision, were an affront. The Court's decision to effectively ignore the allegations of the abuse that Daigle had suffered in formulating its ruling sent a clear message to women in similar situations across the country:

Domestic abuse was not considered an important issue, and certainly not a strong legal defense. The fact that Daigle *chose* to stay in an abusive relationship was presented as unproblematic.[27]

The Daigle case was deeply disturbing for many Canadian women and motivated extensive pro-choice mobilization. Donna Greschner (1990, 755) attempted to capture the mood surrounding the case in Quebec when she said, "Women followed every move of Tremblay and the courts, anguished with [Daigle], talked amongst ourselves late at night about the pain and horror she must be feeling, concurred with each other that she should ignore the court injunction, and participated in some of the largest pro-choice demonstrations ever held in Canada as a sign of our support." Ultimately, despite the troubling shortfalls of the case, the pro-choice movement came to stress the significance of the ruling, turning the focus from the Court's treatment of Daigle to the precedent, which, as the movement framed it, further confirmed women's rights to abortion access.

Another noteworthy case in this context occurred almost a decade later. Attempts to control women's reproduction through litigation have not been restricted to women wishing to terminate their pregnancies; the rights of women choosing to carry their pregnancies to term have also been in dispute. The case of a pregnant Manitoban woman with a drug addiction is perhaps the most infamous. In *Winnipeg Child and Family Services (Northwest Area) v. D.F.G.* (1997), the group in question was seeking legal backing to allow it to have a pregnant woman incarcerated against her will, to prevent her from consuming drugs that could harm the development of her fetus. Although the Supreme Court ultimately ruled that "an addicted woman could not be detained against her will in order to protect the health interests of her fetus" (Kaposy and Downie 2008, 300), the ruling was not unanimous. One justice dissented, arguing that "once a woman has chosen not to have an abortion and to continue her pregnancy, she must be responsible for the foetus's well-being, and the state may justifiably act to ensure the foetus's health if the woman cannot or will not do so" (ibid.). Chris Kaposy and Jocelyn Downie correctly point out the problematic assumption on which this reasoning is based, namely that "women who continue to be pregnant must have rejected the abortion option" or that the decision to remain pregnant requires the forfeit of bodily autonomy (ibid.).

Although far from an exhaustive list of litigation, the above cases are often cited as pivotal moments in the pursuit of women's reproductive rights. To be sure, each has helped validate women's claims to bodily autonomy. However, when evaluating the role of litigation in promoting rights claims, it is important to evaluate them with clear reference to the social contexts in which they were interpreted, and to avoid overstating their role in bringing about change. By looking at the specific wording of these decisions, including dissenting opinions, we gain insight into the grounds on which rulings were made and the pervasive views about women's reproduction that underlie them.

Problematic understandings of choice and autonomy are present in each of the cases discussed above. The notion that women must forfeit their autonomy as soon as they become pregnant, regardless of whether they choose to carry the pregnancy to term, suggests an unsettling interpretation of both concepts. Moreover, none of these cases actually validated a positive right to abortion access. That many of these cases have been read as if they do is a result of concerted social movement activism rather than of the cases themselves. Such troubling understandings of women's place in society reveal deeply rooted views of women's roles and the fear associated with their equality – views clearly illustrated by the man who once served as the figurehead for fetal rights in Canada: Joe Borowski.

When Morgentaler was in court with the Ontario government, in the early stages of the case that would decriminalize abortion in Canada, a would-be challenger was also fighting to take on the Criminal Code in court. Joe Borowski, a former MLA for the Saskatchewan New Democratic Party (NDP), was in his home province arguing for public standing to challenge Canada's abortion regulations. Borowski asserted that the TACs created by Trudeau's 1969 Criminal Code amendment were too lenient because the fetus had a "right to life."[28] His case was shifted between courts, owing to uncertainty about which court should be trying the case, and was appealed numerous times. In 1981, his appeal reached the Supreme Court – but not to try the case itself; rather, Borowski had to appeal to the highest court in an attempt to secure standing.

The issue of standing was central to his case, as Borowski, neither a woman nor a doctor, was not directly affected by abortion policies. In a surprise ruling, the Court found, with a vote of seven to two, that Borowski did have standing. Justice Ronald Martland wrote for the majority, validating Borowski's ability to bring the case forward on the grounds that those who were directly affected by it (i.e., women, physicians, and hospitals) were unlikely to challenge a law that protected them from criminal sanctions (Morton 1992, 102). Justice Martland also found, foreshadowing cases like that of *Tremblay v. Daigle*, that the partners of women seeking abortions would be unable to make it through the court system before their claims were rendered moot through either abortion or birth, and that a fetus, whom the defendant argued was the most interested party, could not speak for itself (ibid.). The dissenting opinion of Chief Justice Bora Laskin on Borowski's standing was that "mere distaste has never been a ground upon which to seek the assistance of a court."[29]

With his standing officially approved, Borowski's case was promptly retried. The lower courts dismissed his claims and, once again, his case was appealed all the way to the Supreme Court. When his appeal finally reached the Court in 1989, the Court refused to hear it on the grounds that the *Tremblay v. Daigle* ruling had rendered it moot.

Borowski's case, had it been tried by the Supreme Court, could have significantly changed the landscape of abortion in Canada today. The fact that the case was untried was simply a matter of timing. Borowski saw fetuses as highly vulnerable, innocent members of society, and as the ultimate underdogs – an opinion rooted in deeply troubling views of women. One particular memo he sent to members of his ministry staff exemplifies his sexist views. In it, he urged his staff members to withhold their support from an organization that funded abortion clinics: "'We are being asked to be accomplices in this medieval act of barbarism,' read the memo, by 'forcing our doctors and nurses to commit murder ... so a handful of cheap, third-rate tramps (and also some good women) can escape the consequences of their actions'" (quoted in Morton 1992, 66).

When the Court ruled that fetal rights had no legal standing in Canada and effectively denied Borowski a federal stage, the pro-choice movement breathed a sigh of relief. Although these victories were hard won, they were far from complete. The Supreme Court had struck down section 251 of the Criminal Code but had stopped short of declaring that women had a right to abortion, expecting the House to create new legislation. Likewise, although rulings such as that of *Tremblay v. Daigle* did not recognize fetal rights claims, they left the House room to do so. Nonetheless, these victories were more significant than the pro-choice movement had dared to hope, and they motivated further mobilization. The losses for the anti-abortion movement were, however, devastating. These decisions were playing out in Court as the House struggled to find an acceptable way to approach the creation of a new abortion law. The pressure on the Mulroney government to impose new restrictions on abortion, and to engage with the anti-abortion language in a way that the courts were increasingly unwilling to, was mounting.

In the wake of the Supreme Court's ruling in *Morgentaler*, the Conservative caucus set out to create a new abortion bill – one it hoped would represent "the party's pro-choice, moderate, and pro-life factions" (Brodie 1992, 97). Unfortunately, any nuance in the legislation, including the use of varying restrictions by gestational age, pleased no one and was particularly problematic for those who held that "life began at conception" (97). Bill C-43, presented by the government on November 3, 1989, was met with resistance from all sides. The bill would once again ban abortion in the Criminal Code, but with exceptions to allow doctors to perform abortions at their discretion should they determine that the woman's health, defined loosely as her "physical, mental and psychological health," were at risk because of the pregnancy (98). In sum, these changes would have "recriminalized abortion unless procedures were performed by a doctor and the life and/or health of the mother were threatened" (Overby, Tatalovich, and Studlar 1998, 383).

On the second vote, cabinet MPs were required to side with the party to pass the bill, though backbenchers were allowed a free vote. The gendered alliance that defeated the Mitges amendment was nowhere to be found.[30] The bill passed with a vote of 164 to 114 and went to committee (Brodie 1992, 99). Despite vehement protest from pro-choice and anti-abortion advocates alike, the government dissuaded the committee from altering the bill, which would have threatened the balance it struck between meeting the "requirements of the Morgentaler decision and the state's interest in protecting the foetus" (107–8). On its third and final vote on May 29, 1990, the bill passed with a vote of 140 to 131.

Bill C-43 moved on to the Senate for its final vetting. In the meantime, abortion providers across Canada began to resign in fear of the impending criminal sanctions they might face. The predictions of the pro-choice movement, "that the mere threat of criminal prosecution would deter many doctors from performing abortions and thereby cause needless delays as well as denying access to women in many regions of the country," were becoming a reality (Brodie 1992, 111). Anti-abortion groups had "remained silent" on the impact of this new bill on doctors, but during committee hearings "they now readily admitted that they would try to persuade women, like-minded doctors, and ordinary citizens to lay charges against doctors performing abortions" (112). Their actions challenged the assurances made by then justice minister Kim Campbell that the law would not impact physicians. After more hearings and deeply troubling reports of the impact that the bill, which had not yet been passed, was already having on access, it went to a vote on January 31, 1991. The Senate, still deeply divided on the legislation, tied with a vote of forty-three to forty-three, which constituted a defeat.

This monumental decision made Bill C-43 "the first government bill that the Senate had defeated in thirty years" (115).

The government made no further moves to present a new bill. Both the pro-choice and anti-abortion movements declared victory. Although the anti-abortion movement felt the defeat provided it with a clean slate "to bring forth good legislation that will protect the *pre-born* child," the pro-choice movement saw its defeat as "an affirmation of women's rights" (Brodie 1992, 116, emphasis mine). Since the Mulroney government's attempt to find a compromise on an issue that both pro-choice and anti-abortion groups understood as a matter of life and death, no government has attempted – at least not overtly – to engage with the abortion debate. Over time, this inaction has reaffirmed the status quo and rendered any future attempts at legislating restrictions to the procedure difficult. No government has taken the risk to their mass appeal of attempting to engage with such a deeply divisive issue.

In the decades after the *Morgentaler* decision, the belief that abortion is a woman's right has grown (Environics Institute 2010, 6; Herman 1994, 268). Access to abortion services is legal and, in many areas, widely accessible. The normalization of these services has come, in large part, from the policy vacuum surrounding the issue, which allowed social movement activists to structure the discourse on abortion. The view that access to abortion is a right is widespread but by no means secure. Nonetheless, the anti-abortion movement has not been silenced by the change in climate; rather, it has changed tactics from overt offence to stealth.

The Pro-life Caucus

Following multiple losses in court and growing acceptance of the view that women have a right to safe and legal abortion services, anti-abortion advocates in the federal government, in line with their social movement counterparts, changed their approach to legislative action against abortion. Initially, advocates pushed for recognition of fetal rights in an effort to capitalize on Charter guarantees. Although these claims are still present in Canada, they are often perceived as resolved through *Tremblay v. Daigle* and unlikely to withstand Charter scrutiny. Moreover, the popularity of this approach has dwindled. Anti-abortion advocates have learned that overt attacks on the morality of women and their place in society were often alienating to those who might join the movement, and so the once central role of such an approach in the debate has diminished (Saurette and Gordon 2013). Nonetheless, both fetal rights and an apparent desire to protect women now characterize federal engagement with abortion, often spearheaded by the so-called pro-life caucus.

Former MPs Keith Martin (Reform Party), Garry Breitkreuz (Conservative), and Ken Epp (Conservative) have all been part of this secretive group. After their party's electoral victory in 1984, Progressive Conservative MPs organized the caucus with the intention to protect "the right to life of a child" (Farney 2009, 247). The caucus held weekly meetings, attended by twelve to fifteen backbencher, all of whom, notably, were male. Indeed, MPs who took anti-abortion stances claimed to do so because they were fathers (ibid.). The caucus has since expanded to include members of both the Conservative and Liberal Parties, though its exact composition is unclear because it remains a guarded organization. The New Democratic Party, Bloc Québécois, and Green Party all run on platforms of choice and do not have any known members in the caucus.

Both pro-choice and anti-abortion organizations have attempted to monitor who might be part of this caucus. A list of anti-choice MPs compiled by the Abortion Rights Coalition of Canada in 2006 identifies a total of 112 overtly anti-abortion MPs, up from 100 after the 2006 election (ARCC 2006a). Anti-abortion MPs are defined as those who "had an anti-choice voting record, or had publicly spoken at or attended events organized by anti-choice groups, or had publicly stated they are 'pro-life' or would support abortion only in limited circumstances." Importantly, an anti-abortion stance does not necessarily signify membership in the pro-life caucus. MPs who stated an anti-abortion stance but said they "would not vote to restrict abortion," and those with uncertain stances, do not appear on the list (ibid.). The current pro-life caucus is likely to have fewer, if any, Liberal members in the aftermath of Justin Trudeau's 2015 victory because of his party's firm pro-choice stance. That said, the exact composition of the caucus remains speculative.

Even though no government has since attempted to legislate the procedure, back benchers have made more than forty-five unsuccessful attempts (since 1988) to introduce bills meant to restrict or re-criminalize abortion (ARCC 2012). None of these motions passed, but their changing content illuminated the evolving rhetorical strategies that anti-abortion MPs employ, reflecting those of the Canadian anti-abortion movement at large. Over time, these bills have changed in character, from clear challenges to the legality of abortion and women's rights to bills that suggest a more woman-friendly treatment of abortion rooted in concerns for women's health and equality, founded in scientific facts rather than religious conviction.

In 1997, the same year as the Winnipeg Child and Family Services (Northwest Area) group went to court seeking to detain a pregnant woman to ensure she did not endanger her fetus by taking drugs, Reform MP Keith Martin proposed a bill that would have imposed criminal charges against pregnant women for fetal endangerment if their lifestyle choices had a negative impact on their fetus (e.g., alcohol abuse, drug use) (Bennett 2008, 58). Similar bills are currently in place in the United States. As of 2013, four states (Wisconsin, Minnesota, Oklahoma, and South Dakota) all have "laws specifically granting authorities the power to confine pregnant women for substance abuse," and "many other states use civil-confinement, child-protection or assorted criminal laws to force women into treatment programs or punish them for taking drugs" (Eckholm 2013). The consequences of these bills have been disastrous both for women's rights and pregnancy outcomes. In 2011, the American College of Obstetricians and Gynecologists affirmed that "incarceration and threat of incarceration have proved to be ineffective in reducing the incidence of alcohol or drug abuse" and that these laws were actually discouraging women from seeking prenatal care that would otherwise help them to avoid complications from substance abuse during pregnancy (ibid.). If the goal of such a bill is to promote fetal health, it would have achieved the opposite had it been ratified.

In April 2002, Conservative MP Garry Breitkreuz called for a new definition of *human being* in the Criminal Code, "to see if the law needs to be amended to provide protection to fetuses and to designate a fetus/embryo as a human being" (Bennett 2008, 58). A new version of this bill made its way into Parliament in 2012 when Conservative MP Stephen Woodworth introduced a motion (Motion 312) to study the concept of human life as treated in the Criminal Code, calling for a committee to assess "what medical evidence exists to demonstrate that a child is or is not a human being before the moment of complete birth?" A vote of 203 to 91 defeated the bill. These attempts reflect an attempt to decontextualize and depoliticize the impact of reproduction on women's lives by exploring reproduction in apparently neutral terms. In this way, scientific facts are presented as a means to discuss abortion without reopening the abortion debate. Most importantly, it suggests that such work should not be seen as an attack on women's rights.

In other instances, women's rights have been positioned as central to calls to restrict abortion. In 2010, Conservative MP Rod Bruinooge introduced a bill to prevent "coerced abortion." Bruinooge stressed that his bill would not reopen the abortion debate or impact existing levels of access, but it would simply "make it a crime to threaten or intimidate a woman into abortion"

(Delacourt 2010b). In a similar vein, in 2012, Conservative MP Mark Warawa attempted to introduce a bill that would ban sex-selective abortion, calling on the House to "condemn discrimination against females occurring through sex-selective pregnancy termination" (Galloway 2012). Warawa was not able to proceed with the motion after a decision by a subcommittee but vowed to continue to "keep speaking out about 'gendercide' outside of Parliament" (Chase 2013). These bills attempt to reframe their goals as woman-friendly, even feminist in nature, without addressing the actual implications of the restrictions they propose. These bills also reflect the changing rhetoric of the anti-abortion movement and its efforts to reframe its attempts to criminalize the behaviour of pregnant women as feminist.

Amid calls for legislation to regulate abortion that is female-centric or strictly medical, calls for fetal rights are also present. Several overt attempts at establishing fetal rights were made in March 2004 and November 2007 by Conservative MPs Garry Breitkreuz and Ken Epp respectively. Both acts would have made it "an offence to injure, cause the death of or attempt to cause the death of a child before or during its birth while committing or attempting to commit an offence against the mother."[31] These proposals did not take into account the status of women during their pregnancies. Notably, Epp's so-named Unborn Victims of Crime Act made no attempts to protect women from violence while pregnant, which is a serious concern, particularly in domestic violence situations. Moreover, there is no evidence that such legislation would prevent violent acts or bring about other beneficial outcomes (ARCC 2008). Identical legislation in the United States has been opposed on the grounds that it is "a flawed response to violence against women" (Mans 2003–4, 304–5).

Thus, abortion has been largely ignored in federal politics since the Mulroney government, and the status quo of a federal-policy vacuum has persisted. Although a determined contingent of the previous government, under Harper, continued to press for legislation to restrict access, they did so amid Harper's regular declarations that he would not seek to reopen the abortion debate and that his government would not create new legislation. Of course, the implication was that inaction should be satisfactory, even though the actions of individual anti-abortion representatives and the negligence of his government threatened existing levels of access in Canada.

The Harper Government

In his bid to become prime minister, and during his subsequent years in office, Stephen Harper consistently reiterated his vow that a Conservative government under him would never endorse anti-abortion legislation (Mayeda and Raj 2011). In so doing, he attempted to distance his administration from conflicts associated with social conservatism that could cost him support. Despite this approach, controversy plagued his administration and the nature of his government's approach to women's reproductive health came under repeated attack.

In June 2010, Canada hosted the G8 summit, an annual meeting of world leaders representing eight of the world's most powerful economic countries, to discuss prominent economic and political issues. The Harper administration announced its plans to take up the focus of past summits on maternal, newborn, and child health in developing countries (Office of the Prime Minister 2011). Exactly what was meant by *maternal health* was inexplicit, and it was unclear whether it included abortion. Pressure for the government to clarify its stance on abortion increased when Foreign Affairs Minister Lawrence Cannon claimed that the initiative did "not deal in any way, shape or form with family planning." He continued, "The purpose of this [initiative] is to be able to save lives" (Clark 2010). In response to the public outcry that ensued, Harper made attempts at damage control, stating that the government would not be "closing doors against any options, including contraception" (CBC News 2010b). Notwithstanding these vague assurances, the government eventually adopted the definition of the World Health Organization, which defines maternal health as "the health of women during pregnancy, childbirth and the postpartum period" (WHO 2012a). This definition does not explicitly list contraception and abortion services, yet they are by no means precluded by it. In fact, the World Health Organization lists "unsafe abortion" as one of the major direct causes of maternal morbidity and mortality (ibid.).

Despite Harper's assurances that his government supported women's health and rights issues, his Conservatives failed to include abortion in either category. This deliberate omission demonstrates their attempts to depoliticize the procedure, denying its significance to women's health and equality. The significance of this move for social movement activists working to improve abortion access worldwide soon became apparent. Conservative senator Nancy Ruth, for example, warned representatives of international aid groups who showed up in Ottawa in the weeks preceding the G8 to "shut the fuck up on [abortion]," lest there be more backlash against women's groups (Delacourt 2010a).[32]

One of the most notable cases of anti-abortion MPs speaking out in recent years is that of Conservative MP Brad Trost, who was recorded speaking to a Saskatchewan anti-abortion organization, congratulating the group on its part in cutting funding to International Planned Parenthood, which had been awaiting news of its funding for over a year and assumed that it been cut off (CBC News 2011). The day after the story broke in the media, Dimitri Soudas, director of communications for the Conservative Party, announced that the government would, in fact, be funding the organization, though it was awarded only $6 million of the proposed $18 million grant (Payton 2011). Soudas made it clear, however, that abortion was not part of the government's "funding criteria," meaning that the organization can work with Canadian funds only in countries where abortion is highly restricted or illegal (ibid.).

It is apparent that the Harper administration continued to push anti-abortion policies quietly, at least through international policy, backtracking only when exposed. It is this careful approach, which attempts to placate anti-abortion groups with small victories while designating support to countries that deny women's rights to abortion, that had many worried. Numerous interviewees expressed concern about the use of stealth tactics by the Harper government. Abby Lippman, a professor of epidemiology at McGill University, observed, "[Harper has] certainly already shown his muscle in not funding groups that are pro-access, pro-choice, whether they are in Canada or outside of Canada."[33] Specifically, she noted the "whittling away at the funding of groups that are progressive in all ways." This trend of removing the foundational institutions supporting women's rights seemed to be part of a process of setting the stage for more dramatic change, possibly with the eventual goal of some degree of recriminalization of abortion. Catherine Megill (2011), a former abortion clinic employee in both Canada and the United States, working toward a degree in medicine at McGill University at the time I interviewed her, echoed these views: "What they have been able to do by cutting funding to groups will do a lot more [than an overt attack on abortion]."[34]

These cases demonstrate the impossibility of the Harper administration's alleged neutrality on abortion; because the realization of abortion access is possible only with active support, the Harper government's inaction was neither neutral nor progressive. At a minimum, access to abortion services requires funding and political backing, as the withholding of either compromises women's equality. Thus, the removal of funding from local and international aid agencies and a failure to acknowledge the importance of abortion for women's equality cannot be constructed as neutrality – rather, they are demonstrative of a backlash against women's hard-won rights to bodily autonomy.

In a 2011 interview, Michelle Robidoux, manager of the Ontario Coalition of Abortion Clinics, stressed that anti-abortion groups "have access to this [the Harper] government in a way that they probably have not had for some time in previous governments."[35] Indeed, the empowerment felt by anti-abortion groups and individuals because of the Harper administration was repeatedly noted by the people I interviewed. For example, shortly after disclosure by the Harper Government that abortion would not be included in the G8's initiative on maternal, newborn, and child health, a representative of the FQPN related the story of Cardinal Marc Ouellet, who was quoted in reference to a discussion of abortion in the case of rape as saying, "There is already a victim [the woman]; must there be another one [the fetus]?" (CBC News 2010a). A representative of FQPN suggested that "the reason he [Outlette] felt comfortable talking so publicly about it was that he sensed an opening in Ottawa that he had never sensed before."[36] Under Harper, anti-abortion sentiment was allowed to flourish, and though the Conservative Party lacks a monopoly on this viewpoint, as is evidenced by the members of the pro-life caucus, they are nevertheless one of its most powerful backers. But is the entrance of a majority Liberal government onto the federal stage likely to change this slow march to create barriers to access, both institutional and rhetorical?

The Trudeau Government

Less than a month after winning the Liberal leadership race in April 2014, Justin Trudeau decreed that all future candidates for the Liberal Party "need to be completely understanding that they will be expected to vote pro-choice on any bills." He initially suggested that this vetting did not apply to current MPs, who were to be "respected to a certain extent in their choices," despite the Liberal Party's policy not to "reopen that debate" (CBC News 2014d). After receiving criticisms from federal NDP leader Thomas Mulcair suggesting that this move had effectively created a two-tier system by allowing incumbent MPs to vote against a woman's right to choose, Trudeau clarified his stance, asserting, "The policy going forward is that every single Liberal MP will be expected to stand up for a woman's right to choose" (LeBlanc 2014).[37]

In the lead-up to the 2015 federal election, Trudeau continued to speak publicly about the importance of abortion, which the Liberals are treating as a Charter right, saying, "We do not accept that a government could legislate away a woman's fundamental rights" (Bryden 2014). During a one-on-one interview organized by the Up for Debate campaign, Trudeau "committed to engaging provinces in discussions regarding their compliance with the Canada Health Act so as to ensure all individuals have access to essential health services, including abortion" (Action Canada 2015b).[38] These promises seem to suggest a willingness to depart from the Harper government's commitment to "open federalism" (White 2014, 166) by engaging with the provinces to protect and promote access to abortion care. However, despite regular reiterations of abortion as a right, the government has continued to frame abortion as a health issue. Although certainly an improvement on failing to engage with barriers to access within the health care system, this classification diminishes the relevance of abortion to women's equality, even as the language used by Trudeau seems to suggest an awareness of its deeply gendered implications. For instance, in the lead-up to his election, Trudeau commented, "It is not for a room full of predominantly male legislators to take away those [abortion] rights from women" (Canadian Press 2014).

Trudeau has also committed to improving reproductive health internationally. In particular, he suggested his hope to address the weaknesses of the Muskoka Initiative on maternal, newborn, and child health, first launched by Harper during the 2010 G8 conference. Recall that this initiative was widely criticized for excluding family planning in its plans for maternal health. To remedy these shortcomings, Trudeau committed to "providing family planning and abortion services as part of the Initiative," while also "increasing Canada's official development assistance, and, more broadly, increasing Canada's engagement on the global stage" (Action Canada 2015b).

Since forming government in October 2015, however, the Trudeau government has taken little direct action on abortion, except to remove the restrictions put in place by the previous government that blocked funding for the performance of abortions overseas (Akin 2016). Indeed, abortion has been markedly absent from key documents.[39] For instance, in the mandate letter for the minister of status of women, MP Patty Hajdu, which Trudeau made public, he outlined the top priorities for this portfolio, but abortion and reproductive health were not mentioned here, or in the body of the letter (Trudeau 2015b). These issues are also absent from the party's platform, though Trudeau has assured the public of his commitment to abortion rights repeatedly.

The reach and force of Trudeau's pro-choice declarations remains to be seen. If abortion is indeed a Charter right, under what section of the Charter does it fall? And what actions does the federal government believe it must take to realize this right? What role does it believe the provinces should play? Will the recognition of abortion as a Charter right be coded in law or in the constitution? Moreover, is it enough to simply strike down challenges to existing access, or does it also have responsibilities to improve access? Although the Trudeau government's acknowledgment of abortion thus far suggests a shift toward improving access and recognizing the significance of abortion to women's lives, its declaration that it wishes to avoid reopening the debate also suggests a desire to preserve the status quo. Only time will tell what changes this new administration can and will bring.

From the House to the Provinces

The federal government's failure to create new legislation regulating abortion has been of considerable value to abortion rights activists. Over time, it became increasingly apparent that the realities of legal abortion access were beneficial to women, both in terms of health outcomes and their status within the community. Attempts to recreate criminal restrictions on the procedure are now synonymous with attacks on women's rights and health. It is, however, important to remember that this was not a predictable outcome of *Morgentaler*. The policy vacuum left in the wake of the decision, even more so than the case itself, proved to be an asset of enormous proportion to social activists working to secure access for women. The lack of a clear legal or political institutional model gave the feminist movement the ability to represent the *Morgentaler* ruling in a more progressive light, as a recognition of the need for reproductive autonomy for women's equality.

The Court case, which is now widely credited with validating women's rights to bodily autonomy, came dangerously close to creating new avenues for the government to restrict women's rights. It was only through massive lobbying against the government's proposed law by feminist groups and physicians alike that this attempt to restrict women's rights failed (Brodie 1992, 110–13). The importance of political and social activism in this case should not be diminished. It was this activism alongside the ruling in *Morgentaler* that led to a largely positive outcome to advance women's right to abortion access, though these rights were never officially recognized. The mobilization around the *Morgentaler* case, and the public discourse it created, contributed to a social climate in which people understood the importance of abortion as a right for women. Indeed, the growing consensus that abortion is a woman's right only increased when the limitations of the *Morgentaler* decision, specifically the extent of fetal rights and the rights of biological fathers, were challenged in court.

The regulation of abortion in the federal government has remained largely unchanged since *Morgentaler*. The fear of losing ground in the regulation of abortion is so strong among many pro-choice activists that the stability of abortion's treatment by federal governments is a mark of pride – and the reasons for this are not hard to find. Anti-abortion legislation, advanced by backbench MPs, is a constant fixture in the House of Commons, where nearly fifty such bills have been defeated in less than thirty years. Although the failure of these bills to pass may seem like a boon, their nearly constant onslaught highlights a looming threat. The bills draw attention to anti-abortion activity as if to warn abortion rights activists that they will always be there, and that pushing for more rights recognitions would only give anti-abortion activists a new soapbox on which to stand. This sentiment in the House has also prevented many abortion rights activists from actively questioning the failure of the House to advocate for women's reproductive rights.

As it stands, the federal-policy vacuum that emerged around the regulation of abortion services, which led to a reclassification of abortion as a health care issue, also failed to provide clear protections for women. Linda White (2014, 157–58) explains that, although "the federal Parliament is responsible for determining the essential legality of an action," such as abortion access, "provincial and territorial legislatures administer the programs," meaning "their cooperation is necessary in order to ensure access to services." Federalism thus creates unique challenges in the realization of rights and services, as demonstrated by provincial responses to their new-found jurisdiction over abortion.

Following *R. v. Morgentaler* (1988), many provincial governments placed unreasonable restrictions on access to the procedure, with some, such as New Brunswick, creating barriers reminiscent of TACs. Others, such as Quebec, made strides to improve access even before it was decriminalized. The way abortion has been regulated in the provinces demonstrates the instability of the federal-policy vacuum that now surrounds the procedure and the dangers of complacency for the protection of women's rights. As the next chapter addresses, many of the restrictions placed on abortion access have since been tested in court and invalidated. Nonetheless, the resulting patchwork of services creates inequalities in access reminiscent of those that led to the decriminalization of abortion in 1988. Without formal recognition by the federal government, amid resistance from the courts to mandate positive political action, access remains vulnerable.

3

Abortion in the Provinces

In the more than twenty-five years since *R. v. Morgentaler* (1988), subsequent federal governments have neither passed new legal restrictions on abortion nor recognized its importance to women's equality. Amid such inaction, the regulation of abortion has fallen under provincial jurisdiction as a matter of health care. Even without a new law, however, the suggestion that abortion is unregulated would be misleading. Each province responded to their powers over abortion differently. Some provinces restricted access to the procedure to compensate for the federal government's failure to do so, whereas others made strides in the creation of widespread access to services. The reasons for these differences vary, but the significance is clear: the ability of women in Canada to access abortion services is hugely dependent on their province of residence.

Such dramatic variation in provincial responses to the *Morgentaler* decision is not the product of any single influence. Deeply held convictions of individual politicians, interventions by the federal government, and the nature of relationships between provincial legislatures and the courts all offer partial explanations for disparities in the treatment of abortion across Canada. When these factors are considered in conjunction with the influences of social movement activists and medical professionals (addressed in later chapters), a more complete picture begins to form. Through an exploration of the interplay between provincial governments and the courts in their regulation of abortion access following the *Morgentaler* decision, this chapter provides a starting point to understanding the nature of access in Canada today.

In the wake of the 1988 decision, most provinces attempted to restrict access to legal abortions in whole or in part. These attempts took various forms, often restricting the allowable locations for the procedure to take place, defining the specializations that providers would require, or setting out requirements for coverage under provincial health insurance. The reasoning for these different responses is not always apparent. *Hansard* transcripts, media interviews, and arguments advanced during legal proceedings do, however, offer insight into the motivations for the varying provincial responses.

After *R. v. Morgentaler* (1988), litigation played an important role in clarifying the responsibilities of the provinces in the provision of access. The rulings in these cases offer important insight into evolving interpretations of the *Morgentaler* decision, as well as into the value of courts in advancing women's rights claims. As will become evident in the cases selected, these decisions have generally protected existing levels of access or prevented extensive state interference in access, but have rarely gone further in suggesting that abortion rights ought to be read as a positive right.[1] In many instances, activist groups have had greater success in securing improved access by engaging with legislative bodies. The successes of these interactions, of course, are themselves dependent on the political climate and receptivity of individual politicians.

The relationships between the courts and provincial legislatures have profoundly shaped the strategies employed by social movements to secure change. Whether or not activists see the courts as the most appropriate venue to advance rights claims varies between the provinces. In Quebec, pro-choice feminist movements developed ties with Quebec nationalists, who placed greater emphasis on political engagement than on litigation as a means of realizing change (Vickers 2010). Quebec's decision to abstain from signing the Charter caused activists in the province to become wary of citing protections from a document that undermined their national identity, preferring instead to engage with politicians who had a progressive history in the regulation of abortion. Ontario, in contrast, has largely deferred to the Supreme Court decision in *Morgentaler*. The province refrained from trying to create substantial barriers once abortion was decriminalized, and much of the activism in the province has focused on maintaining the status quo rather than pushing for change. In sharp contrast, activists in New Brunswick, where major restrictions to abortion access were put in place shortly after the *Morgentaler* decision, have long faced governments with strong anti-abortion agendas that are resistant to recognizing abortion as a right. As a result, until recently, activists in New Brunswick devoted significant energy to litigation as a means of securing change, though recent events in the province have led to increased engagement with the legislature.

As we have seen, provincial politics differ from federal politics in their relationship to the Charter. Both levels of government have responsibilities to uphold the Charter, but whether they embrace rights discourse or defer to the courts (or, in the case of New Brunswick, neither) depends on the political climate. The history of abortion regulation by the federal government demonstrates a willingness to defer the potentially controversial issue to the courts, though provinces have generally not taken the same tact.

Understanding the diversity of provincial political climates in Canada and the approaches to activism that have resulted from them helps expose the reasons abortion access in Canada became disparate in the wake of the *Morgentaler* decision. Such an exploration also highlights the deficiencies of different avenues of rights recognitions in the realization of substantive access, suggesting the need for provinces to take their rights obligations seriously.

New Brunswick

With the exception of Prince Edward Island, which only announced plans to begin offering surgical abortions on the Island in 2016, New Brunswick has long been one of the worst provinces in Canada in terms of abortion access. The province is not only home to enduring restrictions on abortion access but is marked by its dogged resistance to improving its policies. Changes to provincial regulations on access have been loosened only within the last few years, and they are far from gone. The reasons for this opposition to the spirit of the ruling in *Morgentaler* are complex and began even before the decision came down.[2]

Resistance to expanded access to abortion services was evident in the New Brunswick legislature years before Morgentaler's Supreme Court victory. The province was not home to an abortion clinic before 1988, and Morgentaler was committed to expanding access to the Maritimes. In 1985, he sent a letter to the New Brunswick legislative assembly, notifying the province of his intent to set up a clinic in the province. In response, then Progressive Conservative premier Richard Hatfield amended the province's Medical Act to stipulate that "physicians could be found guilty of professional misconduct if they were involved in performing an abortion elsewhere than in a hospital approved by the Minister of Health" (Dunsmuir 1998). Abortions at this time were still illegal in Canada unless first approved by a therapeutic abortion committee (TAC), yet this change to the provincial act empowered the provincial government to remove Morgentaler's licence if he attempted to open and practise in a private clinic in the province. As a result, if Morgentaler had gone ahead with his plans to open a clinic, the government would have been able to interrupt his practice rather than having to wait for a hearing on his breach of the Criminal Code, which provincial precedent from Ontario and Quebec suggested would legitimize his attempts to challenge existing restrictions on the procedure.[3] If this was indeed the goal of the amendment, however, it was quickly rendered moot.

Shortly after the amendment was entrenched, abortion was decriminalized by the Supreme Court and jurisdiction over the procedure shifted to the provinces. The New Brunswick government made no immediate response to the decision. No attempts were made to alter provincial regulations governing abortion services, and Hatfield's amendment stayed on the books. Soon after, Morgentaler launched the first of what would be many court cases against the province to challenge its regulations on abortion. As these cases developed, a troubling pattern emerged in the government's responses to them. After losing to Morgentaler twice in court, the legislature largely avoided any debate on the subject, a pattern that it has maintained. Asserting its right to jurisdictional authority over health care as a sufficient justification for the status quo, the legislature has long refused to engage with the substance of Morgentaler's claims, either within its own walls or in court. Only as recently as 2014 has this pattern begun to change, twenty-five years after Morgentaler's first trial in the province.

Morgentaler first challenged the New Brunswick government in 1989, less than a year after his Supreme Court victory, when he sought reimbursement for performing abortions on three New Brunswick women in his Quebec clinic. At the time, there was no formal legislation to regulate the performance of abortions by doctors outside the province. The only legislation in place was Hatfield's 1985 amendment that labelled performing an abortion outside a registered hospital facility as professional misconduct. Morgentaler argued that he should be reimbursed under New Brunswick medicare for his services because the policies in place that restricted abortion access did not explicitly apply to services rendered outside the province.[4]

Leading up to the case, a provincial election was called, leaving Morgentaler to face off with the newly formed Liberal government of Premier

Frank McKenna.[5] In response to Morgentaler's claims, the McKenna government asserted that it indeed had a policy that restricted the classification of abortion as an entitled service under medicare: "Unless it is determined by two doctors to be medically required and is performed by a specialist in an approved hospital." The government maintained before the court that the policy was in effect, but it was forced to concede that the policy was legally indefensible because it had never been formally adopted. In its ruling, the court stated that "whether such a regulation would be valid cannot be determined unless and until it is made," and the existing regulation in the Medical Act was found to have "no application to members of the profession in other provinces."[6] As a result, Hatfield's amendment to the Medical Act was declared invalid for doctors practising outside the province. Morgentaler had won his first court battle in the province.[7]

Rather than appealing the decision, the government moved to fill the legal loophole the court had identified in its policy. In 1989, the McKenna government made an amendment to the Medical Services Payment Act that mimicked the policy the government claimed to have put in place after the first provincial *Morgentaler* decision. Abortion was included in Regulation 84-20 under the Medical Services Payment Act as an unentitled service, save under certain circumstances, specifically, if the abortion is "performed by a specialist in the field of obstetrics and gynaecology in a hospital facility approved by the jurisdiction in which the hospital facility is located and two medical practitioners certify in writing that the abortion was medically required" (Government of New Brunswick 1984, 38). According to Liberal MLA James Lockyer, who spoke about the amendment in the legislature at the time of its enactment, "These regulations will ensure that the conditions under which payment is made for services provided within New Brunswick will be the same as for payment for service provided to New Brunswick residents outside the province."[8]

Years later, in spite of the McKenna government's new restrictions on abortion access, Morgentaler fulfilled his promise to open a freestanding abortion clinic in the province. In 1994, Morgentaler opened a clinic in New Brunswick's capital city of Fredericton. In response, McKenna threatened him with "the fight of his life."[9]

Given his strong opposition to Morgentaler, McKenna quickly gained standing as an anti-abortion figurehead; many activists interviewed in the province suggested that his actions were rooted in his personal opposition to abortion. Alison Brewer, former leader of the New Brunswick NDP (2005–6) and the first director of the Fredericton Morgentaler Clinic, suggested that McKenna was not only motivated by his personal convictions but bolstered by anti-abortion sentiment among some of his fellow MLAs.[10]

Liberal MLA George Jenkins, for example, was clear that he would oppose abortion even if he was alone in holding the viewpoint. As he said, "To me, abortion involves an absolute moral value"; "it is in debate on moral issues that judgment supersedes interests, be they political or otherwise."[11] He, like many other representatives, saw his personal convictions as outweighing the rights of women. Progressive Conservative MLA Brent Taylor also spoke about his convictions in the legislature, where he stressed the rights of "the unborn" but failed to address the rights of women:

> We who did go to that march were there to tell all of New Brunswick about our attachment to the rights of the unborn child. We quietly marched in front of the proposed site of the clinic, of the abortuary, and we then dispersed peacefully. I hope our witness there on Saturday will, at the very least, help give other members of this House and of the government the courage that they may lack as they prepare to join in the battle for the sake of the unborn child.[12]

True to McKenna's word, his government invoked Hatfield's 1985 amendment the day the clinic opened, forcing the clinic to close to await a hearing. The government also pressured the New Brunswick College of Physicians and Surgeons to suspend Morgentaler's medical licence, which it promptly did. Later that same year, 1994, Morgentaler faced off with the New Brunswick government in the Court of Queen's Bench. Taking into consideration that the Hatfield amendment dated from a time when abortion was considered a criminal offence, the court ruled that it was unconstitutional.[13] In its ruling, the court stated that the creation of the amendment was not in the interest of ensuring the highest quality of care for women in the province, but that it was designed to "prohibit the establishment of free-standing abortion clinics and, particularly, the establishment of such a clinic by Dr. Morgentaler."[14] The decision was upheld on appeal and the Supreme Court declined to hear the case (Richer 2008, 8). Victorious again, Morgentaler's licence was reinstated and his clinic was permitted to remain open. The regulation was removed, but as far as the government was concerned, it was not the only one on the books: McKenna's amendment to the Medical Services Payment Act was still in effect.

It was some years later before Morgentaler returned to court to challenge Regulation 84-20. In the meantime, his clinic continued to operate in

Fredericton without the benefit of any provincial funding.[15] Finally, in 2002, Morgentaler made a public statement in which he accused the New Brunswick government of being "sexist, male chauvinists [and] of victimizing and oppressing women" (quoted in Moulton 2003, 700). He went on to assert that, through its continued failure to pay for all abortion services, "the New Brunswick government has been saving money on the misery of women." In response, then justice minister Brad Green expressed his confidence in the government's position and his willingness to defend it "as far as the Supreme Court of Canada" (ibid.). Despite this boast, the government did everything in its power to avoid engaging with Morgentaler's claims, either in court or in the legislature.

On July 16, 2003, Morgentaler sued the New Brunswick government, this time challenging its provincial funding restrictions. His filing stated that he was suing on the grounds that the government's amendment to the Medical Services Payment Act was unconstitutional because it "erects a barrier to abortion services that violates rights guaranteed to women under s. 7 ('Life, Liberty and Security of Person') and s. 15 ('Equality') of the *Canadian Charter of Rights and Freedoms*."[16] He further argued that the amendment was not only inconsistent with but actually violated the Canada Health Act because the province was not providing services that were "an integral component of women's necessary reproductive-related health care."[17] Unfortunately, the government and anti-abortion groups worked to ensure that the substance of these claims would never be heard in court.

There seemed to be an awareness that a straightforward court case against Morgentaler would not be successful so, rather than preparing their defence, the government and anti-abortion interest groups attempted to stall the case. In 2004, the Coalition for Life and Health applied for intervenor status on the Morgentaler case but was denied on the grounds that it had "no more direct interest in issues pleaded than any other taxpayer and demonstrated no special expertise not otherwise available."[18] The coalition appealed the case in 2005, but the verdict held. It was subsequently denied leave to appeal to the Supreme Court.

The case was delayed further still when, in 2007, the province challenged Morgentaler's standing. The government argued that a woman would be better suited to bring the case forward.[19] Morgentaler responded by arguing that, although others were more directly impacted by the legislation, there were many barriers that might prevent them from challenging it, and moved to be granted public interest standing in the case.[20] The New Brunswick Court of Queen's Bench looked to precedents set in other cases involving vulnerable populations and stated in its ruling, "There are many valid reasons why women who have had abortions at the Fredericton Clinic would not or could not bring this challenge. Dr. Morgentaler is therefore a suitable alternative person to do so."[21] Morgentaler was subsequently granted public interest standing. The government appealed this decision in 2009, but the verdict was upheld.[22]

In subsequent years, the New Brunswick government took no further action on this case, likely owing to Morgentaler's advanced age and failing health. On May 29, 2013, Morgentaler suffered a heart attack in his home and died at the age of ninety. The case has since been officially dropped. University of New Brunswick law professor Jula Hughes, in an interview conducted two years before Morgentaler's death, explained the government's reasoning in approaching this case:

> The provincial government know perfectly well that they have not got a legal case, so they do what governments sometimes do when they do not have a legal case: they throw their litigation resources at delaying it – in this case, with the evil intention of waiting for Dr. Morgentaler to die – or for him to run out of money. I do not have a lot of sympathy for that. It seems to me that if the government has a case, why not put it forward and be done with it?[23]

The government's reluctance to engage with the accusations Morgentaler was attempting to bring forward was not unique to this case. It also failed to engage with a similar criticism in the form of a human rights complaint.

Challenges to the province's regulation have not been confined to the courts. In October 2008, a female doctor, referred to only as A.A. for her protection, filed a complaint with the New Brunswick Human Rights Commission.[24] The complaint was twofold: first, it alleged that the "procedural hoops" that she, as a female physician who regularly provided sexual health services, was forced to contend with in helping her patients access funded care amounted to sex discrimination.[25] Regulation 84-20 forces physicians to provide services that are not in keeping with the Canadian Medical Association's position on abortion, which suggests that there "be no delay in the provision of abortion services" and, most importantly, that "induced abortion should be uniformly available to all women in Canada" (CMA 1988, 2). Central to A.A.'s claim was her perception that, as a female doctor providing sexual health care, she was subject to uniquely negative treatment as a result of the regulation.

A.A. brought the second claim on behalf of women seeking abortion services, alleging sex discrimination by the province as the result of its restrictive regulations. Since pregnancy is an inherently gendered issue, A.A. argued, women were being "denied a service on the basis of sex," which contributed to the risk of "psychological harm."[26] The Labour and Employment Board ruled that A.A. could proceed only on the first complaint because the Human Rights Act allows only individuals from a specific group that is being discriminated against to bring forward a claim. Because A.A. did not "allege that she is a member of the class of persons who have made a decision to have an abortion," the board found that she could not represent women in her complaint.[27] Despite the fact that other legal disputes have allowed individuals to represent groups to which they are external, on the grounds that a member of the group in question may face barriers in bringing a case forward, the Labour and Employment Board is "a creature of statute" and does not provide for representative complaints.[28]

Before her first complaint could proceed to a hearing, the Province of New Brunswick filed an action against the New Brunswick Labour and Employment Board, the New Brunswick Human Rights Commission, and A.A. in order to challenge the board's standing to render a decision on the case (New Brunswick Human Rights Commission 2014, 15). The province challenged the board's authority to rule on either one of A.A.'s original complaints, despite her claim of discrimination against women having already been found outside the board's purview to try. In the case that followed, A.A. and the commission used this platform to argue that both complaints should be heard before the board. The judge upheld the original ruling of the board on A.A.'s inability to represent women but considered the validity of the board's involvement in the second claim. However, in May 2013, Justice Paulette Garnett ruled against the board, quashing the case and removing it from court. Her judgment was based on the case's inability to meet the standard of reasonableness; that is, although the complainant was found to be an aggrieved party, the standard of evidence was not met (ibid.). Specifically, Justice Garnett found that the case fell outside the purview of the board because A.A. "wasn't directly affected by the abortion policy" and "lacked sufficient information to show the problems with accessibility" (CBC News 2013a).

The case was not appealed but, as Hughes (2014) explains in a blog post, this failure to challenge the decision itself reflects a lack of sympathy for the challenges of bringing such a case forward:

> The complainant physician [A.A.] was not able to appeal the Court of Queen's Bench decision before the expiry of the appeal period, fearing

reprisal if her identity became known. A motions judge of the Court of Appeal refused to extend time. In the course of so doing, he ridiculed the difficulty of the complainant in finding legal assistance to appeal by stating that "other than expressions of discouragement and an unwillingness to pay a large retainer, A.A. offers no explanation for her failure to respect the time limits."

Cumulatively, the above cases demonstrate attempts by the province to keep challenges to the regulation of abortion access within strictly jurisdictional terms, avoiding the rights debate altogether when justifying its activities in the legislature and in public statements. Members of the legislative assembly have also endorsed these moves, using the rhetorical tools of the anti-abortion movement to suggest that challenging abortion in the legislature would risk what access does exist in the province. Unfortunately, such sentiment in the legislature failed to dissipate in the years after the *Morgentaler* decision. In December 2004, Liberal MLA Stuart Jamieson asked of the legislature: "Why are we allowing the rights of mothers to outweigh the rights of that human life inside a womb?"[29]

Women's rights to equality and security of the person, as well as their right to access safe and legal medical services within the parameters laid out by the Canada Health Act, have been raised time and time again in New Brunswick. Despite this, discussion of their significance has been virtually absent in the provincial courts and legislature. When abortion access is mentioned, the government has historically defended existing services.

Brewer characterizes government officials in the province as consistently "quite disingenuous in their responses to abortion access," suggesting that there is no need for a clinic so long as "abortions are being performed in at least one hospital," regardless of the hospital's ability to meet demand. Rosella Melanson, former executive director of the New Brunswick Advisory Council on the Status of Women, which was dismantled in March 2011, also commented on the unwillingness of the government to discuss abortion access. She said that, in response to any suggestions made by the council, the most it was told was that the government was "satisfied with the policy" as it stood.[30]

It has only been in the last few years that big changes have begun to happen in New Brunswick. A newly formed activist group, Reproductive Justice New Brunswick (RJNB), has pressured the new government to initiate change, building on the efforts of other activists in the province.[31] The group formed after the Morgentaler Clinic, which performed more than half of the abortions in the province annually, closed owing to a lack of provincial funding (CBC News 2014b). The abrupt loss of access to abortion services was a turning point in the mobilization of activists in the province, who have lobbied tirelessly for the repeal of Regulation 84-20 (ibid.).

RJNB's first act was to organize a crowdfunding campaign to help fund a new clinic.[32] The campaign was a resounding success, receiving support from across Canada and raising more than $125,000 to help open a new clinic on the same site (CBC News 2015b). At the same time, the group began to organize demonstrations and talk to the media about Regulation 84-20, which it hoped to have repealed. Whether by chance or design, the formation of the group aligned with an upcoming provincial election, which RJNB used as a platform to pressure the legislature for change.

Because of RJNB, abortion access became a central issue in the provincial election. The sudden significance of access to the outcome of the election led Liberal leader Brian Gallant to vocalize his pro-choice views throughout his campaign. Indeed, the Liberal Party made two resolutions leading up to its eventual victory, which called for "access to a full range of publicly funded family planning information and services" as well as improvements to "access to reproductive health services that meet national standards and respect the Canada Health Act" (CBC News 2014a).

Shortly after the 2014 election, the new Liberal government amended Regulation 84-20.[33] Although the regulation is still in place, the requirement that a specialist must perform abortions is gone, and women no longer require written permission from two doctors to access services. The provision that abortions must be performed in hospitals is, however, still in place. At present, three hospitals in the province, one in Bathurst and two in Moncton, now perform the procedure, with one of the Moncton hospitals serving as the sole site for English speakers in the province (C. Smith 2015).[34] No publicly funded services are available in the province's capital city.

RJNB was also successful in helping fund a new clinic. Clinic 554, a family practice that also provides abortion care, now operates on the former site of the Morgentaler Clinic in Fredericton. Unfortunately, the provinces' regulations exclude abortions at the clinic from coverage under provincial health insurance.

The recent changes to New Brunswick's abortion regulations demonstrate the value of concerted social activism to pressure governments to engage with the issue of abortion. The reality that these changes were made so quickly in the wake of over two decades of litigation in the province also speaks to the significance of the social climate when appealing to the government. Timing was a huge factor in the success of RJNB's campaign. Were it not for the election and the clinic closure, whether it would have had such immediate success is unclear. These factors contributed to a social climate in which the pressing need for improved access was difficult to ignore. However, despite these changes, the long history of tolerance for these policies in the province suggests that activists there have a long road ahead. Although many people within the province are supportive of improved abortion services, the general climate is not necessarily a receptive one. As such, even with improvements to services, many women are still unlikely to feel that they are exercising a right in seeking abortion care. Many will simply be thankful for having a chance at getting any services at all – even if they have to travel halfway across the province to access them.

Ontario

Ontario's treatment of abortion stands in stark contrast to that of New Brunswick. After the *Morgentaler* decision, Ontario's approach was to treat abortion as a medical issue. The government made no attempts to block access, either through funding or physicians and facility restrictions; indeed, the addition of abortion to other health care responsibilities in the province was almost routine. When contrasted with other provinces, extensive litigation and legislative debate on the topic is noticeably absent.

The medicalization of abortion – that is, treating abortion as a solely medical issue insulated from social and political concerns – has allowed for the creation and maintenance of reasonable access for many Ontarians, but others continue to face barriers in their attempts to access care. Even though access is quite good in large urban centres, rural access to services continues to be a problem. In a province as large as Ontario, both geographically and in terms of population, such a disparity is noteworthy. Treating abortion as a health care procedure has largely obscured the centrality of services to women's citizenship.

Political and legal activity surrounding abortion access issues in Ontario has been markedly less prevalent than in New Brunswick, effectively ceasing after the *Morgentaler* decision. Nonetheless, the activity that has taken place in the province has been instrumental in shaping the landscape of abortion access in Canada today. Although the Ontario government has never overtly stated that the provision of abortion services is necessary for women's equality, provincial regulation treats abortion as a health care issue and, at least in this respect, access is widely thought of as a right.

The 1988 *Morgentaler* decision originated from a legal challenge in Ontario, where Morgentaler opened a clinic in 1983, when abortion was still regulated under section 251 of the Criminal Code. When abortion was decriminalized five years later, the Ontario government was compliant with the ruling, treating abortion as a matter of health. Coverage for abortion services was included in the provincial health-insurance program for both hospital and clinics.

In the midst of these changes, a small amount of overt anti-abortion sentiment was vocalized in the Ontario legislature. This sentiment was only apparent in the years following the *Morgentaler* decision, when abortion was still being debated in the House of Commons. Liberal MPPs Carman McClelland and Michael Murray Dietsch, for example, both spoke out in February 1988, encouraging the federal government to create new legislation "to provide protection for the unborn."[35] However, these views did not seem to be widely held, and abortion has rarely been a topic of debate in the legislature, except for one notable Ontario court case: *Murphy v. Dodd* (1989).

This case, which was the Ontario equivalent of *Tremblay v. Daigle*, concerned an Ontario man, Gregory Murphy, who sought an injunction to prevent his former partner, Barbara Dodd, from getting an abortion.[36] Murphy claimed to be the undisputed biological father of Dodd's fetus, despite his knowledge that she had been intimate with another man. He also signed a sworn affidavit that he had "conferred with Ms. Dodd's gynecologist who was of the opinion that a 'third abortion' could represent a serious risk to [Dodd's] life' while 'a pregnancy did not constitute such a risk to her'" (Shaffer 1993–94, 59n2). Dodd subsequently provided "an affidavit from her doctor who swore that the alleged conversation never took place" (ibid.). Ultimately, since the injunction was granted on fraudulent grounds, the case never went to court. The injunction, however, was an area of contention in the legislature.

In response to the court's decision to grant Murphy an injunction, NDP MPP Richard Frank Johnston stated that it was "an outrage to women in the province [and], an affront to their sense of autonomy" that "a third-party male should be able to make a decision which would hamper a woman's right to have an abortion," calling the decision a "reversion to notions of women as chattels."[37] In response, Liberal MPP Dalton McGuinty reiterated the *Morgentaler* decision's allusion to "the need to achieve the socially imperative balance between the rights and interests of women and the equally important rights and interests of unborn children."[38] Despite these passionate reactions to the case, the use of a language of rights appears only in these isolated statements. Neither a strong pro-choice nor anti-abortion position has been pushed in the Ontario legislature, which continues to remain relatively neutral on these debates, attempting to treat abortion as a straightforward medical question.

In general, abortion has become a virtual nonissue and is rarely raised in provincial politics. When it is discussed, concerns regarding the way abortion is regulated in the province have tended to focus on the distribution of services. The greatest political concerns in the province pertaining to abortion access relate to deregulation of services and the enactment of policy at a service level. The actions of Mike Harris's Progressive Conservative government are a prime example.

In 1995, the Harris government took dramatic steps to curb health care spending, delisting many services, particularly those dealing with quality-of-life issues (Armstrong and Armstrong 2001). Michelle Robidoux, manager of the Ontario Coalition of Abortion Clinics (OCAC), spoke about these cuts in an interview:

> Several years ago, the Ontario government delisted a whole range of procedures, ranging from reversal of tubal ligation to removal of port wine stains that people are born with to the provision of prosthetic testicles for men who have testicular cancer. Small, cosmetic things that can make a difference for a person who is in that situation – and they just cut it. We saw it very much as part of a process of whittling away at things that are considered part of essential health care.[39]

Robidoux went on to define essential health care as procedures that are necessary to defining "your sense of yourself as a person" – that is, "your mental health, as well as what's immediately necessary." The anti-abortion movement, however, continues to see abortion as falling outside the realm of essential health care.

Anti-abortion groups in the province have tirelessly reiterated their belief that abortion is not a necessary medical service. Consequently, there is fear that abortion care could also face funding cuts, particularly if the politicians masterminding these decisions are anti-abortion. Indeed, Robidoux identified this kind of potential attack on abortion services, which has already manifested in New Brunswick, as part of a greater challenge to "what's seen as a right, what kind of healthcare is seen as your right, and what's seen as your private responsibility, or a luxury, or trivial."

This push by anti-abortion groups to reframe abortion as a lifestyle issue – a procedure of convenience, chosen frivolously by women – rather than as a medical issue or a right has been a major area of concern for abortion rights advocates. Pro-choice advocates feared that abortion might also be delisted. In the end, the Harris government abstained from cutting abortion, but attempts by social movements to redefine what constituted a necessary medical service exposed the potential pitfalls of relying on a rigid health care framework to realize women's equality.

An expert panel on abortion service provision in Ontario, assembled by Echo, an agency of the Ministry of Health and Long-Term Care with a focus on women's health, underscored concerns that abortion services in the province are vulnerable (Echo 2011, 2). As a result of health care reforms that shifted from a model relying on hospitals to one relying on clinics, concerns arose that abortion services and their importance have become "poorly understood and [are] dependent upon a relatively small group of providers" (ibid.).[40] Without formal recognition as a right, provinces are largely free to treat abortion like any other health care service. The report made several recommendations based on continued stigma around the procedure, including improvements to the system of reproductive health care designed to increase the quality of services, and better training for providers to ensure their "alignment and adherence to [the] ethical and legal obligations" they must meet as health care professionals (ibid., 3).

Despite concerns about delisting, limited facilities, and a lack of providers, interviewees in the province generally perceived access to be quite good. This is in no small part owing to the stability of abortion provision in Ontario, which has meant that individuals within the province generally feel that access is relatively secure. Interestingly, when interviewees in Ontario articulated their concerns for the future of abortion access in the province, they were most often focused on external threats rather than provincial; namely, the actions of the federal government.

The influence of the Harper government, in power at the time the interviews were undertaken, was widely cited as a concern by interviewees in the province. The increasingly vocal anti-abortion sentiment in the federal government seemed to overshadow issues of provincial politics. For instance, a representative of Planned Parenthood Toronto explained that, although in previous years the organization felt relatively secure in the notion that abortion access was "here to stay," the Harper federal government has threatened this view. "Within the political atmosphere," she elaborated, "a lot of the political leaders still see it [abortion] as murder, and they still see it as wrong. It's always going to be jeopardized as long as there are people with that mentality running the country."[41] Robidoux echoed this sentiment, stating that she believes the Harper government had "quite uniform and quite dominant opposition to abortion in their caucus." She drew particular attention to the role of Conservatives in anti-abortion legislation, relating that on recent backbencher bills designed to restrict women's rights to abortion, "the bulk of the people who voted for those laws were Conservatives." Even though the "Conservatives stand out on the political landscape" in terms of anti-abortion policies, Robidoux did not express trust in the Liberal Party either. She explained that, "historically, the laws that existed which restricted abortion were probably in place as long under Liberal governments as they were under Conservative governments," stressing that she does not "have any great faith that we are protected from such things just by the fact of a Liberal government." She did, however, clarify that although she had no "confidence that the Liberals have a strong commitment to it [abortion access], in the sense of really fighting for it," the Conservatives were of particular concern because they are "really, really opposed to it."

The absence of enforceable rights to abortion access for women is an ongoing concern in Ontario, despite the absence of any provincial restrictions on the procedure and virtually no litigation since *R. v. Morgentaler* (1988). Keeping abortion strictly within the realm of health care has left it vulnerable to cuts and disputes over what constitutes a medically necessary service. It also leaves the regulations of the procedure largely outside provincial politics, since nonstate actors chiefly control the training of future providers and the inclusion of abortion in medical school curriculum. Although abortion is a health care service, its taboo status has meant that it is not always treated as such. Thus, in spite of Ontario's policies being far from regressive, without formal recognition of abortion as necessary to women's equality, women's rights remain at the discretion of doctors rather than women themselves.

Quebec

Quebec is a standout case when it comes to abortion access. The progressive treatment of abortion in Quebec began long before it did in the rest of the country; Quebec was the only province to liberalize its regulation of abortion *before* the Supreme Court voted to decriminalize the federal law restricting it. The acknowledgment of abortion as a matter of women's rights is evident in all aspects of Quebec society, including its National Assembly. Although some legal and political activity on the subject has taken place since 1988, the result has always been a reassertion of abortion as a right necessary for women's equality. Quebec is home to over half of Canada's abortion clinics (Reid 2013).

The majority of legal activity in Quebec relating to abortion access occurred before the *Morgentaler* decision. Indeed, it was the refusal of Quebec juries to convict Morgentaler that contributed to public acceptance of abortion as a woman's right; a belief held even more deeply in the province today (Kennedy 2012). As is true of many activities in the province, to understand Quebec's treatment of abortion, it is helpful to situate pro-choice activism within the Quebec nationalist movement.

The Parti Québécois (PQ) was first elected in 1976, the same year Morgentaler was granted his third acquittal for the performance of illegal abortions in Quebec. Then justice minister Marc-André Bédard wasted no time in granting immunity to doctors performing abortions, effectively decriminalizing the procedure in the province (FQPN and CFC 2010, 15). This immunity exempted doctors from legal action if they failed to seek consent from therapeutic abortion committees or performed abortions in a facility other than a registered hospital, the requirements set by the federal government in 1969 that women were required to meet before being allowed legal abortion services (ibid.). Bédard justified this action by referring to Morgentaler's multiple acquittals, suggesting that "the abortion law had become inapplicable" (Desmarais 1999, 142, translated by author). The PQ even went so far as to vote for "free abortions upon request" for Québécois women at its 1977 party convention, but Premier René Lévesque vetoed the results of the vote (Bauch 1977; *Ottawa Citizen* 1977).

When questioned, Lévesque said that his veto was not the result of any opposition to abortion but of his belief that "public opinion had not been prepared for discussion of the issue," as well as his wish not to be divisive. He also pointed to the fact that the Criminal Code fell under federal jurisdiction and his government was unable to remove the procedure from it (*Ottawa Citizen* 1977). Nonetheless, he spoke out later that year, saying that abortion would eventually be decriminalized, and that it was time to "get out of the dark ages, admit that abortion exists, and start to do something positive in the area" (*Montreal Gazette* 1976).

Jill Vickers (2010, 430) explains that Québécois women were able to benefit from strong nationalist sentiment in the province "by combining discourses about the liberation of women, Quebec, and society." By linking gender equality to a nationalist narrative, pro-choice activists were able to champion abortion access through the National Assembly. As a result of their success at the provincial level, Vickers explains, Quebec feminists are "more deeply invested in provincial politics, which they can influence more than English-Canadian women, especially in provinces with conservative governments" (ibid., 426).

This pattern has held true over time. When abortion was decriminalized at the federal level in 1988, little changed in Quebec, as the province had already adjusted its policies following its own legal battles. The lack of political backlash may largely be because of the dominance of more left-leaning parties in the province. Since 1976, the provincial government has shifted between the Liberal Party and the Parti Québécois; the last right-wing party to hold power in Quebec was the Union Nationale, which was defeated in 1970. Although the political parties in power are not a clear determinant of political regulation of abortion, as evidenced by New Brunswick's history of abortion regulation, a lack of socially conservative values seems to have contributed in government to openly pro-choice views, which recognize women as equal citizens and abortion as necessary for women to exercise their equality.

The necessity of abortion access was interpreted in keeping with an understanding of abortion as a positive right. When the procedure was de facto legalized in 1973, it was also funded, at least in most cases. Abortions were covered in hospitals, but limitations were placed on funding in private clinics and women's health centres; women were required to pay the supplementary fees, which ranged from $40 to $350 in the early 2000s, when accessing abortions (FQPN and CFC 2010, 32). Although the government was not clear about its rationale for restricting clinic funding, interviewees in the province suggested that the decision not to fully fund private clinics was likely in keeping with Quebec's support of more socialist policies rather than a desire to restrict abortion access. The government, they suggested, may have been attempting to prevent the proliferation of a two-tiered health care system – a cause with clear social justice foundations.

Regardless of the motivation, pressure to fund services in all facilities grew as wait times in the public sector rose (to approximately three to four weeks), causing women to resort increasingly to clinics for service (ibid., 33). L'association pour l'accès à l'avortement (the Association for Abortion Access) filed a class action lawsuit against the government of Quebec for its failure to pay these fees in private clinics and women's health centres between 1996 and 2005. The Quebec Superior Court released its judgment in 2006, ruling in favour of the plaintiff.[42] The government was required to reimburse women who paid out of pocket for abortion services during that nine-year period.[43]

In total, the province was required to pay out $13 million. A program was set up to reimburse women but was generally unsuccessful. According to a representative of the FQPN, "Most people didn't ask for a refund, probably didn't even know that they could or didn't understand exactly how they could go about doing that so most of that money is still left over."[44] In an effort to reach more women, the reimbursement program was reopened in the fall of 2010 until mid-January, but much of the money has yet to be claimed. Despite this legal victory, a representative of the FQPN noted that "there was some division within the movement about whether or not this [the lawsuit victory] was a good thing, whether this was going to lead to a greater privatization of our healthcare system, things of that sort."

Unfortunately, although the women in question in the class action lawsuit who had received abortions between 1996 and 2005 were granted reimbursements, future Québécois women were denied the same guarantees. In an effort to address this issue, the Quebec Ministry of Health and Social Services first attempted to "increase the public system's capacity to meet the demand for abortion" through an increase in the number of facilities performing abortions and a bigger budget (FQPN and CFC 2010, 34). The intention was to "reimburse abortion services provided in private clinics and at the CSFM [Centre de santé des femmes de Montréal] in cases where the public sector was not able to provide services within a reasonable time" (ibid.).[45] A coordination centre was created to guide women seeking first trimester abortions to the appropriate facilities. At the same time, an agreement was negotiated with private clinics and the CSFM, which would allow them to provide services covered in full under their provincial health care plan. When the agreement took effect in January 2008, women were able to access abortions covered under their health insurance at hospitals and clinics, and at the CSFM.

Not only did the province take pains to ensure that women would have access to abortion services in the future, going beyond the requirements set out by the courts, but unlike other provincial governments, the National Assembly of Quebec has not remained silent on the issue of abortion. Most recently, the 2010 G8 summit was a catalyst for provincial outrage for its exclusion of abortion as a maternal health consideration. In response to the federal government's treatment of abortion, a motion was put forward in the assembly, which read:

> THAT the National Assembly reaffirms the rights of women to freedom of choice and to free and accessible abortion services and asks the federal

> Government and the Prime Minister of Canada to put an end to the ambiguity that persists in relations to this question; and that the National Assembly reaffirms the fact of supporting the rights of women to an abortion must in no way be adduced by the federal Government as a reason to cut subsidies to women's groups.[46]

The motion passed unanimously and received national coverage. This symbolic gesture reaffirmed Quebec's commitment to treating abortion as a right necessary to women's equality.

Despite this commitment, however, in 2009, the National Assembly of Quebec put forward a bill that had the potential to compromise existing services. The bill would have elevated the standards for abortion care beyond what was necessary. Bill 34 proposed strict guidelines for all private clinics that would have effectively turned abortion clinics into operating rooms (CBC News 2009). The Quebec college of physicians denounced the bill, recommending that it be significantly amended or thrown out altogether. The proposed amendments would fail to improve the quality of care in private clinics, according to the Fédération des médecins spécialistes du Québec – rather, they would create "cumbersome organizational and bureaucratic requirements" (FMSQ 2009). These changes would have been particularly damaging to abortion clinics: "Building a sterile operating room is costly, too costly for the Morgentaler Clinic, Fémina, and Alternative, the three Montreal clinics that have said publicly they will stop offering abortions if the rules remain. About one-third of the thirty thousand abortions performed in Quebec each year are done in private clinics" (Picard 2009). After extensive lobbying, abortion clinics were made exempt from this new bill.

With this history in mind, it is not surprising that activists in the province continue to appeal directly to their legislature to improve access. Indeed, a representative of Le Conseil du statut de la femme (the Council on the Status of Women), a Quebec governmental organization that consults on issues of women's equality and rights interviewed for this project, explained that the group was unable to see how the government could have a vision that did not recognize the autonomy of women.[47] Even those who expressed concern about the ease with which the political climate could shift – for example, the dramatic federal win of the NDP in the province in 2011 – seemed optimistic about the outcome. A clinic representative in the province, for example, noted that, despite "everything that has happened, [the outcome] has always been positive."[48]

As in Ontario, concerns about the Harper government's interference with the regulation of abortion were greater than fears of provincial action. Many interviewees expressed concern that a rise in right-wing politics would lead to less support for abortion rights, and dwindling access to abortion care. Some individuals interviewed in the province also expressed concern about the activities of the federal government in shaping access. A Quebec clinic representative, for example, said that, despite the large pro-choice movement in the province, "the rise of the right in the States, [and the subsequent] rise of the right in Canada," could lead to a similar situation in Quebec.[49] Despite these concerns, the general sentiment was that any real anti-abortion activity would have to occur at the federal level – and if it did, Quebec would not stand for it.

When asked to describe the political climate that surrounded abortion in 2011, most interviewees drew attention to the Harper government, showcasing the unique role of federalism in Quebec politics. Although interviewees in Ontario and New Brunswick also identified fear of federal interference, this concern was coupled with the possibility of provincial restrictions on abortion, a fear not shared in Quebec. Some felt strongly that the government would attempt to reopen the debate, likely through stealth. Quebec interviewees expressed not only fear that the Harper government would attempt to restrict abortion federally but also a keen awareness that it had already taken action against pro-choice and reproductive justice views.

Patrick Powers, former president of the Sexual Health Network of Quebec, had said that Harper was unlikely to reopen the debate, even with a majority government: "He's realized that it is a political hot potato, it could hurt him in the polls, and he's a coward. He's an out and out coward."[50] Powers also felt that Harper's desire to stay in power was stronger than his socially conservative values, especially those that could harm him in the long run. He did, however, note the work that Harper's administration has done to cut funding to progressive groups in Canada and abroad, though Powers felt that, ultimately, Harper "couldn't touch Canada," at least not without threatening his position. Certainly, the slow chipping away of abortion access abroad seemed to be a feature of the remainder of the government's mandate, and is one that the Trudeau government has already addressed by removing the "restriction that prevented federal foreign-aid dollars being used for abortion services in other countries" (Akin 2016). Of course, whether Trudeau will continue to take strides to address access issues remains to be seen.

Reflecting larger health care issues in Canada, many of the concerns expressed in Quebec relate to worries that austerity measures will compromise access. If safe access to abortion services is reduced and becomes accessible only to those who are either fortunate enough to live close to a facility or those who have the means, then not all women can act as equal citizens, let alone believe themselves to be. Regardless of the nature of the actions taken by the federal government, the response from Quebec to any that restrict abortion was resoundingly clear: "We would fight."[51]

Making the Case for Positive Rights

In each of the above cases, both legislatures and courts have affected the nature of access to abortion services. In some instances, the courts either mandated state action or served as the catalyst for this action (for better or for worse). At other times, direct engagement with government, often by social movements activists, was responsible for change. The utility of these approaches is difficult to evaluate in isolation, as the success of these strategies also varied by province and was clearly influenced by their respective social and political climates. As such, it is difficult to argue that there is only one correct path toward change. In advocating for a more holistic understanding of abortion, however, I have asserted that governments need to take responsibility to create positive rights to abortion access. Although I do not suggest that litigation relating to abortion is necessarily to be avoided – indeed, I would be hard pressed to make such an argument, given the improvements to access that have resulted from such claims – I have attempted to show the limitations of the courts in creating positive rights.

Rounding out the case studies discussed above, I want to focus on two decisions considered significant in the advancement of abortion access in Canada, to drive home this argument. Both the Supreme Court decision in *R. v. Morgentaler* (1993) and *Jane Doe et al. v. Manitoba* (2004) created precedent that continues to inform the regulation of abortion in Canada and may even foreshadow future cases. The precedent set in these cases, however, while important, is also inherently limited. Courts have generally avoided interpreting Charter rights as positive rights. Emmett Macfarlane (2014, 59) suggests that "justices are properly reluctant to impose major spending commitments on governments" because they lack the democratic legitimacy to do so. He explains the reason behind this assertion: "There is a principled logic to ensuring that the same institutional actor that spends public funds is the one responsible for collecting them; otherwise, incentives to manage and redistribute scarce resources are distorted" (ibid.). As a result, even when legal decisions seem to favour protecting a right to access, it is important to recognize that these rights are often interpreted with a negative character. In practice, these rulings have stopped governments from blocking access in important ways, but they have failed to mandate that governments fundamentally improve access.

The creation of new policies to restrict access to abortion services for women was widespread after the 1988 *Morgentaler* decision. In 1989, the government of Nova Scotia approved a regulation that prohibited the performance of an abortion "in any place other than a building, premises, or place approved by the Minister of Health and Fitness as a 'hospital.'"[52] When Morgentaler subsequently opened a clinic in the province, he was charged with fourteen breaches of the Medical Services Act.[53]

A Nova Scotia judge promptly acquitted Morgentaler on the grounds that the province was "in pith and substance" attempting to legislate criminal law, which falls outside its jurisdiction.[54] The province appealed the case all the way to the Supreme Court, making it Morgentaler's third Supreme Court appearance. The Court ultimately upheld the trial judge's acquittal, finding the government's actions to be an "indivisible attempt by the province to legislate in the area of criminal law."[55] The Morgentaler Clinic in the province has since closed, but the Nova Scotia government amended its legislation to allow for private clinics. Like cases in other provinces, such as *New Brunswick v. Morgentaler* (1989), this case turned on jurisdictional claims rather than rights issues, leaving women's rights vulnerable and failing to engage with the foundations of women's claims to abortion access.

It was these very foundations that would come to the fore in the next case, *Doe et al. v. Manitoba* (2004). Two women, whose identities were kept confidential for their protection, initiated the case after difficulties negotiating provincial barriers to access abortion services in Manitoba. These women were also permitted to testify on behalf of other pregnant Manitoban women requiring abortion care.[56] Their case challenged the constitutionality of Manitoba's refusal to cover clinic abortions under the province's health insurance plan, using three sections of the Charter: conscience (section 2(a)), equality (section 15), and security of the person (section 7). Jane Doe 1 and Jane Doe 2 argued that "the right to reproductive freedom is central to a woman's autonomy and dignity as a person" and, further, that "the ability to assert that autonomy and to exercise self-determination regarding one's own body is fundamental to the preservation and protection of a woman's dignity."[57] They further asserted that the law violated section 2(a) of the Charter, which guarantees freedom of conscience, because "the impugned legislation interferes with a woman's ability to make a moral or ethical decision as to whether or not she wishes to terminate a pregnancy," and moreover, that delays in access to funding violated Charter rights guarantees to security of the person.[58] The lower court judge ruled in favour of the complainants:

> I declare that Section 2(28)(a) of Manitoba Regulation 46/93 and sections 116(1)(h) and 116(2) of The Health Services Insurance Act of the Province of Manitoba are of no force and effect insofar as they pertain to therapeutic abortions because they are in violation of the rights and freedoms as guaranteed by sections 2(a), 7 and 15 of the Charter and do not constitute a reasonable and demonstrably justified limit on those rights and freedoms within the meaning of s. 1 of the Charter.[59]

Even though this case was quickly set aside on appeal on the grounds that it was not found to be "an appropriate case for summary judgment," for which "a trial is warranted," it remains a notable precedent in the recognition of positive rights to abortion access.[60] The apparent failure of the challengers to provide compelling proof of the stress they suffered as a result of delayed access to services and increased physical risk was centrally important.[61] Joanna Erdman (2007, 1108) stresses that the 1988 *Morgentaler* decision "set an onerous evidentiary burden under the threshold requirement of section 7," which made further litigation difficult. The vulnerability and resources of the individuals in question, resulting from the placement of this substantial evidentiary burden on them or other women who would bring forward charges, is troubling (ibid., 1115).

Despite their apparent interest in the implications of such a decision, the provincial and federal governments have failed to make efforts to research the consequences of delayed public access – notably, no Canada-wide study of abortion access has been commissioned since the Badgley Report (Erdman 2007, 1109). Without government support, and with the burden of a narrow legal definition of what constitutes an acceptable source of truth, the bar set by the courts is unlikely to be met.

Another issue also gave the appeal court pause when ruling on this case. The lower court found that the law in question was unconstitutional on the grounds that it created barriers to access, despite it being, by definition, "positive in character" (ibid., 1114). That is, the law was intended to grant some coverage, but it fell short of setting out to create universal coverage. Indeed, the interpretation of section 7 of the Charter in all the

Canadian provinces solidified this interpretation, as it has never been used to enforce a positive right to health (ibid.). Despite these shortcomings, Macfarlane (2014, 50) has argued that similar cases at the Supreme Court level, even when they adopt a negative rights approach, may employ judicial reasoning that "actually supports a constitutional obligation for provincial health delivery of these services even while the courts explicitly avoid a positive rights application of the charter." He goes on to suggest that these cases may be exceptional, since they otherwise advance an incoherent logic from a policy perspective, but also that they ought to be "a warning to the elected branches to give more explicit attention to their charter obligations" (ibid., 51).

To date, courts have been reluctant to recognize positive rights. Although many court cases have been important catalysts for government action and social movement mobilization in the provinces, the cases themselves are limited in scope. It is crucial, then, when considering potential avenues to protect and promote women's reproductive rights, to recognize the boundaries of potential approaches to these ends. The courts have been a valuable tool to advance rights claims in Canada, but they alone are unlikely to recognize a positive right to abortion access. As such, we ought to consider the value of looking to democratically elected bodies to recognize these rights, without neglecting the significance of social activism in creating a climate in which these rights claims are well received.

From Policy to Practice

The Canadian provinces have used their jurisdiction over health care to regulate abortion in different ways, effectively recreating the patchwork of services that led the Supreme Court to strike down the 1969 law on abortion as unconstitutional. As evidenced by the above cases, provincial governments have interpreted their obligations in the provision of abortion services in various ways; Ontario has attempted to uphold the spirit of the Charter in its provincial policies by treating abortion as a health care issue, though Quebec has gone further, recognizing a right to abortion access. Other provinces, such as New Brunswick and Nova Scotia, have a history of erecting barriers to service provision. These differences reflect diverse political climates as well as provincial governments that maintain different interpretations of the Charter and their role upholding its provisions.

The variety of provincial Charter jurisprudence following the 1988 *Morgentaler* decision illustrates the value of the courts as a venue for rights discussions when provincial governments are resistant to addressing them.

That said, courts are constrained in their ability to create access. Courts may keep rights discussions on the agenda and in the public consciousness, but they are unlikely to recognize a positive right to access in the provinces. These changes are more likely to emerge from political action, though such action seems unlikely to take place without the concerted efforts of social movement activists.

These sometimes dramatic variations in provincial responses to jurisdiction over abortion access demonstrate the problems inherent in assuming that the treatment of abortion as a medical issue can fill the policy vacuum left in the wake of the *Morgentaler* decision. Although abortion itself is a medical procedure, the ability to choose whether to carry a pregnancy to term is a deeply personal decision rooted in social expectations of women and their place in society. To deny women the right to make this choice, particularly under the guise that their ability to do so is apolitical, is an attempt to obscure the power relationships that underlie it.

4

Abortion as Health Care

Provincial jurisdiction over abortion is grounded in a federal division of powers that grants the provinces primary authority over health care. When these powers were initially granted at Confederation, health care lacked substantial political weight, as did most provincial powers.[1] The Fathers of Confederation had a largely unitary state in mind and failed to anticipate that a provincial rights movement would lead to the creation of a "thoroughly federal country" by the end of the nineteenth century (Russell 2004, 34). Moreover, they would have been unable to predict that public health care would become foundational to the Canadian national identity, or that many Canadians would come to view health care as a citizenship right (Maioni 2010, 226).

Public health care was first introduced in Saskatchewan in 1962, spearheaded by Premier Tommy Douglas, leader of the Co-operative Commonwealth Federation. The federal Medical Care Act later followed it in 1966, formally establishing publicly funded health care, albeit within strict parameters (Health Canada 2012). If they wished to receive federal money, "provincial programs would have to be universal, portable, publicly administered, and cover all services provided by physicians" (Maioni 2012, 169).[2] Over time, public health care has become widely accepted as a principal social good, and funding for more comprehensive care has increased, split between the provinces and territories and the federal government. Indeed, Antonia Maioni (2010, 165) suggests that the treatment of health care in

Canada captures "the essence of the successful model of Canadian federalism: decentralized jurisdictional responsibility (that allows provinces extensive policy-making capacity) combined with flexible federal intervention (that ensures equity across political boundaries)."

In order to fund health care, the federal government implemented a series of evolving health care transfers. Initially, these payments, which first took the form of the 1966 Canadian Assistance Plan, covered both health care and social services.[3] Eventually, in 2004, in an effort to "improve the transparency and accountability of federal support to provinces and territories (Department of Finance 2014)," the existing funding was split into two transfer payments: the Canada Social Transfer and the Canada Health Transfer. The latter is an annual transfer payment consisting of both a cash and a tax credit, for redistribution to the provinces to cover health care costs, while the former is a block payment in support of post-secondary education, early childcare, and social programs. Cumulatively, these funding streams have provided the provinces with the necessary tools to tailor health care systems to the needs of their citizens. The creation of regulatory frameworks governing these transfers also established clear inroads for federal influence on health care, but it is up to individual governments whether they wish to use them.

Although the federal government had always had influence through funding, in 1984, new legislation was enacted with the aim of clarifying the terms of its involvement. The Canada Health Act, a piece of legislation outlining the conditions under which the provinces could expect to receive the allotted funds, further elucidated the role of the federal government in health care. The act contains five central principles to which the provinces must adhere in order to receive financing: public administration, comprehensiveness, universality, portability, and accessibility. (Appendix A outlines specific ways these principles have been used to frame the regulation of abortion in Canada.) Under the act, the province must fund all physician and hospital services deemed to be medically necessary in accordance with these principles. The Canada Health Act does not, however, provide a definition of *medical necessity* or, for that matter, of *health*. The lack of clear terms in the act has proven a stumbling block for the creation of funded abortion access. At present, the interpretation of *necessity* is left to "negotiation between the particular provincial/territorial Ministry of Health, and the professional group representing the physicians of the province or territory" (Kaposy 2009, 303). The closed-door negotiations between these stakeholders provide guidance to physicians by classifying certain procedures as medically necessary, but individual physicians are left with ultimate discretion in their dealings with patients, which can mean a wide variance in access to care both between and within provinces (Collier 2012, 1770). When a procedure that is in any way stigmatized, such as abortion, enters this system, it can lead to disputes about the necessity of the procedure.

Nonetheless, pro-choice groups have consistently framed abortion as a medical necessity (ARCC 2013; NAF, n.d.), and this understanding has also been the foundation for legal challenges to provincial regulations (e.g., *Morgentaler v. New Brunswick* [2009]). Some governments have also adopted this view, but the force of this framework is dependent on larger federal arrangements.[4] Martin's Liberal government (2003–6), for example, attempted to crack down on provinces that had created regulations contravening these principles (ARCC 2007), although the Harper government's adherence to "open federalism" (White 2014, 166) meant that the Liberal government's previous investigations into violations of the Canada Health Act were not pursued. Trudeau, however, has committed to reopening discussions with the provinces on their adherence to the Canada Health Act (Action Canada 2015b), which could lead to resurgence in the use of the act to enforce access to abortion services in the provinces.

The resulting jurisdictional disputes over health care have come to characterize much of today's abortion debate in Canada, in which social activists pressure the courts and various levels of government to ensure that women's rights to abortion are recognized. What is often overlooked in this equation, however, are the added complexities created by the organization of health care in Canada. Provincial governments are "responsible for the management, organization and delivery of health services for their residents" but are not alone in shaping the nature of these services (Health Canada 2010). Provincial colleges of physicians and individual physicians have considerable influence on the delivery of services. It is true that provincial governments create regulations that may constrain the activities of physicians, but physicians are largely exempt from answering directly to legislatures; rather, they are subject to the will of provincial colleges of physicians and surgeons.[5] Moreover, though colleges are responsible for disciplinary actions against physicians, they often leave physicians the discretion to use their professional judgment in difficult circumstances. For these reasons, the medical profession in Canada is best thought of as highly atomistic – a reality with the potential to completely undermine women's equality rights claims to abortion access. After all, if women can exercise their rights only through nongovernmental actors who both regulate themselves independently of government and articulate a right to refuse services according to their conscience, how are we to decide whose rights take precedence?

Within this organizational labyrinth, other factors, including the availability of facilities and trained providers in a given province, as well as the types of abortion services available, further complicate the ability of women to access appropriate services. It is not surprising, then, that the multiple loci of authority over the provision of abortion services has created a profound variance in the ability of women to access services both within and between provinces. Even when women are denied services, the lack of transparency in the regulation of health care means that they are unlikely to understand their rights as patients, often because the scope of these rights has not been made explicit.

By showcasing the variance in access that results from the policy vacuum surrounding abortion, this chapter aims to highlight both the strengths and limitations of restricting abortion to the realm of health care. Although abortion is, unquestionably, a medical procedure, its treatment in law and policy, as well as motivations offered for expanding or restricting its availability, belies such a straightforward framework. Rather, its treatment suggests that the regulation of reproductive bodies is part of a larger history of women's inequality that requires rights recognitions to address. The complexity of health care regulation in Canada, especially when physicians' rights are considered, demands an increase in transparency generally, and a recognition of women's rights to abortion access specifically. Ultimately, classifying abortion solely as a medical issue obscures the relationship between women's reproductive choices and their status as equal citizens.

The Shortcomings of Health Care

Canada's commitment to a national medical program is a testament to the importance the country places on the health of its citizens. Nonetheless, scholars studying abortion disagree as to whether the procedure ought to be treated as a straightforward matter of health care. One reason for this skepticism concerns the use of this framework in practice. Although access to abortion services has improved in some provinces as a result of its classification as a health care issue; in others, this very classification has been used to justify restrictions on access. Until recently, New Brunswick, to take one prominent example, used its jurisdiction over health care to create barriers to accessing services. When questioned about its regulations, the province cited its jurisdictional authority to make the health care decisions it deemed best for its citizens, even if those decisions meant creating barriers to abortion access without any medical rationale. These restrictions can also occur at the practitioner level when women encounter physicians who object to performing an abortion, or even object to offering guidance or referrals to assist them in making a choice.

Shelley Gavigan (1992, 127) points out that feminists have long been wary of classifying abortion as a medical procedure because of the contradictory justifications this necessitates. To be sure, classifying abortion as a medical issue has undesirable implications. Understanding abortion as a straightforward health issue obscures its links with the status of women in society. Certainly, my claim about the need to understand abortion as a positive right extends beyond a purely medical framework to a more robust view of equal community membership. However, the need to see abortion in its proper context does not preclude the provision of abortion services within medicine. Indeed, the significance Canada places on universal health care has "fuelled the pro-choice movement" in the aftermath of *R. v. Morgentaler* (1988) (ibid.). The promise of comprehensive, funded access to necessary medical services has been a powerful tool to advance women's claims to abortion as a right, even as it risks depoliticizing the issue.

When making claims for ensuring abortion is a funded and accessible procedure, however, it is important to recognize that not all medical procedures in Canada have a claim to public funds. According to the Canada Health Act, in order for a procedure to be guaranteed coverage under a province's health insurance plan, it must first be classified as *medically necessary*. Yet the specific requirements for this classification, as detailed above, are undefined, which has given activist groups and physicians alike room to critique the inclusion of abortion in this category, even though all the provinces and territories in Canada do classify abortion as a medical necessity.

Nonetheless, anti-abortion advocates have used the concept of medical necessity to dispute the appropriateness of classifying abortion as a health care procedure. They contend that abortion often happens for social reasons rather than purely medical ones and should therefore not be considered a required medical service. Of course, this critique depends on a narrow definition of health that seems to exclude both mental health and social determinants of health. Even though the Canada Health Act does not provide a clear definition of health with which to dismiss these claims, as Chris Kaposy (2009) explains, the anti-abortion dismissal of abortion as a required service can still be reasonably rejected on two grounds. First, what if we take a broader definition of health, like that adopted by the World Health Organization in 1948, which frames it as "a state of complete physical, mental, and social well-being and not merely the absence of disease or infirmity" (WHO 2003). If we adopt this definition, "abortion for social reasons is medically necessary because social well-being is part of health"; moreover, "a procedure cannot be regarded as medically unnecessary if women's health, in the sense of social well being, is compromised by not having the procedure" (Kaposy 2009, 304). Second, if we consider social determinants of health, the anti-abortion stance does not hold up. "Abortion," Kaposy (2009, 304) says, "is a tool that can enable women to avoid many of these social ills [e.g., physical and sexual abuse, poor education, poverty, inadequate housing], and barriers to abortion access place women in peril of experiencing them." Such a definition of health, which seems more reflective of the health care system in practice, suggests that health is something more holistic than simply being free of disease. Indeed, the preamble to the Canada Health Act lists well-being, prevention, and "collective action against the social, environmental and occupational causes of disease."[6]

Critiques of this view might suggest that a more expansive definition of health means the inclusion of a range of procedures, treatments, and other considerations that currently exist outside the realm of publicly funded medicine. This critique is not without merit. Although it may be ideal to provide the most complete care possible for all Canadian citizens, this is not feasible in the existing system, and so the provision of services is carefully weighted and considered; offering one service often means forgoing another. In the allocation of health dollars, the objective is to get the best health outcome for the dollar spent. In this way, abortion is as straightforward a procedure as they come. Abortions are safe, inexpensive, and require minimal physician training. In this respect, the suggestion that abortion should be treated as a core, medically necessary service is uncontroversial. Given the substantive constraints on health care dollars, this is an important point.[7]

Bearing these practical implications of treating abortion as a health issue in mind, we return to the question of why the treatment of abortion as a matter of health is so often contested. Certainly, abortion is far from the only medical procedure with deep social implications. The consequences of being denied any number of medical procedures or being unable to access them in a timely manner can dramatically impact people's lives and interactions with their communities. Neither is abortion alone as a medical procedure that is highly stigmatized. Accessing gender reassignment surgery, for example, though it is a comparatively rare procedure, may also come with stigma. Likewise, stigma often accompanies illnesses such as AIDS and other infections that may be sexually transmitted. What distinguishes abortion from other stigmatized issues in health care is its uniquely gendered implications.

Although not all women can become pregnant, only those with female reproductive organs can experience pregnancy, a biological reality that is inextricably tied to deeply held gender role expectations that continue to structure women's lives, regardless of whether they chose to have children.[8] Kaposy (2009, 307) stresses that failing to provide public funding for abortion care "is also a denial of self-determination" that would "leave some women unable to make choices about whether or not to bear a child, which is one of the most profound life-changing events anyone experiences."[9] Treating abortion solely as a medical issue may disconnect it from a larger discourse on the role of women's reproductive lives in the realization of equality. For instance, if access to abortion services is measured merely in terms of the mother's health, physical or mental, the sociopolitical implications of an unwanted pregnancy are obscured. Indeed, the nebulous definition of both *health* and *necessity* within the Canada Health Act further complicates the use of medical necessity. Although many physicians may take a woman's own choices into account when providing services, they are not mandated to do so. Moreover, in practice, many physicians opt out of helping women access abortion and other reproductive health services, even if the procedure is required.[10]

The gendered implications of this treatment are especially compelling when we consider the reality that, "unlike abortion, all provincial public health plans insure prenatal, maternity, and neonatal intensive care without condition," despite the significant cost associated with these services (Erdman 2007, 1144). Indeed, the costs and dangers associated with childbirth "are not considered an unreasonable burden on the public health system" (ibid.). Why, then, would a comparatively safe and inexpensive procedure that helps safeguard the physical and mental health of women not be considered a necessary service? Pregnancy, after all, can be physically dangerous (in rare cases, even fatal), and the desire to terminate an unwanted pregnancy in the absence of medical assistance can often lead women to dangerous back-alley abortions or even self-harm (MacQuarrie, MacDonald, and Chambers 2014). The health implications of pregnancy are not negligible, yet the health considerations associated with abortion are often framed as a matter of choice, whereas carrying a pregnancy to term is not. Why the discrepancy? Simply put, because abortion is one of the grounds on which the political battles over women's rights are fought.

Moreover, implicit in the belief that abortion access can be achieved solely by locating abortion in the realm of medicine is that access to health care itself is a constitutionally protected right. Despite the fact that "most Canadians have come to consider health care, in common parlance, a right of citizenship" (Maioni 2010, 225), Canadians do not have a constitutionally protected right to health care. Although public opinion polls "reveal that Canadians, encouraged by politicians and the media, believe they have a constitutional right to receive health care ... no such right is explicitly contained in the Charter" and no other "Canadian law specifically confer[s] that right" (Parliament of Canada, Standing Senate Committee on Social Affairs, Science and Technology 2002). Put simply, in spite of government support for publicly funded health care, denial of services does not necessarily constitute a rights violation.[11] Moreover, as a matter under provincial jurisdiction, the provinces, and more specifically individual physicians, have discretion over what services are provided in specific circumstances, though they risk having federal transfer payments docked if they fail to conform to the Canada Health Act. Of course, this is without considering international protections meant to safeguard access to abortion services.

Erdman, Grenon, and Harrison-Wilson (2008, 1764) identify the International Covenant on Economic, Social and Cultural Rights as entitling Canadian women (by virtue of Canada being a signatory to the covenant) to "available, accessible, and acceptable reproductive health care, including abortion care." Likewise, international organizations in which Canada is active, like the United Nations, affirm women's reproductive rights broadly, and their rights to access safe abortion services specifically. These rights recognitions are important for the realization of women's equality but, as is true of Canadian law, without enforcement or social acceptance, they cannot ensure it. Moreover, when these issues are framed as matters of health rather than equality, abortion risks being treated as an apolitical issue, disconnected from its implications for the status of women in Canada.

Both Erdman (2007) and Gavigan (1992) make important points about the treatment of abortion as a health service. Abortion is considered a medically necessary service in Canada, but we should also be wary of limiting it to a health issue. Mandating expanded access through recognition as a medical necessity will certainly have important knock-on effects that will further legitimize the procedure, but it will not resolve many of the ongoing elements of its troubling treatment. After all, most provinces today do consider abortion a medical necessity, yet barriers persist, including stigma and harassment of women and abortion providers. It is only through governments' more holistic understanding of abortion, as fundamentally connected to women's gender role expectations in ways that implicate their status as citizens, that both the federal and provincial governments will begin to make lasting and substantive progress. The classification of medical necessity may seem to offer an easy answer to the access problem, and it does have significance, but provincial recognition of a need for access does not go far enough in recognizing the significance of the procedure to women's equality.

Whether individuals understand abortion from their personal belief systems and moralize the procedure or treat it as a necessary right for women's equality, its regulation across Canada reflects how it is socially perceived. In essence, relegating abortion to the realm of health care has left access to the procedure vulnerable. Some provinces, such as Quebec, have created exceptionally progressive services under the umbrella of health care; others, including New Brunswick, have used a health care framework to restrict access to the procedure. Without women having some form of rights protections to ensure at least a minimum level of services, keeping abortion solely in the medical sphere leaves women's equality largely to the discretion of physicians.[12] To truly comprehend this vulnerability, it is important to appreciate the multiplicity of rights claims at play in the provision of health care across Canada and to understand the sequence of events that led to provincial jurisdiction over abortion provision. The first dimension of this relationship concerns the dynamics of federalism in structuring provincial access.

The Role of Federalism in Health Care

Canada's universal, publicly funded health-insurance program is designed to ensure that "all residents have reasonable access to medically necessary hospital and physician services, on a prepaid basis." Instead of a national program, individual provinces and territories handle insurance, "all of which share certain common features and basic standards of coverage" (Health Canada 2010). Provinces must comply with the five basic tenets of the Canada Health Act. Failure to adhere to these principles may warrant a denial of the maximum amount of federal funding to the provinces through the Canada Health Transfer, though the force of this mechanism depends on the political will of federal governments to employ it.

Linda White (2014, 165) stresses that, as a result of the manner in which constitutional authority over abortion has been divided, "the federal government has few levers to compel provincial governments to deliver services, save for using the federal spending power." Previous governments have been willing to withhold transfers to provinces that refused to fund abortions in private clinics, yet White notes that Harper's Conservative government was loath to use its authority to pressure the provinces into action (ibid., 166).[13] The blurry division of authority between the federal and provincial governments in the regulation of abortion makes it especially difficult to challenge existing policies. An example of this problem is evident in the federal government's attempts to intervene in New Brunswick's refusal to fund private clinics.

In 2005, then federal Liberal health minister Ujjal Dosanjh initiated a dispute avoidance and resolution (DAR) action against the province for its refusal to "reimburse the cost of abortions carried out in private clinics" (Eggertson 2005, 862). DAR is a process created in 2002 to resolve "disputes related to the interpretation of the principles of the Canada Health Act" (Health Canada 2013, 171). This process is launched in the event of disagreements over the application of the Canada Health Act by different levels of government. The process begins with "government-to-government fact-finding negotiations," which a third party can take over on the request of either the federal or provincial minister of health, though the "final authority to interpret and enforce the Canada Health Act" falls to the federal minister (ibid.). Should the levels of government be unable to come to an agreement on the issue in question, the noncompliance provisions of the act can come into effect. Noncompliance can result in a "deduction from federal transfer payments under the CHT [Canada Health Transfer]" proportional to the "gravity of the default" (ibid., 6).

The response from the New Brunswick government, then under the leadership of Bernard Lord, a Progressive Conservative, was not conducive to productive negotiations. New Brunswick minister of health Elvy Robichaud publicly stated that the provincial government would not "bow to pressure" from the federal Liberals (Richardson 2011). Judy Burwell, the former director of the Fredericton Morgentaler Clinic, recalled the difficulties that the federal government faced in its dealings with the province: "The New Brunswick government was just the most arrogant ... they wouldn't return calls, they just ignored them, because they know they can."[14] The province failed to comply with the fact-finding component of DAR, so Dosanjh announced he would appoint a third-party panel. But before any resolution could be achieved, a federal election took place and the Liberals lost to Harper's Conservatives. The new Conservative minister of health, Tony Clement, appeared "reluctant to continue [the] dispute resolution process with New Brunswick" and soon announced: "The federal government does not intend to pursue the matter of abortion funding at the NB clinic," stating that the "issue is 'off the radar'" (ARCC 2007, 3). During their time in office, the Conservatives did not use DAR to sanction any province restricting abortion access services. Although the door remains open for the newly elected Liberal government, under Justin Trudeau, to reinitiate this process, no action has yet been taken on this front. There are, of course, other federal mechanisms in effect that are meant to ensure that all Canadians receive equal access to necessary medical procedures.

Reciprocal billing agreements are another example of an attempt to ensure more uniform access to medical services for Canadians – in this instance, for residents requiring care outside their home provinces. All provinces and territories have signed on to reciprocal hospital agreements that ensure all "insured hospital services are payable at the approved rates of the host province or territory" when provincial medicare cards are presented (Health Canada 2007, 266). This system does not require the patient to pay out of pocket or wait for reimbursement for services. The reciprocal billing agreement, which makes physician services accessed by individuals outside their home province payable to the host provinces, was entrenched four months after the 1988 *Morgentaler* decision (CIHI 2007, 1; ibid., 267). Every province, with the exception of Quebec, is part of this arrangement, and it covers most health care services. This means that patients can present their health cards anywhere in Canada and have the services they receive billed to their home province. However, a small number of services were made exempt from this act in 1988. Abortion services were excluded, alongside plastic surgery for appearance and psychoanalysis (CIHI 2007, F-1). These excluded services were considered to be either not time sensitive or still experimental, or to have less costly alternative treatments. The rationale for excluding abortion under the reciprocal billing agreement was not made explicit.

Since the procedure was excluded from reciprocal billing arrangements, many provinces made efforts to ensure that their citizens still have access to abortion services outside their home province. Often, access was organized through arrangements with specific hospitals and clinics outside the province. However, information regarding reciprocal billing policies for abortion in Canada is difficult to access, as there is no federal or provincial database. For women in need of these services, the lack of a centralized format poses considerable difficulty. Fortunately for women in need of care, abortion was quietly removed from the list of prohibited services in 2015. According to Dawn Fowler, Canadian director of the National Abortion Federation, as of June 18, 2015, "abortion is now included on the inter-provincial billing agreement."[15] She explains that, "since health is a provincial mandate, the notices have been sent via bulletins to physicians through each provincial/territorial system for informing physicians of changes in billing practices," but no public statement was made about this change or the motivations for it. As such, many women are likely still unaware that these barriers are no longer in place.

Whether the federal government is willing to enforce the Canada Health Act through available mechanisms highlights the role of federalism in shaping access across Canada. But the power of federalism extends beyond government bodies; physicians have also organized nationally.

Physicians

Organizations – including the Canadian Medical Association (CMA), which provides professional and ethical reports outlining the rights and responsibilities of physicians, and the Society of Obstetricians and Gynaecologists of Canada, which creates procedural guidelines detailing "safe and effective methods for the termination of pregnancy" (CMA 1988; David 2006, 1014) – have attempted to provide a degree of uniform, national structure for physicians. Collectively, these organizations offer procedural, ethical, and professional guidelines for doctors working in all provinces and territories. Unlike the federal government, however, they lack recourse should physicians opt to disregard these guidelines, as provincial colleges maintain disciplinary power over physicians.

Every province and territory has its own medical association and college of physicians and surgeons. The provincial and territorial medical associations are divisions of the CMA, though they are "autonomous, with specific responsibilities in their provincial/territorial jurisdictions" (CMA 2012). Provincial medical associations thus represent "the professional interests of the Society's members [including] the advancement of medical science [and] physician work-related issues" (College of Physicians and Surgeons of New Brunswick 2005). Each province also has a college of physicians and surgeons responsible for licensing doctors who fall under its jurisdiction. The college is responsible for enforcing regulations and ensuring adherence to professional ethical standards. This includes issuing sanctions and other disciplinary actions when required. These organizations work in conjunction with provincial governments to deliver health care. As a result, if we are to understand how medicine is delivered in each province, it is necessary to focus on the provincial colleges rather than national bodies as the regulators of individual physicians.

Although health care falls under provincial jurisdiction and is funded largely through federal transfer payments, physicians are responsible for providing the health care services *on the ground*. The regulatory framework of medicine in Canada means that, even when provincial colleges share the same guidelines as national bodies, they are responsible for enforcing their own rules of conduct. The implications of these organizational structures inform the nature and scope of abortion access in the provinces.

Medical schools are heavily subsidized in Canada, with provincial governments contributing significant sums to guarantee seats for residents from their own provinces, though students are still required to pay tuition.[16] For example, Prince Edward Island pays $800,000 annually to secure four seats at Memorial University medical school for PEI students (R. Ross 2013). These arrangements are common, with many provincial governments hoping that this investment will pay off if students return to practise in their home provinces.

Yet, despite these government subsidies, medicine is a self-regulating profession, and the specifics of how physicians are trained and what they learn is at the discretion of nongovernmental bodies. The Committee on the Accreditation of Canadian Medical Schools (CACMS) was created in 1979 and worked alongside the US–based Liaison Committee on Medical Education to establish Canada-wide standards for medical schools. Only those schools "demonstrating compliance are afforded accreditation, a necessary condition for a program's graduates to be licensed as physicians" (Association of Faculties of Medicine of Canada 2008). These committees are jointly responsible for standardizing, among other things, medical school curricula.

Even with these standards in place, the content taught at schools across the country varies considerably. Not all Canadian schools currently teach their students how to perform abortions, either in the classroom or during residency. Without this training, a shortage in trained physicians is anticipated, particularly in rural areas, which risks rendering the *Morgentaler* (1988) decision irrelevant (ARCC 2005; Blackwell 2013). The reasons for these training gaps are often unclear, but a range of issues – from fears of violence or harassment to personal moral opposition to abortion – may be motivating factors. In response, chapters of Medical Students for Choice have formed across the country to advocate for the inclusion of abortion in the curricula as well as for the creation of residency opportunities.[17] These chapters have been successful in influencing some schools, but the need for students to lobby for such change is troubling, particularly as abortion is a safe and simple procedure that one in three Canadian women will access in their lifetimes.[18] A study by Medical Students for Choice in Canada and the United States revealed that "nearly 40% of the more than 50 schools surveyed do not teach any aspect of abortion in the preclinical years." It went on to note that, "on average, more class time is dedicated to Viagra than to abortion procedures, pregnancy options counseling, or abortion law and policy" (Koyama and Williams 2005, 4). Of course, even if students do learn to perform abortions in medical school, their rights when they become physicians may free them from the obligation to perform the procedure.

As a result of the ethical debate about abortion, the CMA attempted to articulate a clear stance on the issue in December 1988, asserting that "induced abortions should be uniformly available to all women in Canada" and covered under provincial health-insurance plans (CMA 1988, 2). It also made it clear that a doctor "whose moral or religious beliefs prevent him or her from recommending or performing an abortion" should be free from compulsion to do so; the CMA holds tightly to the belief that "the decision to perform an induced abortion is a medical one, made privately between the patient and her physician" (ibid., 1).

The stress placed on the ability of physicians to refuse to participate in abortions implicates conscientious objection, a concept that refers to the right of doctors to refuse to provide services that would require them to act against their own moral compass. The right of physicians in Canada to conscientiously object to providing abortion services, barring emergency circumstances, is recognized by the CMA, though the specifics of this right are left to the discretion of the provincial colleges. Notably, according to a representative of the CMA, a woman's desire for an abortion, even if she has encountered barriers to access that have delayed the procedure, does not constitute such an emergency.[19] In order to contravene a physician's objection, the situation would have to be one of life and death.

A woman whose doctor refuses to provide a referral can seek the help of another doctor, though she may be unaware of this recourse.[20] And even if she is able to make an appointment with another doctor in a timely manner, there are no guarantees that the next doctor will agree to help her access an abortion. In other words, although abortion is a recognized medical procedure, there is no legal requirement that the medical sector make such a procedure available in an accessible and timely manner. This model takes the onus off physicians to ensure that their patients receive care and creates unreasonable barriers for women attempting to access a safe and legal medical procedure. The rights of practitioners are protected above those of women seeking to terminate a pregnancy, though these rights have been met with scrutiny.[21] The significance of conscientious objection for the outcomes of patients becomes all the more stark when the reality that many Canadians do not even have access to a family doctor is considered.[22]

The force of the belief in conscientious objection was evidenced by responses to a guest editorial written for the *Canadian Medical Association Journal* in 2006. *Abortion: Ensuring Access* was written with the intent of educating physicians on the still precarious nature of abortion access in Canada. It drew attention to some of the tactics taken by anti-abortion physicians to block access, noting that "health care professionals who withhold a diagnosis, fail to provide appropriate referrals, delay access, misdirect women or provide punitive treatment" are committing malpractice and breaching the CMA Code of Ethics, which "prohibits discrimination on the basis of sex, marital status and medical condition" (Rodgers and Downie 2006, 9). Despite its progressive message, which was in keeping with CMA position statements, the editorial received criticism from anti-abortion physicians concerned about the apparent professional obligation to provide referrals (Blackmer 2007, 1310). These concerns pushed the CMA to clarify its position on referrals for abortion services. It suggested that not referring was acceptable so long as the doctor did not further "interfere in any way with [the] patient's right to obtain [an] abortion" (ibid.).

These disputes demonstrate a lack of clarity about conscientious objection. Indeed, a recent collection on conscientious objection in *Bioethics* found that, in addition to the CMA's vague policy, other bodies "have policies concerning refusals that govern physicians but are at times inconsistent, and yet they provide no indication of which policy takes priority in the face of an inconsistency" (McLeod and Downie 2014, ii). At the moment, provinces also vary in their guidelines around the policy: "the College of Physicians and Surgeons of New Brunswick states that referral in the case of moral objection is 'not an obligation' but 'preferred practice,'" whereas in Quebec, "physicians are not only required to refer patients but also to inform them of the 'possible consequences of not receiving such professional services'" (Glauser 2014, E483). And the Ontario College of Physicians and Surgeons recently reviewed the college's policy on conscientious objection, voting twenty-one to three to prevent the "moral or religious convictions of a doctor" from obstructing "a patient's access to care" (Kirkey 2015). Important considerations going forward involve the implications of the conflict between physicians' rights and patients' rights.

Physicians' rights to religious or moral beliefs can be curtailed when they infringe on the rights of others, such as the right to access services without discrimination, said Barbara Hall when she was chief of the Ontario Human Rights Commission. The college's policy "could clarify that limiting services based on moral or religious grounds could be *prima facie* discrimination." For example, a physician who provides birth control to married women but objects to providing contraception to unmarried women may be found by a tribunal to be discriminating based on marital status (Glauser 2014, E483).

Ontario's new policy requires that physicians provide referrals for prescriptions or procedures to which they conscientiously object while upholding the existing requirement that doctors must perform necessary procedures in an emergency, "regardless of their beliefs," on pain of professional misconduct (Kirkey 2015). Although this policy may signal progress for some, the province's medical association has yet to come out in support of it, "arguing that it forces physicians to do something that may conflict with their fundamental beliefs."[23] The Ontario Human Rights Commission, in contrast, writes that the policy "is in line with legal principles set out in court rulings," and went on to recognize that "rights can be limited by the rights and freedoms of others" (ibid.).

Physicians, then, have considerable power to shape the provision of abortion access on the ground. Even the gestational limits for abortion are at the discretion of doctors. Although government-funding restrictions and the availability of appropriate facilities may impose practical time limits on the procedure, such limits are not codified in law. The services provided by the provinces reflect the preferences of practitioners to perform abortions up to a certain number of weeks of gestation, as well as the CMA's policy statement on induced abortion, which allows for termination of pregnancy only before fetal viability (approximately twenty weeks), barring "exceptional circumstances" (CMA 1988, 2). The significance of this discretion over abortion becomes more apparent when the different types of abortion are considered.

The Procedure

Although often talked about as a single procedure, different types of abortion are, in fact, available. The procedures can be divided into two groups: medical abortions and surgical abortions. The choice of method depends on several factors, including availability, gestational age, and the woman's preference. Medical abortions, for instance, may seem preferable, since part of the procedure can often be carried out at home and does not necessarily require a woman to go to an abortion clinic or hospital, since general practitioners can provide them. However, the experience itself is more prolonged than a surgical abortion, requires a follow-up appointment, and can be accompanied by cramping and bleeding, which may be a deterrent. On the other hand, surgical abortions may be seen as desirable because – especially in the first trimester, when the vast majority of abortions are performed – they are relatively quick and have a short recovery period. It is, however, still a surgical procedure, which some women may feel is invasive. Of course, not all women in Canada have a full range of choices available to them. Ensuring that the correct equipment, medication, and training is available for a given procedure across Canada can be highly politicized.

Without any legal limitations on abortion, the specifics of the procedure are left largely to the discretion of physicians, but that does not mean the consequences of these decisions are apolitical. The choices of these non-governmental actors may profoundly affect the ability of women to exercise their rights. Different types of abortion (detailed below) may require longer recovery times, involve significant travel, or necessitate multiple visits to clinics, hospitals, or physicians – the result of any of which may be an insurmountable barrier to access.

Although they have considerable discretion, physicians may also feel limited in the kinds of procedures they are able to perform. Governments often place restrictions on the locations in which abortions can be performed, and by whom. Whether protections are granted for physicians who feel threatened by demonstrators at work is also left to the discretion of governments, who can chose whether to create bubble zones around certain facilities. As well, governments may determine, directly or indirectly, the types of technologies available on the Canadian market, as revealed through controversy on a new form of medical abortion (discussed below). Cumulatively, the influence of these actors has real consequences for women's experiences when seeking abortion services.

During the first trimester, either surgical or medical abortions can be performed. In the first fourteen weeks after the first day of a woman's last period, the method of surgical abortion used is called vacuum aspiration. The National Abortion Federation, the professional association of abortion providers in North America, produces annually updated clinical guidelines for providers. Its guidelines describe the procedure as follows:

> Suction (from either a machine or a hand-held pump) is used to remove the pregnancy through the cervix (the opening to the uterus). This procedure is very brief, usually 5–15 minutes. Although women's experiences with

aspiration abortion vary, many say that it is "uncomfortable but bearable." Most women return to their daily activities the day after their abortion. (NAF 2015a).[24]

After fourteen weeks, surgical abortions normally take the form of a dilation and evacuation (the same procedure used for late-term miscarriages), though second-trimester procedures can be medically induced.[25]

Medical abortion is also available in the first trimester, but normally only in the first seven weeks of pregnancy. The details of the procedure depend on the type of medication used. Before Health Canada announced that a new drug, Mifegymiso, had been approved and would be on the market in 2016, a combination of two drugs – methotrexate and misoprostol – was used. The first medication, methotrexate, is taken at the facility. A few days later, as directed by the facility, a second medication, misoprostol, is taken. Typically, pain, cramping, and bleeding similar to that of a heavy period occur a few hours after taking misoprostol (the second medication), and the abortion itself, which resembles a miscarriage, usually occurs within twenty-four hours (NAF 2015a). Importantly, women who use this form of medical abortion must return for a follow-up visit to verify that the termination was successful. Although the procedure has a 95 percent to 98 percent success rate, these drugs can cause birth defects when they are not successful and require that the patient has follow-up care, which may include the necessity of a surgical abortion.

This drug combination is only available "off label," meaning the drugs are available separately and were approved by Health Canada for different indications. Neither (alone or in combination) was formally approved for use as an abortifacient. Although this drug combination has been a staple of service provision in Canada for decades, the fact that it was not approved for the purpose of inducing abortion also means that it is not bound by the same Health Canada guidelines as drugs used for their indicated purpose(s). It is these very guidelines that have created controversy around a new drug on the Canadian market – Mifegymiso – a drug widely used in European countries that is considered to provide a safer and more effective option for medical abortion.

Mifegymiso is a combination of two existing drugs: mifepristone (commonly called RU-486) and misoprostol.[26] This drug combination is the "internationally recognized 'gold standard'" of abortion care (Dunn and Cook 2014, 13) and, when it is available, is recommended for use instead of methotrexate in clinical guidelines (NAF 2015b).[27] It differs from methotrexate (plus misoprostol) in two ways. First, it is safe for use up to nine weeks of gestation, thereby creating a larger window for women to choose a medical abortion (WHO 2012b, 3). Second, unlike methotrexate, Mifegymiso is not teratogenic, meaning it does not cause fetal abnormalities that require follow-up care and a possible resort to surgical abortion if it is unsuccessful (WHO 2012b, 46). These advances in medical abortion are noteworthy because they necessitate "less technical skill and simpler health care infrastructure," meaning they can be "delivered in a broader range of health care facilities and offered by a more diverse and larger set of providers" (Erdman, Grenon, and Harrison-Wilson 2008, 1764).

Despite its potential benefits, Mifegymiso was delayed in coming to the Canadian market. The wait to approve the drug has been "attributed to the Canadian drug approval process, which can be initiated only by application from a pharmaceutical company" (Erdman, Grenon, and Harrison-Wilson 2008, 1767). The government received an application on November 14, 2012 (Health Canada 2017). Yet, even amid assurances from the deputy minister of Health Canada that the application "would go faster than normal applications" owing to the drug's widespread use, the approval process was noticeably protracted (Grant 2014a). When questioned about the delay, Health Canada spokesperson Leslie Meerburg said: "Timing for the review of drug submissions varies depending on the information provided by the manufacturer, as well as [on] whether or not requests for additional information or clarification are needed" (Action Canada 2015c).

This vague explanation, in combination with the political weight of the decision, has contributed to speculation that certain politicians may have had a hand in delaying the process. NDP leader Thomas Mulcair observed that "[Health Minister Rona Ambrose] has a history on this particular file, so I hope her personal opinions are not stopping a health solution for some women who want to have [a medical abortion]." Further, referring to Ambrose's history of voting in favour of anti-abortion bills such as Stephen Woodworth's 2012 motion to reexamine the definition of *human being*, he remarked, "I certainly hope that politics is not in play" (Payton 2014). As of yet, however, there is no hard evidence.

Notwithstanding the delay, and requests for more information from the drug company that would be manufacturing the drug (Grant 2014b), Mifegymiso was eventually approved in July 2015 and was expected to be on the market in 2016, but encountered delays on the supply end, only entering the market in January of 2017.[28] It has been approved for use on the Canadian market until seven weeks of gestation.[29]

According to a Health Canada monograph on Mifegymiso, the drug faces numerous restrictions now that it is on the market. First, it will be accessible only through physicians and can be supplied only by those who have first taken a six-hour online course to educate them on the drug. This likely means that the distribution of the drug will be limited to specific physicians – if you conscientiously object to medical abortion, why have the drug in your office, let alone take the time to complete the module? There is also concern that some physicians, particularly those in small, rural practices, the very areas that would benefit most from access to this drug, do not have the experience or means to stock and sell drugs to their patients (Lunn 2016).[30] Moreover, some provincial colleges of physicians and surgeons "don't allow doctors to dispense drugs, so doctors in those provinces would have to get special permission to prescribe and dispense Mifegymiso," adding another obstacle to its provision (ibid.). Despite the safety of the drug and its potential to improve access to abortion Canada-wide, this restriction could dramatically reduce availability.

Other medical professions, including pharmacists, the established experts in drug therapy and distribution, have also expressed concern regarding these restrictions on the distribution of Mifegymiso. Indeed, a statement by the Canadian Pharmacists Association (CPhA) on the approval of Mifegymiso by Health Canada reveals that the "CPhA is disappointed that access will be limited at this initial stage through distribution only at clinics through physician dispensing, despite the key role community pharmacists play in the distribution and patient care associated with medications" (Canadian Pharmacists Association 2015). The statement goes on to say that

> access to abortion services in Canada is often an issue, with geography a substantial barrier, particularly in rural or remote communities. Pharmacists can play a key role in the distribution and patient care associated with this medication to ensure it is provided in a safe, convenient and timely manner. Including community pharmacists in the dispensing and counselling for medical abortion, in collaboration with the prescribing physician, enhances the care that a woman receives, improves access and follow-up. (Ibid.)

A representative of the CPhA further revealed that the organization "has been in discussions with both Health Canada and key stakeholders regarding how Mifegymiso will be prescribed and dispensed."[31] The sentiments of these talks have also been supported by other organizations. In response to the decision to allow Mifegymiso onto the Canadian market, Action

Canada for Sexual Health and Rights has expressed the hope that "Canada will eventually follow the World Health Organization's recommendation that health-care providers other than doctors – midwives and nurse practitioners, for example – be allowed [to] provide the pill" (Goodyear 2015). Although Health Canada has since clarified that pharmacists could still be responsible for filling a prescription for Mifegymiso, provided it is delivered directly to the doctor's office to be administered rather than to the patient, the only justification offered for this mandate is a desire to "help reduce risks to patients" (Health Canada 2016).

A second restriction on the drug is the requirement that a woman must undergo an ultrasound to determine gestational age and to identify risk factors associated with its use (such as ectopic pregnancy), before the medication may be administered. Other countries do not require an ultrasound before drug usage. Moreover, in rural areas, where the advantage of more effective medical abortion could lead to dramatic improvements in access, ultrasounds may not be readily available. Since this requirement is not consistent with the practice in other countries, and may limit the use of the drug where it is most needed, it is troubling. Indeed, commenting on these requirements, the president of the National Abortion Federation in Canada and the United States said, "There's no evidence to support that an ultrasound is necessary to provide safe and effective abortion care. So it's unfortunate that they're making it a requirement, and [that it] may impede some women's access to the care" (Paperny 2016).

Finally, physicians are able to require a woman to take the first dose of the drug while under their supervision. Dr. Supriya Sharma, Health Canada's senior medical adviser, says that this option was meant to verify that the patient, first, was seeking the drug for themselves and, second, did not delay its use until later in their pregnancy, when its use could result in complications (Kirkey 2016). Dr. Wendy Norman, a member of the Society of Obstetricians and Gynaecologists of Canada, called this requirement "medically unnecessary and demeaning to Canadian women," since there is "no evidence in any jurisdiction that women would seek and obtain a mifepristone prescription, yet not use it" (ibid.). Others pointed out that this requirement is offensive because such a requirement is typically used to prevent drug trafficking, and there "is no evidence women who want to terminate a pregnancy would try to sell Mifegymiso on the streets" (Picard 2016).[32]

Because abortion can take multiple forms that are suited to a variety of circumstances, decisions about what types of abortion will be available have profound consequences for women's citizenship. As such, these decisions must not be perceived as somehow apolitical. Although the medical profession may be insulated from politics in important ways, they are still subject to political influence. Moreover, even if physicians were completely shielded from government power, their role in shaping access to a procedure necessary for women's equality would necessitate their recognition as political actors in certain respects, regardless of whether they want to be.

Facilities

Just as specific forms of abortion impact women's choices, so too do the available facilities. Different abortion procedures require different facilities, equipment, and levels of expertise. Today, abortion services in Canada can be accessed at various institutions, including hospitals, specialized clinics, private physician offices, women's health centres, and, in Quebec, des centres locaux des services communautaires (local community service centres, or CLSCs) (Echo 2011, 2; FQPN and CFC 2010, 5).[33] (Appendix B offers a list of the facilities that provide abortion access across Canada.) A full array of facilities is not available in every province, and some provinces will fund services only when they are performed at specific facilities. New Brunswick, for example, will fund only those abortions performed at "registered medical institutions," while refusing to grant abortion clinics this status. Ontario and Quebec cover services performed at all aforementioned locations, though clinics have only recently been fully funded in Quebec.[34] Where abortions should be performed continues to be a contested topic in many provinces. New Brunswick is resistant to expanding services beyond hospitals, and there is concern in Ontario and Quebec that abortion services are increasingly being relegated to clinics, CLSCs, and women's health centres, leading to a concentration of access in urban centres.

Hospitals used to be the primary facilities providing abortion services in Canada. In 1996, hospitals performed 66.7 percent of abortion services in the country; this percentage steadily fell to 51.9 percent by 2005 (Statistics Canada 2005, 10). In 2013, hospitals performed only 42.2 percent of abortions nationally (CIHI 2013). The rationale for this shift is multifaceted and includes budget cuts, a push toward privatization by some provinces, and hospital amalgamations.

Hospital amalgamations in Canada, in the face of budget cuts, have contributed to a reduction in reproductive health services, including abortions. Today, only 16 percent of hospitals in Canada offer abortion services. The consolidation of secular and religious hospitals (typically Roman Catholic) may be one reason, since it has contributed to "the elimination or curtailment of many family-planning health services including abortion services" (Palley 2006, 581–82). Howard Palley notes that "between 1997 and 1998, the number of Catholic-operated hospitals increased by 11 percent, whereas the number of secular public-run hospitals decreased by 2 percent. Of the 127 hospital mergers between 1990 and 1998, 50 percent resulted in the elimination of some reproductive services" (ibid., 582).

The services provided in a given hospital in all provinces are at the discretion of hospital trustee boards, composed largely of community members rather than doctors. A board with a strong anti-abortion presence, or a board that is ill-informed of the importance of abortion provision to the women in the community it serves, can easily impede access. Of even greater concern is the fact that hospitals are not responsible for ensuring services are provided elsewhere if they are unable or unwilling to meet demand. Indeed, this is a problem that Action Canada for Sexual Health and Rights is now investigating. In an interview, executive director Sandeep Prasad shared the organization's intention to explore the concept of institutional objection to abortion in light of the fact that five-sixths of hospitals in Canada do not offer abortion services: "The whole exercise of conscientious objection [by physicians] exists because there is a freedom of conscience, freedom of thought and conscience, so you, as an individual provider, can assert that you're not going to provide a service if it's not an emergency" – though one still has a "duty to refer." However, he went on, "institutions have no conscience – buildings and groups don't have collective consciences that can be legitimately claimed under human rights laws," so the rights of hospital boards to refuse to provide services on these grounds necessitates investigation.[35]

Even though hospitals remain important facilities for the provision of services, particularly in rural areas that cannot support clinics, they are not without their problems. The sheer size and variety of services available at Canadian hospitals mean that the provision of a high level of care, understanding, and support tailored to specific services can be difficult to achieve. Women encounter numerous staff members when accessing hospital services, and there is rarely screening at every level to ensure they are encountering personnel who will treat abortion as a standard medical procedure. The presence of anti-abortion personnel can cause serious problems for providers and women seeking abortions.[36] In fact, women are sometimes misinformed or redirected to anti-abortion groups when calling hospitals to make appointments (Shaw 2006). The Canadians for Choice *Reality Check* report recounts difficulties women face in attempting to access abortion services in Canada.[37] Women reported being misinformed and treated with disrespect by hospital personnel and by the anti-abortion organizations – to which some hospitals, perhaps unwittingly, had referred them (ibid.).

Moreover, even when hospital staff are pro-choice, the volume of services provided in hospitals can inadvertently expose women to difficult situations. Judgment by staff and patients alike can deter women from seeking to terminate their pregnancy in a hospital. Anne Marie Messier, general director of the Centre de santé des femmes de Montréal, recounted stories of women being refused standard doses of painkillers to ensure that they would be "reminded" of their apparent wrongdoing.[38]

Amid increasing pressures to improve and expand health care services across the country, particularly given Canada's aging baby boomer population, provinces have made attempts to redistribute and cut services. With constant pressure to reduce health care spending wherever possible, abortion services are constantly at risk. Indeed, the Fédération du Québec pour le planning des naissances (FQPN) noted "a gradual withdrawal of government and a transfer of collective responsibilities toward the private sector" in the 1990s and 2000s, which caused some reproductive services to be rolled back (FQPN and CFC 2010, 29). Two clinics were forced to close, and two hospitals had to reduce services, all while demands for services increased (ibid.).[39] As noted earlier, Ontario faced similar pressures to delist services under the Harris government.

Despite their shortcomings, hospitals remain important facilities for the delivery of abortion care. A representative of the FQPN noted that, although hospital services can be "problematic," they must nonetheless be defended.[40] The rationale for maintaining hospital abortion services is to ensure widespread access for women across the country. It is not financially viable to set up private clinics in small regions, so the continued provision of services by rural hospitals in particular will remain crucial, albeit not ideal. Quebec, for example, has two forms of public medical facilities: hospitals and CLSCs. CLSCs are community health centres run by the provincial government. These centres provide a wide array of services, including abortion services at many locations (Shaw 2006, 33). The prevalence of these centres enables greater access for women in outlying areas that may lack the population base to sustain a hospital or clinic.[41]

In recent years, clinics have become the primary providers of abortion services in Canada. In 2013, 57.8 percent of pregnancy terminations were performed in clinics, up from 33 percent in 1996 (CIHI 2013; Statistics Canada 2005, 10–11). These specialized facilities are more cost-effective for the provision of abortion services than hospitals and are known for their sensitive and respectful approach to care. According to one representative of a Montreal clinic, "The basic advantage of the clinic is staff that are dedicated to the pro-choice movement, dedicated to providing empathic and nonjudgmental care."[42] Concerns about privacy may also make clinic services preferable, at least in some cases.

Privacy is a serious concern in a province such as New Brunswick, which Judy Burwell, the former director of the Fredericton Morgentaler Clinic, characterized as reminiscent of a small town in which "everybody knows everybody else." She explained that women sometimes express concern about their anonymity in hospitals, where their friends or acquaintances may work, as well as concerns about facing anti-abortion staff. Clinics may be a more comforting option for these women, as staff there are screened, and confidentiality at all levels of the process, from appointment bookings to the procedure itself, is stressed. Women who enter the clinic are in a nonjudgmental, supportive space. Clinics ensure that their staff are pro-choice and understand the difficult decisions women seeking procedures often have to make, as well as the barriers they encounter in exercising their choices. Burwell characterized the former Morgentaler Clinic as "a pleasant place to come in a difficult situation."[43]

Several clinics in Quebec have taken their attempts to create a comforting environment even further, operating under a strictly feminist approach. The Centre de santé des femmes de Montréal is one of three clinics in Quebec offering services that embrace this approach, aiming to create a procedure that shows respect for women and their experiences. In so doing, facility staff and practitioners create a comfortable atmosphere in which women can seek care without fear of judgment. For example, if a woman comes to the clinic certain of her conception date, she is exempt from having a sonogram. Anne Marie Messier, the clinic manager, explained that women who were certain of their dates were typically more accurate than the sonogram.[44] By treating women as aware and competent participants in the process, the medical hierarchy is obscured, and women often feel both more empowered and at ease. Unfortunately, this ease does not necessarily translate to their experiences entering abortion clinics.

Abortion clinics in Canada have a long history of anti-abortion activists demonstrating outside the facilities. When considered in conjunction with the history of violence against facilities and providers in the provinces, these demonstrations pose a threat to patients and providers alike. Although rarely discussed today, the Toronto Morgentaler clinic was destroyed after being firebombed in the middle of the night in 1992 (ARCC 2006b, 2). Two years later, a sniper shot physician Dr. Garson Romalis in his Vancouver home, the first of three shootings carried out on Canadian abortion providers in the mid-1990s, which included physicians in Hamilton and Winnipeg (ARCC 2006b, 2; Mickleburgh 2014). All of the physicians survived these attacks, but with serious wounds.[45] Romalis suffered damage to his leg but continued to practise, surrounding himself with heightened security. Despite these precautions, he suffered another attack six years later, when he was stabbed in the back at his clinic (Mickleburgh 2014). He survived. Indeed, the National Abortion Federation, which records incidents of violence and disruption against abortion providers, noted a sizable increase in "hate speech and internet harassment, death threats, attempted murder, and murder" in recent years (NAF 2015c, 1).[46]

It is unsurprising, then, that violence continues to be a factor that influences who is willing to provide abortions and in what context. A representative of Toronto Public Health, Tracey Methven, pointed out that it is difficult to find physicians who will go to clinics to perform services because "they're scared, and rightly so."[47] "Nobody," she went on to say, "wants to have to hear of somebody coming and hurting them or their family or their staff" (ibid.). Brewer shares this sentiment:

> A lot of doctors, even pro-choice doctors, won't perform abortions because it can be dangerous. If people in your practice find out then suddenly you've got people picketing outside your house. One of the nurses at the [Fredericton Morgentaler] clinic was harassed in front of her kids on a number of occasions. Someone would go to her house and harass her. There are not a lot of doctors who want that kind of stigma, so it's difficult to get doctors to perform abortions.[48]

Threats to safety are a powerful disincentive to provide abortions, even in a hospital setting. An Ontario physician noted that the rooms in which abortions are performed in hospitals are generally locked, and the gynecology wings of hospitals often need to remain under surveillance.[49] Although doctors practising in hospitals can more easily remain anonymous than those working in clinics, given the size of the institution and the many different procedures they perform, making it difficult to single them out as abortion providers, they are routinely reminded of the potential for violence.

Security threats are also on the minds of those working with physicians. Although she worked at clinics in both Fredericton and Toronto, Peggy

Cooke explained that the clinic layout meant she was less concerned about violence while in Ontario:

> There's probably less chance of it in Fredericton, but in Fredericton I worked in reception, so I was sitting at the desk, and there's a panic button under the desk – so it's always there and you're always thinking about it. And I was the one buzzing people in, whereas at our clinic here in Toronto we contract out to a private security company, so the person at the front desk buzzing people in and out is a trained security person. The Toronto clinic is way better set up for security; there are more panic buttons and mantraps.[50]

This sense of security, Cooke went on to say, was not shared by everyone. Specifically, she mentioned that the workers who had been at the Toronto clinics when it was firebombed "have a more heightened sense of what the risks are."

In light of these problems, some provincial governments have taken steps to handle issues with protesters. Ontario, for example, has had some success in creating protections for women and physicians facing harassment. In 1994, a temporary injunction was granted to prevent "protesting within a certain distance of clinics and doctors' homes, and from circulating information about abortion providers," but only remains in force in a few urban centres (Downie and Nassar 2007, 161).[51] Injunctions are now in place in Toronto, London, Brantford, Kitchener, and North Bay, but unfortunately, without police cooperation to enforce them, these protections are relatively meaningless (ibid.). A pro-choice activist in Ontario noted a "real lack of effort on behalf of the province to intervene on matters like [the injunction]. The clinics can call the police, but the police just come and say, 'I'll tell the person to go away' – and they come right back."[52]

These injunctions have also been limited by other factors. The type of building a clinic is located in can pose problems in creating and enforcing legislation to protect women and physicians entering clinics. Not all clinics are stand-alone buildings. The Women's Care Clinic on Lawrence Avenue West in Toronto, for example, is a multi-office building. Protesters still block the entrance but often do so indiscriminately. Early in 2011, Michelle Robidoux, manager of the Ontario Coalition of Abortion Clinics, noted that a group of roughly twenty-five protesters "were harassing not just women of reproductive age, but just anybody going into the building where this one particular clinic is housed."[53]

In Quebec, those clinics that do have issues with protesters have, in some cases, been able to secure injunctions to prevent anyone from demonstrating directly in front of the facility and blocking access. Notably, although anti-abortion activism still exists in Quebec, interviewees in the province did not cite it as a major barrier to access. A representative for the FQPN pointed out that "protesting here is not a problem. It just hasn't reached Quebec in the same way."[54] Still, where there is protest, its new-found tendency to mimic the language and tactics of the US anti-abortion movement is a major concern.[55] By all accounts, the number of anti-abortion demonstrators has seen a lack of perceptible change and even been reportedly decreased in some areas, yet the high levels of organization and funding of these demonstrators allow them to accomplish more.[56] Several interviewees expressed concern that Canadian anti-abortion groups were receiving funding from the United States, specifically from religious rights groups.[57] This funding was of particular concern to interviewees as it pertained to crisis pregnancy centres, which appear in Quebec, as they do across the country.[58] According to an FQPN study on abortion services in Quebec:

> With names like "Care Center" or "Pregnancy Options," these centers generally present themselves as being neutral and as providing support to women in their decision-making. In reality, some of these centers try to discourage women from choosing abortion." (FQPN and CFC 2010, 65)

Similar facilities exist throughout Canada (Shaw 2006, 15). In a 2008 study, Canadians for Choice counted 197 crisis pregnancy centres across the country, as compared to 151 abortion facilities (J. Smith 2010).[59]

These centres are known for providing misinformation on abortion in an attempt to dissuade women from accessing the procedure. Some of the most troubling messages that a woman might receive are assertions that she "puts herself at great risk of developing breast cancer" and that she may become infertile as a result of the procedure (ibid.). Both statements lack any medical foundation. Furthermore, women are commonly told that abortion is "far more dangerous than carrying a baby to term," an argument that is patently false (ibid.). One counsellor interviewed by the *Star* defended this approach, saying, "(Women) aren't told the truth (at the abortion clinics) either, so not to say I'm lying, but there's a lot of hidden truths everywhere and hidden stuff that people need to know" (ibid.).

These centres, which commonly employ the language of clinics and the pro-choice movement in their materials, are often difficult to distinguish from clinics – that is, until the women seeking an abortion enter them. Although, to date, no Canadian government has made any attempt to regulate these facilities, allowing them to spread misinformation and misdirect women who struggle to access services, a movement has recently begun in the United States to regulate these centres. The New York City Council approved legislation in March 2011 that would require the centres "to clearly disclose the types of pregnancy-related services they provide, including whether or not they have a licensed medical provider and provide prenatal care, abortions and emergency contraception" (Griffee 2011). Such legislation has yet to be introduced in Canada. Given the reality that these centres continue to outnumber abortion facilities in Canada, and that hospitals have been known to direct patients seeking care to these centres (Shaw 2006, 26), the urgent need for governments to hold these facilities to account is clear.

In sum, the nature of available abortion services, the willingness of physicians to provide them, and the likelihood that new physicians will be trained in them is dependent in large part on the availability of facilities. These facilities, in turn, affect the experiences of women in seeking care. Therefore, the interrelationship of all these factors must be taken into account when considering how to improve access to abortion.

The Future of Abortion Care

Moving toward a solution that creates substantive access for women across the country, the role of both state and non-state actors in achieving these ends is paramount. The multiple loci of authority over the provision of abortion services certainly complicates attempts by women to access procedures. It also highlights the potentially conflicting rights claims advanced by the federal government, provinces, physicians, and women alike. Who ought to have the power to influence the nature of care in the provinces? Or to decide whether a woman can access abortion services? A careful unpacking of the power dynamics at stake does not illuminate the answers to these questions; rather, existing dynamics uncover the absence of any recognized consensus on the matter. Within the current system, it is simply unclear who does, or should, have control over matters of access. Given the significance of abortion access to women's status as equal citizens in Canada, this finding requires us to rethink the scope of the claims by each of the relevant groups, and the very classification of abortion as a health care issue.

Despite federal organization of funding criteria and professional and ethical guidelines for physicians, the regulation of health care in Canada is largely at the discretion of provincial governments, provincial colleges of physicians and surgeons, and individual physicians. Each of these bodies and individuals has the discretion to treat abortion in different ways, powers that have contributed to a patchwork of services across the country. In some instances, the discretion left to the provinces and doctors has led to dramatic improvements not only in levels of access but also in the nature of services. Quebec is a standout example of this phenomenon, with a number of clinics pioneering new approaches to the provision of abortion, and reproductive health care more broadly, in ways that emphasize both sensitive and dignified care. In other cases, this grey area has been used to restrict access to services and create obstacles, rooted in a desire not to improve women's health but to limit the performance of a safe and legal procedure deemed undesirable by the government or individual medical personnel.

Regardless of which path is taken, it is apparent that treating abortion as a straightforward medical matter leaves the procedure vulnerable. The taboo nature of abortion has only complicated this matter. Certainly, not all doctors who refuse to perform abortions are necessarily doing so because they feel morally opposed to the procedure; a history of violence against abortion doctors and clinics in Canada, alongside continued demonstrations and threats of harassment, are enough to deter many physicians. Although governments need to do more to safeguard against such threats, the continued treatment of abortion as controversial only exacerbates the problem. Forcing physicians to provide abortions when they feel their safety would be at risk for doing so is certainly problematic, but leaving women without a safe and reasonable means to terminate an unwanted pregnancy is also unacceptable.

Requiring that physicians make referrals in the event that they are unable to perform abortions is a promising step toward a solution, but more needs to be done. The creation of more points of access in family health centres and hospitals, as well as bubble zones around clinics (to create a perimeter within which protesters are not allowed to demonstrate), would help alleviate these fears, as would increasing access to medical abortions by allowing pharmacists to distribute Mifegymiso. Normalizing the procedure by requiring it be taught at medical schools and during residency across Canada would also help improve access. Given the relative simplicity of the procedure and its frequency, it should come as a shock that it is not a compulsory subject. Such changes, of course, would not necessitate that abortion access be reclassified as a right necessary for women's equality; they simply necessitate clarifications regarding the rights and obligations of both the provinces in regulating access and the medical profession in providing it. These changes are important, but they are also inadequate.

Even if classifying abortion as a health care right could guarantee more points of service across the country, such protections fall short of guaranteeing quality or dignity of care, which continue to be significant barriers for women. Nor would they necessarily protect women against other barriers to access, including threats of violence and harassment. Confining the conceptualization of abortion to medicine means its significance to women's equality is obscured, diminishing the relationship between women's reproductive abilities and their place in society.

Of course, recognition of access to abortion services as necessary to women's equality in no way removes abortion from the realm of health care. Abortion is a medical procedure and will always be located in this sphere to some extent. That said, if the procedure were treated as a right, it would be possible to create substantive protections for women through service provision. Importantly, these changes do not require that the relationship between provincial and federal governments be undermined, or that provinces lose control over health care provision; many of these modifications can easily be implemented in each province without a dramatic change in political culture or major changes to infrastructure.

There are many avenues of change available to improve services and create more substantive equality for women in Canada. For example, the creation of a minimum bar under which services cannot fall in the province would help ensure relatively equal access across the provinces. Such a change, however, is unlikely to come into being without external pressures on the provinces. Indeed, the recognition of abortion as a right necessary for women's equality might result in the reclassification of the procedure at least partially outside of health care, creating space to rethink its regulation in the country. There are, of course, other means of creating improvements. One such suggestion I encountered in my research addressed questions of health care in Canada more broadly, and suggested the need for greater transparency in health care administration and funding so that governments could be held accountable for their choices, and so that individuals could see how other provinces dealt with similar issues.

In an interview, Dr. Carolyn Bennett, a former family physician and now the federal minister of indigenous and northern affairs, explained that a more transparent health care system in Canada could facilitate such a project. She suggests the creation of a "pan-Canadian quality audit" that would create a comparable set of health care data between the provinces.[60] At present, no such comparison is possible, meaning citizens are in the dark about the success of their province's health care strategies. If health care services were more transparent, it would be possible not only for citizens to judge their provincial health care objectively and demand specific change but also for provinces to learn from one another's successes. The realization of such a system would make the creation of a set of minimum standards for the provinces much easier while also opening the door for myriad other improvements to the delivery of health services.[61]

Bennett and other interviewees, including Messier, also suggest that the creation of health centres tailored specifically to women's health needs might improve women's access to abortion services in addition to improving their personal and reproductive health more broadly. One of the noteworthy strengths of moving toward such a facility model would be its potential to safeguard providers and patients against anti-abortion protesters outside facilities.[62] There is no guarantee that demonstrators will not convene outside these facilities, but the varied nature of services within would make it more challenging to single out individuals for harassment. Enforced bubble-zone legislation to protect patients and physicians should this actually occur would also be an important step.

Of course, many areas of Canada cannot reasonably be expected to support such facilities. Clinics require an urban population to be cost-effective, and many communities in Canada do not even have nearby hospital facilities. Alternatively, nursing stations and private practitioners supply services to many areas of Canada. Importantly, these variations in facility access may cease to pose a substantive barrier now that Mifegymiso, a reliable and effective abortion drug, has entered the Canadian market. Training in administering this drug could create a much more expansive network of abortion services in Canada, especially if some of the restrictions on the drug were relaxed.

Achieving Balance

To say that the organization of health care in Canada is difficult to navigate is something of an understatement. When individuals are attempting to access a procedure that is frequently seen as taboo, this complexity often becomes insurmountable. Issues in accessing service are not, however, rooted only in a lack of transparent policy; they are rooted too in ongoing debates about the extent of rights possessed by the actors involved.

Although provincial governments have clear jurisdictional authority over health care, their continued reliance on federal funds to maintain these systems has meant that the federal government can exert some influence over the nature of health care in the provinces. This influence is exemplified by the requirement that provinces adhere to the principles laid out in the Canada Health Act. Governments, however, are able to exert only a limited influence on physicians, who have laid ground rules of their own.

Physicians maintain a right to conscientiously object to performing procedures to which they are morally opposed. Although these rights have been widely critiqued, physicians there still commonly use them to deny women access to reproductive health services, especially abortion. Given the obstacles that patients now face in Canada to access a family doctor in a timely manner, let alone multiple doctors, this is a serious obstacle. Moreover, many women may be unaware that seeking another physician is an available recourse should they be denied care.

The barriers created by these rights claims and disputes mean that attempts to access abortion services for women in different parts of Canada have the potential to be deeply challenging, if not impossible. Some advocates suggest that recognizing abortion as part of a larger right to health care might address these difficulties, but this option seems lacking, in part because formal recognition of a right to health care does not exist. Furthermore, the uniquely gendered nature of abortion and its broader implications for the role of women as citizens would be obscured in such a model. Instead, I advocate that governments need to recognize abortion as necessary to women's equality, and to implement services that will allow all women to realize these rights.

In making this argument, I do not mean to imply that there is a need to overhaul the health care system, though there is certainly a general need for greater transparency in health care, nor do I wish to completely undermine the different right claims at play. Rather, I suggest that these rights must be balanced in pursuit of the larger project of women's autonomy. To say that women need abortion access is not to say that governments must forfeit total control over the allocation of funds or facilities, or that all physicians must be willing to provide abortions in all circumstances. Instead, it suggests the need to create a certain baseline under which services cannot fall, and requires the validation of women's experiences in seeking out these services. Moreover, it suggests a need to rethink the barriers to access that women face, whether they result from race, class, age, location, identity, ability, or other factors.

Notably, none of the changes to access that interviewees in the provinces or social activists recommend require dramatic institutional change;

they can be achieved without totally compromising provincial jurisdiction over health care and without expensive changes to existing infrastructure. Indeed, the changes necessary to create more even access to abortion care across Canada are relatively minimal. Moreover, they are rooted in a broader desire to create a more transparent health care system, which includes clarifying the rights and responsibilities of physicians and patients, to the benefit of health care in Canada more generally.

Even though these changes must take place predominately in the realm of service provision, the multiple points of authority, both political and private, mean that abortion access continues to be deeply impacted by social perception. Whether abortion is stigmatized or celebrated has a real impact not only on physicians and lawmakers but also on the way women view themselves and their relationship to the community. The way women experience their attempts to access the procedure, then, are illuminated by the role of social activists in shaping provincial attitudes toward abortion.

5
Social Movement Activism in the Provinces

The realization of abortion access as an equality right requires not only political and legal action but also social acceptance. Although rights are often conceived in purely legal terms, choices only become rights "in so far as a duty binds another to respect [them]" (Cook, Dickens, and Fathalla 2003, 156). Without social support, even entrenched rights can quickly become moot. In the same vein, a public consensus on the existence of a right can alter social expectations and influence state actors even without formal recognition. In the case of abortion, widespread belief that *R. v. Morgentaler* (1988) validated a right to abortion access has given teeth to this assertion in law, politics, and medicine, even though such a right has yet to be entrenched.

Even before the *Morgentaler* decision came down, Janine Brodie (1992, 60) argued that the "'court of public opinion' had forged a tentative social consensus" on abortion, favouring improved access to abortion services. Acceptance of the need for access has grown steadily since the decision. Canada-wide polls demonstrate that the small majority of those supporting a right to abortion has steadily increased in recent decades, with three-quarters of Canadians now in support of a woman's right to choose (Environics Institute 2010, 6).[1] These shifts in public sentiment influence the nature of public discourse surrounding abortion, which in turn informs the actions and decisions of actors providing services and creating policies. In the case of abortion, resistance to addressing controversial issues in many public and official forums may have given social activists an unforeseen advantage.

A combination of luck and institutional wariness to address abortion has meant that social movements have gained a surprising amount of influence in dictating the terms of the abortion debate since *Morgentaler*. After the Mulroney government's new abortion law was defeated in the Senate, subsequent federal governments have largely stayed away from the subject of abortion, as have many provincial governments. Although abortion was reclassified as a matter of health care following the 1988 decision, its treatment in the provinces, which ranges from attempts to recriminalize access to recognition that abortion access is a right, failed to conform to such a straightforward understanding. Even the provinces that restricted access after the decision tended to remain mum about their actions after the fact, addressing them only when forced, typically as a result of litigation. Social activists wasted no time in exploiting this silence.

Pro-choice activists and, more recently, reproductive justice advocates have used this space to reframe abortion as a social necessity and a woman's right. Central to these claims is often the portrayal of the *Morgentaler* decision as the final battle for reproductive rights in Canada – the fight that affirmed women's rights to abortion access. The void also left room for anti-abortion advocates to spread their own message. Indeed, significant changes in the movement's approach to securing influence, discussed at length in Chapter 1, highlight the success of the pro-choice movement in shaping the tone of the debate. Nonetheless, anti-abortion groups continue to adapt their strategies in an effort to recriminalize abortion access or, as they are more likely to frame it today, to encourage women not to choose abortion.

Some of the strategies anti-abortion groups have employed to deter women from seeking abortion services have remained fairly constant. These approaches include regular appeals to government in the form of petitions and letter-writing campaigns, which are evidenced in the frequency of anti-abortion backbencher bills in the House. One of the most well-known tactics used by these groups comes in the form of public demonstrations, which are very commonly held outside of medical facilities. In some cases, individuals within the movement have also been known to threaten patients, physicians, and workers at these facilities.[2] Given the history of violence against abortion providers in Canada, as well as the destruction of facilities, these threats are not taken lightly.

Focusing on manifestations of social activism and perceived stigma, this chapter looks at the influence of social movement activities on provincial social climates. In so doing, it attempts to shed light on how women internalize their rights to abortion services in the provinces, if they believe they are entitled to such services at all. Fear of judgment, exposure, and violence prevent many women from attempting to access services, just as threats and demonstrations deter health care professionals from providing care. Likewise, public support and recognition of abortion as a right creates an environment where women are more comfortable taking ownership of their rights.

Social attitudes contribute to the creation of social climates in which women either perceive themselves to be full citizens or see themselves as social exceptions in need of sympathy and support. When women internalize their worth, they are more able to act as empowered citizens. They are also more likely to react with incredulity to caricatures of femininity that seek to restrict their rights, demanding progressive social change. An enforceable right to abortion access is necessary for women to realize their equality, and such a right can be created only in a society that respects the value of women as equal citizens.

New Brunswick

New Brunswick's enduring resistance to creating accessible abortion services seems to be founded in a social climate that is, at best, wary of abortion and, at worst, openly hostile to it. Alison Toron, at the time of my interview with her a volunteer escort at the Fredericton Morgentaler Clinic (which closed its doors in July 2014, citing a lack of government funding), characterized provincial attitudes as a "sort of 'don't ask, don't tell'" on abortion issues. That is to say, individuals may or may not have a stance on the issue, "but we [New Brunswickers] just don't talk about it."[3]

According to Toron, the motivation for this silence has multiple roots, including the prevalence of groups with religiously motivated, socially traditional views. These views go beyond abortion to include reproductive rights and sexual health at a broader level. She attributes the dominance of this rhetoric to a kind of "mass inertia" whereby "people just don't discuss the issue, and so it's able to not move forward by reasons of silence." In some respects, this silence has given a relatively small anti-abortion movement a platform to be heard, though the closure of the Fredericton Morgentaler Clinic in 2014 has since created resurgence in pro-choice and reproductive justice activity in the province.

Without a strong public discourse, the anti-abortion movement was able to create an illusion of domination, particularly when some of its strongest supporters are in positions of power (such as members of the legislative assembly). This sense of power through silence afforded the anti-abortion movement some boldness in their actions and dramatically influenced discourse on the issue, but is ultimately limited by its small member base. The main anti-abortion group in the province, New Brunswick Right to Life, focuses its energies on challenging provincial policy by organizing marches and collecting signatures for petitions in addition to, historically, attempting to disrupt the function of the Fredericton Morgentaler Clinic. To this end, the group purchased the building next to the clinic to serve as their base of operations, converting it into a crisis pregnancy centre called the Mother & Child Welcome House. Crisis pregnancy centres are anti-abortion facilities that market themselves using the language of clinics, advertising help for women facing unplanned pregnancies to help them better understand their *choices*, but are known to provide misinformation about abortion and to attempt to dissuade women from accessing it. The Mother & Child Welcome House also acted as a home base for the protesters who demonstrated in front of the Morgentaler Clinic when it was open. Indeed, the constant presence of anti-abortion demonstrators became so problematic that the clinic decided to organize volunteer escorts for women entering the building – both to shield them from protesters and to guide them into the correct building, as many women who booked appointments at the clinic mistook the Mother & Child Welcome House for the Morgentaler Clinic, given its proximity and the language used on its signs.

According to clinic staff, these protesters, who typically numbered between four and eight, employed various tactics to dissuade women from seeking abortions. These included silent vigils, the use of placards, and verbal harassment, but came short of physical violence. A former employee of the New Brunswick clinic now working at a Toronto clinic, Peggy Cooke, recalled in 2011:

> No one was ever physically violent, but they were physical. I have seen them use their bodies. There is one particular individual who will throw herself in front of cars or move so she's between the escorts and the patients, so she will use her body to get closer to people, but I have never seen anybody push or hit or anything like that.[4]

Even absent physical violence, the harassment women endured attempting to enter the clinic was a serious barrier. Toron recounted some of the most oft-uttered phrases by the demonstrators, which she ranked from mild (reiteration of other options, such as adoption) to extreme – for example, "Don't kill your baby," "If you have an abortion, you might not be able to have a baby someday," and even "Abortion is linked to breast cancer."

The clinic had little recourse against the protesters. It was situated in a stand-alone building, and patients needed to be buzzed into reception, but the area outside was unprotected without an injunction or bubble-zone legislation that would require demonstrators to keep their distance. Threat of violence to employees, women, and the building itself were ever present. When the clinic was open, the protesters were a fixture, a constant reminder for women, doctors, and the community at large that abortion is a contested right – one which any woman trying to exercise risked being threatened, harassed, guilted, or frightened into forfeiting.

Demonstrations outside the legislature and supportive words from allied officials only served to reinforce these barriers to access while subverting discussion of abortion as a woman's right. The result is a muted public discourse, which often frames abortion as a moral issue. As Toron explained:

> For the general populous [in New Brunswick,] it is a moral issue almost in the abstract. That is the problem with the kind of discourse that exists around abortion in this province. People talk about it as a black or white moral issue, at least in public; I think things are different in private, but in public it is framed as an abstract moral issue in that it does not actually seem to relate to actual women who need to get those services.

The silencing of women's rights claims is, according to many interviewed in the province, rooted in socially traditional ideals, many of which are supported by dominant religious groups there, specifically, the Catholic Church.[5] According to a law professor at the University of New Brunswick, "There is a strong tradition of both Irish Catholic and French Catholic influence on the public discourse," which is notably "misogynist in its rhetoric," alongside a competing Protestant view, which operationalizes its "[anti-abortion] doctrine as being deeply felt."[6] According to Hughes, the combination of an "emotional sense of righteousness, [a] doctrinal sense of exclusion of women, and conservative politics" have made up "this brew of ideology that becomes very silencing for a large number of New Brunswickers." Toron echoed these views in her assessment of demonstrators outside the Fredericton Morgentaler Clinic: "If you question any of the protesters about their broader views, it becomes clear that their views are deeply rooted in notions of social traditionalism. They are often anti-contraception and believe women belong in the home."

However, although a deeply held emotional response to the issue, which rejects rights-based equality claims, accounts for some anti-abortion sentiment in the province, it may still fail to shed light on broader social perceptions of abortion. Are a majority of New Brunswickers in fact anti-abortion, or does the nature of public discourse merely obscure their sentiments? Interviewees in the province seemed inclined to believe that the province was more pro-choice than it first appeared. As Toron said, "Looking at our incredibly repressive policies, you would think that this must be a socially conservative province where everyone is against abortion, but I really don't find that that's the case when I actually talk to people about the work that I do at the clinic."

She stressed that the traditional understandings of conservatism as falling along urban/rural or young/old failed to account for views on abortion. Certainly, as the original Morgentaler cases in Quebec in the late 1970s revealed, women who were the most vulnerable in cases of unwanted pregnancies were poor, rural women who could not afford abortion services. Many women in rural New Brunswick certainly remember the struggles associated with unwanted pregnancy; even today, services in the province are few and far between and are fraught with barriers, a reality all the more apparent to these demographics. According to Hughes:

> There are lots and lots of people who are actually pro-choice, somewhere in the spectrum, or at least not so anti-woman that they really want it to play out in this way [as it has in New Brunswick]. You get people who want to see abortion restricted in some fashion but wouldn't go quite to the kinds of extremes that are sometimes contemplated here. So I suspect that the majority of people in New Brunswick are as pro-choice as the rest of Canadians but they wouldn't say it, because the public discourse is so controlled.

The general lack of dialogue on the subject has also influenced the sense of entitlement to abortion services among New Brunswick women. Cooke contrasted the attitudinal differences between women in Toronto and women in Fredericton:

> They [Torontonians] take it for granted that the access is there, especially with payment, because it is covered under OHIP here. So people come in and we get them to sign all this stuff. I get them to sign a billing agreement,

and I explain that "this gives us permission to use your health care, but it also makes you liable if it's rejected." People often say, "Well, it's not going to be rejected, but just out of curiosity, how much is the payment?" And I reply, "Well, it depends how far along you are, but it's going to be at least five hundred dollars," and people are shocked. Absolutely shocked. They cannot believe it. It is a lot of money, but in New Brunswick everyone is paying this, sometimes six hundred. Everybody. So people just have no concept at all that there is a world outside of Toronto and things do not come as easily.[7]

The media has only contributed to the silence on abortion in the province. According to Rosella Melanson, former executive director of the New Brunswick Advisory Council on the Status of Women, when the media does deal with the issue of abortion, "it's not medical, it's moral, it's right and wrong."[8] The media's sparse coverage of abortion politics, Melanson suggests, fuels a lack of discussion. The problems associated with biased news reports or a general absence of reporting on the issue is of particular concern in New Brunswick, where a single family owns the three English-language dailies: the *Fredericton Daily Gleaner*, the *Moncton Times & Transcript*, and the *Saint John Telegraph-Journal*. Recent expansions have also meant that it now also controls five French-language weeklies: *Le Madawaska*, *La République*, *La Cataracte*, *L'Hebdo Chaleur*, and *L'Étoile* (Steuter 2004). The resulting absence of dialogue can contribute to a widespread lack of knowledge and accountability on the part of social movement activists, providers, and politicians.

The lack of dialogue on abortion in public, in the media, and at the legislature, combined with the presence of a vocal anti-abortion movement in the above-mentioned forums, has made the exact nature of the populous views on abortion difficult to ascertain. What is clear is that the anti-abortion groups in the province exercise power over the social climate. This power has created fear rather than widespread consensus. However, recent events have curbed their power.

The closure of the Fredericton Morgentaler Clinic in July 2014 served as the catalyst for a dramatic resurgence in reproductive rights activism in the province. The sudden removal of one of the main points of access in New Brunswick, which performed more than half of abortions accessed in the province annually (CBC News 2014b), made the precarious nature of abortion access in the province impossible to ignore. Moreover, fear that pushing for better policies might have a negative impact on existing levels of access, an anxiety also felt by federal advocacy groups, ceased to be a central concern. Reproductive Justice New Brunswick (RJNB), which identifies as "a collective of individuals from across New Brunswick dedicated to ensuring publicly funded and self-referred abortion is available in the province," formed in response to the clinic closure (RJNB 2014).

RJNB has been incredibly active since its inception. The group crowdfunded over a hundred thousand dollars through an online campaign to reopen the clinic, and it continues to raise awareness through local and national media, including social media campaigns and rallies.[9] RJNB succeeded in keeping abortion on the agenda leading up to a provincial election, and ultimately pressured the government to make a significant amendment to Regulation 84-20. As a result of RJNB's campaigning, the government of New Brunswick removed the requirements that abortions be performed by a gynecologist and that two doctors deem, in writing, the procedure to be medically necessary in order for it to qualify under provincial health insurance. Despite these momentous steps, the portion of 84-20 that requires abortions be performed in hospitals is still in place, and concerns about violence and harassment persist.[10]

To be sure, there is still work to be done in the province, where the long-term impacts of these movements have yet to appear. Optimistically, a change in the social climate will occur and abortion will no longer be considered a taboo subject. Regardless of the outcome, however, a comment made by Judy Burwell, former manager of the Fredericton Morgentaler Clinic, during a 2011 interview, about the tireless and frustrating nature of the struggle that characterizes reproductive rights activism in the province continues to ring true:

> It just wears you down in this province. I mean, for eleven years now I have been working specifically on this issue, both as a clinic manager and also as a board member for AARC [Abortion Rights Coalition of Canada], and it just wears you down, and you think, "Why do we bother?" but then you don't stop bothering because you don't stop bothering. You just keep trying.[11]

Ontario

Ontario, the province from which the *R. v. Morgentaler* (1988) decision originated, handled the decriminalization of abortion by attempting to regulate abortion like any other medical issue. Today, abortion is still largely treated as a nonissue in the province. In many respects, the availability of services has seemingly reduced concerns about how abortion is perceived.

In essence, so long as the service is available, women's rights are seen as having triumphed, and universal acceptance of the equality rights frame is thus often seen as unnecessary.

To be sure, the 1988 *Morgentaler* decision was a huge boon to pro-choice groups, satiating the movement to a large degree. In its wake, many pro-choice groups turned their focus to ensuring that abortion services were available and accessible to women, rather than focusing on the large-scale consciousness-raising campaigns of previous decades. This focus is reflected in efforts by these groups to pressure governments to create and maintain accessible services, including holding the provinces accountable for adherence to the Canada Health Act, attempting to get new technologies (i.e., RU-486) to the Canadian market, and supporting and maintaining abortion providers and clinics. These efforts have been critical to the creation and maintenance of existing levels of access. At the same time, however, Morgentaler's victory served as a catalyst for increased anti-abortion mobilization.

Despite the continued work of these groups, interviewees in the province expressed concern that a general lack of public openness about abortion, including the consequences of illegal abortions, has contributed to an ambivalent public that is often uninformed – and even misinformed – on the matter. Still, many interviewees remained positive about the nature of individual views in Ontario. One activist in the province suggested that, even where people were personally opposed to abortion, "most people understand that, if you're in that position [of having an unwanted pregnancy], it should be your choice."[12] The activist went on to reveal the experiences of being in a university class that dealt with the issue of reproductive choice:

> Lots of the students came from very religious families and all different kinds of religions – Jewish, Christian, Islamic – and had heard of the debate about abortion but hadn't necessarily had to talk about it, because it's not something they needed to access or not something that was right in their face. But very few people were in favour of making it illegal. Some said, "You know, I think it's wrong, I think it's against what God wanted," even that "it's murder," but that they would never interfere with a woman's right to choose that because they've never been in that position.

Michelle Robidoux, manager of the Ontario Coalition of Abortion Clinics, suggested that Ontarians are generally ambivalent but, "when push comes to shove," are likely to express staunchly pro-choice views.[13] Others, like Tracey Methven, a sexual health promoter for Toronto Public Health, were concerned about how easily the rights of women can be revoked. Canadian women, she argued, are not "necessarily as emancipated or as feminist as we think we might be." She explained that "equality issues [may not be] as strong as lots of people seem to assume they are" and, further, that the fight for equality is "a really fragile, hard-fought, unacknowledged battle that people have just taken for granted."[14] Fear about the potential consequences of ambivalence is understandable, especially given the means through which gains in the feminist movement were realized historically. Robidoux explained that pro-choice mobilization has been crucial to the success of the movement, socially, politically, and through litigation:

> That's how we got here [mobilization]; it wasn't just some legislation that came in. The Supreme Court would not have thrown this thing out in 1988 without the *Morgentaler* decisions; the jury decisions, the reversal of the jury decisions, him [Morgentaler] going to jail, it created a climate where people got it.

Moreover, she maintains, in the years preceding the *Morgentaler* decision, when debates were being held in small towns in Ontario, it was the proximity of the populace to the consequences of unwanted pregnancies and back-alley abortions that contributed to public support:

> We [OCAC and CARAL] went to all these small towns before the law was overturned. There were constant debates in Midland, Ontario, or Peterborough, or wherever about abortion, and there would be somebody representing the anti-abortion groups and one of the people from OCAC or CARAL or one of those groups. And over and over and over again, all these women who you'd think, "Oh, here we go, some elderly woman coming up and she's going to chastise us for, you know." No. "You don't want to go through what we suffered. I saw it. I witnessed it. I experienced it." And just spelling it out, over and over again, and not just to women, but to men and women. That's the other thing. It's just that it's so clear for people what the consequences of an unwanted or unplanned pregnancy are in conditions where you don't control your income, you don't have access to child care, you're studying, or whatever, it's devastating. It's such a step forward for women to actually be able to make those decisions themselves.

Robidoux's experiences are demonstrative of the power of information in the abortion debate. The messaging of the anti-abortion movement today, including assertions that abortion harms women, has only become possible as the memories of illegal abortion have begun to fade. However, those individuals who lived through the time before legal abortion services were available, and who experienced the consequences of having to seek out, or watch a friend seek out, an illegal back-alley abortion, understand the consequences of women's inequality. Their support of access to abortion services, as Robidoux reported, is unconditional given their remembered experiences.[15] A lack of discussion about abortion in the public discourse has distanced people from the realities of its illegality. Anti-abortion groups have worked hard in this environment to subtly rescind women's hard-won access. Although Ontario has both hospital and clinic services covered under its provincial insurance plan, social barriers have made some of these services difficult to access.

The prevalence of abortion clinics in Ontario have made protesters in the province a pressing concern. The province has a history of violence toward clinic staff and past destruction of facilities that has contributed to a climate of fear. Steps have been taken to protect staff and patients at the clinics with the most consistent and threatening protesters. Limited bubble-zone legislation, which creates a perimeter around certain facilities that demonstrators cannot legally breach, has proven calming for some employees. Still, individuals who worked at clinics around the time the Morgentaler Clinic was firebombed are much more conscious of the risks.

Robidoux also expressed concerns that anti-abortion violence in the province is once again on the rise, involving both "implicit [and] explicit threats of violence." She noted an increase in picketing outside at least one prominent Toronto clinic, and related stories of protesters forcing their way into clinics to harass patients in the waiting room. A representative of Canadians for Choice (2011), now Action Canada for Sexual Health and Rights, also commented on this trend, noting the way the anti-abortion movement has revved up their organization in recent years.[16]

Another interviewee suggested that a diversity of cultural backgrounds, languages, and religions in Toronto has influenced social views. A representative of Planned Parenthood Toronto commented that individuals seem to form their views about abortion at a very personal, emotional level, which is "very dependent on their cultural upbringing and their religious beliefs," as well as on the way "their friends feel about abortion and how society feels about abortion."[17] Despite the continued existence of stigma surrounding abortion, the attitude of most Ontario women Cooke has encountered, especially those in large urban centres, has been, quite simply, "entitled" – which, she was quick to point out, "is a good thing, because we should have these rights." The disbelief that women express when told they cannot be seen in a timely manner or that they must drive long distances to access services is completely reasonable and should be taken as a positive sign. It suggests that women in this position feel they are truly equal citizens and are shocked to be denied services necessary for that equality.

Recently, many pro-choice groups in Ontario have begun to incorporate principles of reproductive justice into their mandates and goals. In so doing, they have been more vocal in connecting abortion to a range of social justice issues, but funding and staffing problems have meant that these groups continue to focus their work on abortion. Nonetheless, increased awareness and respect for the broader mandate of reproductive justice may signal a renewed commitment to shifting public perception and advocating for increased protections for abortion access as a woman's right.

In sum, Ontario is something of a hodgepodge of entitlement, stigma, and pro-choice deference, with pro-choice groups focused on maintaining access rather than on pushing for improvements. Interviewees characterized the resulting social climate as one of widespread ambivalence, bordering on apathy, especially among those who assumed abortion rights were already secure. According to a representative of a government-affiliated organization created to promote women's health, "Organizationally there's a lot of recognition that this [abortion] is a legal service, it's a needed service, it's a service that women value, but there's also tremendous recognition of there being a similarly strong segment of the population that wants the service less available, limited."[18] Methven too acknowledges the prevalence of discord in public discourse on abortion: "I would like to think that it's an accepted practice, but I know that it's not; it might be accepted, but not openly."[19]

Quebec

Quebec, the only province to respond to its new-found jurisdiction over abortion by endorsing a rights-based understanding of the procedure, is characterized by a progressive stance on the issue of abortion. The topic is not out of bounds in the province; indeed, it is taken for granted that the rest of Canada is less open to and supportive of a woman's right to equality. The differences in the way that women in the province understand their status as equal citizens is marked. Women in Quebec, where abortion is a clear-cut rights issue, see themselves not as victims of an unwanted pregnancy but as entitled citizens exercising their rights.

Before the Quiet Revolution, Quebec was a devoutly Catholic province, and the Church had a powerful hold on women, particularly relating to expectations around reproduction. Catherine Megill, a former clinic employee and medical student when I interviewed her, said, "Not that many years ago people [in Quebec] remember having fifteen kids. My grandma was one of nineteen."[20] Large family sizes were the norm, so much so that there was even concern historically by English Canada that French Canadian families were attempting to "outbreed" the English, as Protestant women, who were predominantly English Canadians, were not expected to have such large families (McLaren and McLaren 1997, 124). The realities of these demands on Catholic women, in the end, seemed to be one of the greatest motivators for their resistance to both the Church and the state during the Quiet Revolution, which changed the nature of the social climate in Quebec dramatically. "I think people here saw the toll it took, they saw what it did," Megill said, and this awareness resulted in "the complete rejection of the Catholic Church and of the patriarchy."

Their resistance was, in large part, a reaction against unsustainable reproductive demands, but their ownership of the issues was what sustained it. Patrick Powers, former president of Planned Parenthood Montreal, noted the fierceness with which Québécois women protect the issues close to them: "Francophone women here [in Quebec] have a notion that their liberation and their issues belong to them, not to anybody else."[21] The advent of oral contraceptives in the 1960s was hugely empowering for women, who now had new avenues to control their reproduction – advantages they were not about to give up. Megill likened the change in attitude and possibilities to a brave new world, saying, "You looked at the way your grandmother lived and you looked at the possibilities you had and it was like 'Wow.' I think that is basically where it comes from – there is this whole mentality of 'never go back, never go back.'"

The fierce protection of women's reproductive rights, firmly rooted in cultural recognition of women as citizens, with rights to fulfilled social and sexual lives, and in acknowledgment of the implications of birth and pregnancy, is as strong as ever in the province. According to a representative of the FQPN, "There was a survey that came out around the G8 lead-up that showed, I think, 96 percent of Quebecers, or something absolutely ridiculous like that, are in favour of abortion services being legal and consider themselves pro-choice. We were completely abuzz about how pro-choice, how strongly pro-choice this province is."[22]

The vocal and protective nature of Québécois women's issues was also noted by Megill, who recounted the incredulity of her female classmates at McGill medical school when anti-abortion attitudes were mentioned: "There were enough women in the class, and enough Québécois French women specifically, that they basically said, 'Excuse me, why are we having this discussion?'" The forceful expression of these attitudes toward feminist issues is common in Quebec.

Social perceptions of abortion as a woman's right have meant that the anti-abortion movement lacks the same foothold in this province as elsewhere, but that is not to say that these groups are absent. Indeed, activists interviewed for this book noted a recent increase in anti-abortion activity in the province. Interestingly, these concerns were based on fears that increased funding is facilitating anti-abortion activity rather than that participation in the movement itself is rising. Central to their concerns is a growth in crisis pregnancy centres. Abby Lippman, professor of epidemiology at McGill University, noted, "There is a huge amount of money being spent by various fundamentalist and religious rights groups on the anti-abortion issue."[23] The manager of the Centre de santé des femmes de Montréal, Anne Marie Messier, shared this concern and also suggested that these centres may be popping up because of external funding, oftentimes believed to be coming from religious organizations in the United States.[24]

Despite the widespread availability of abortion services, interviewees also expressed concerns regarding difficulties in maintaining confidentiality in rural areas, as well as a lack of publicly available information. As in other provinces and territories, there is an urban-rural divide in services in Quebec. Lippman drew a parallel with the provision of Plan B (the morning-after pill) in small towns:

> It was one thing to have Plan B be available, but if I'm living in a rural region and I know I can get it from the pharmacy, does that help when the pharmacist is likely to be my uncle? In a small town, I know everybody in that town, so it's not as if I can take the metro and walk into a pharmacy in a region of Montreal where no one knows me. In a small town, I don't have that sort of access. So I think there are a lot more constraints on choice of all kinds outside Montreal, or outside of any big city.

The majority of social barriers identified in the province were relatively minor in comparison with other provinces and territories, including the confidentiality of services in smaller towns and the difficulties in negotiating the system because of a lack of information.

A long history of reproductive oppression was successfully challenged in an incredibly short period thanks to the conviction by a majority in the province that reproductive control was a rights issue. Clear connections between the naturalization of women's care roles and reproduction have made this battle all the more compelling. By politicizing reproductive autonomy, Quebec was able to create a favourable social climate that both facilitated access to abortion and recognized the political nature of reproductive rights writ large. To attempt to classify abortion as anything but a rights question in this province is to be met with challenges about all aspects of women's community membership, and rightly so.

Setting Social Precedent

The instrumental nature of activists in securing legal and policy reform while influencing social norms is clear. In this way, activists have profoundly impacted whether services are offered, safe to access, and funded. But it is important to remember that activism also helps shape the social climate in a given city or province and can deeply affect the ability of individual women to access services. After all, some of the most significant obstacles women face when attempting to access abortion services, including social stigma and harassment, manifest outside the formal political sphere.

Variance in attitudes toward abortion in the cases discussed throughout this book demonstrate that not all Canadian women experience their equality in a uniform way; rather, their experiences are conditioned by the social perceptions of abortion in their home province. Public support or tolerance of anti-abortion views, or ambiguity toward women's rights, allow for more than mere interference with women's attempts to access services. Perhaps even more importantly, they can lead women to internalize the belief that they are not, in fact, equal citizens. Whether societies accept abortion as a political issue and, fundamentally, a question of rights, speaks to larger understandings of women's social roles and value as citizens.

6 Never Going Back

Nearly thirty years after the decriminalization of abortion in Canada, access to abortion services remains tenuous. Many women must negotiate complex bureaucratic hoops and threats of harassment in the hopes of obtaining abortion services covered under provincial medicare plans. Those unable to access services in the public system may have no option but to pay out of pocket to access a health care service that is both safe and legal, assuming they have the means to do so. Failing that, some Canadian women have been forced to seek out back-alley abortions or tried to self-induce abortion – the same horrors faced by women when abortion was considered a criminal offence (MacQuarrie, MacDonald, and Chambers 2014).

In this book, I have endeavoured to show that the reclassification of abortion from a criminal offence to a matter of health has not resulted in equal access across the country. Many provincial governments have used their authority over health care to restrict or block access, while successive federal governments have largely denied any responsibility to intercede. Coupled with serious deficiencies at the level of service provision, the result is a patchwork of services across Canada that is reminiscent of the same uneven access the Court deemed unconstitutional in 1988. It is apparent that classifying abortion as a matter of health is insufficient to ensuring women are able to access safe, legal, and dignified abortion care, regardless of their province of residence. Moreover, this framework obscures and depoliticizes the relationship between women's reproductive abilities and their status as Canadian citizens.

Conclusion

Looking to the history of political activity, litigation, social movement activity, and medicine, I have argued that governments have a responsibility to fulfill their Charter obligations by recognizing abortion access as necessary for women's equality. However, taking seriously the contributions of the reproductive justice framework, I have also suggested that rights recognitions should not be understood as ends unto themselves. Rights, especially negative rights, are limited in scope, and overstating their reach risks disregarding in the process other issues that impact women's reproductive lives. After all, abortion is not a stand-alone issue insulated from a woman's social and political life; to the contrary, its study is so important precisely because it sits at a challenging crossroads in sociopolitical thought, blurring the boundaries between the public and private, and shedding light on the many factors that are implicated in the ways women experience attempts to access services. Recognizing the context in which women seek abortions is crucial both to appreciate its significance as an equality right and to confront the continued barriers faced by women attempting to access the procedure.

Reproductive justice advocates provide such a framework by locating reproduction in larger social justice claims. Keeping the lessons of this framework in mind, abortion is best thought of as one of numerous reproductive health issues necessary for women's equality, albeit a highly stigmatized one. As such, although its recognition as a right would be a significant boon for women's equality, it would be a mistake to think of the path toward improving access as somehow insulated from other concerns. An array of issues shape not only the way individual women experience abortion access but also how the issue is viewed in politics, in the courts, and by society at large. To conclude this study, I turn to an emerging case to illustrate the continued rhetorical and strategic value of rights in Canadian abortion politics, that of Prince Edward Island.

The province, widely recognized as having the most restrictive abortion policies in all of Canada, is lately in the process of undergoing substantial modifications to the way it regulates abortion. These changes are the product of focused activism on the Island. Importantly, many of these changes have occurred since the election of Trudeau's Liberal government.[1] As such, the responses of the federal government to the actions of Island officials serve as a starting point for an evaluation of the Trudeau Liberals' response to unequal access to abortion across the country. In addition, the means through which these changes were brought about help illustrate the evolution of social activism described in Chapter 1, in which pro-choice groups are increasingly adopting a more holistic view of abortion, in keeping with the lessons of reproductive justice.

Prince Edward Island

Prince Edward Island has been a long-time hold out when it comes to providing abortion care, having blocked access to surgical abortions since 1982 (Fraser and Sinclair 2016), when the procedure was still regulated by the Criminal Code.[2] Importantly, this failing is not a product of inaction by the legislature but one of design. In February 1988, immediately following the decriminalization of abortion in *R. v. Morgentaler* (1988), the province enacted Resolution 17, which asserts that "life begins at conception, and any policy that permits abortion is unacceptable" (CBC News 2013b). Legislators justified this resolution through an assertion that a majority of Islanders believe life begins at conception, a fact that Lori Brown, Shoshanna Ehrlich, and Colleen MacQuarrie (forthcoming) note was not substantiated by any systematic engagement with the public. Until very recently, this resolution stood out "as PEI's only legislative response to abortion" (ibid.). That is not to say, however, that there has been no action on this issue.

In keeping with his work in other provinces, Morgentaler challenged Prince Edward Island's abortion regulations in the mid-1990s. In *Morgentaler v. Prince Edward Island (Minister of Health and Social Services)* (1995), Morgentaler questioned the constitutionality of the province's abortion policy, specifically targeting the requirement that an abortion be deemed medically necessary by a medical advisory committee composed of five physicians, all appointed by the Hospital and Health Services Commission, before it could be covered under medicare. The procedure would then have to take place at a hospital, even though no hospitals on the Island performed abortion, rendering this process redundant.[3] He also pointed out that this policy, much like the policies he successfully challenged in New Brunswick and Nova Scotia in the preceding years, was "made for an authorized purpose"; that is, it had no clear medical purpose but was intended to prohibit abortion.[4] Morgentaler won his case, with Justice David Jenkins noting that the province's policies "contain all of the trappings and have the practical effect of inhibiting or thwarting access to legal therapeutic abortion based on what the executive perceives to be socially and morally undesirable conduct."[5]

This victory was short-lived, however, as the decision was overturned in a two-to-one verdict on appeal the following year. The appellate court ruled that the legislature did, in contradiction to the lower court ruling, have the authority to give the Prince Edward Island Health and Community Services Agency power to rule on the conditions under which abortion could be funded according to the province's 1988 Health Services Payment Act, despite the intent of the policy.[6] Notably, while Morgentaler was in the process of appealing the decision to the Supreme Court, the government of Prince Edward Island negotiated a compromise behind closed to doors to avoid the case by altering its existing policy. The province would "refer women to the QEII hospital in Halifax, Nova Scotia," but only under very narrow circumstances (Brown, Ehrlich, and MacQuarrie, forthcoming). In order to access an abortion in Halifax, certain criteria had to be met, specifically, "women needed referral by an Island physician to a physician in QEII, be less than 15 weeks, have had an ultrasound, and not have a previous referral for abortion" (ibid.). Importantly, the steps women needed to take to access these services were not made available to the public.

In the years that followed, successive governments have held fast to Regulation 17, even in the face of shifting attitudes at the federal level. Indeed, in 2014, after an announcement by Trudeau that all future members of the Liberal Party would be expected to vote along pro-choice lines, Prince Edward Island's Liberal premier Robert Ghiz defended the province's anti-abortion stance, saying that he believed "the status quo [on abortion] is working" (TC Media 2014). It was in this political climate that Colleen MacQuarrie, Jo-Ann MacDonald, and Cathrine Chambers began a large-scale, community-based research project at the University of Prince Edward Island, exploring the regulation of abortion on the Island.

The study, which began in 2010, set out to assess the impacts of the province's abortion policy on women. MacQuarrie explained that the impetus to start this research was the desire to create evidence-based policies to influence government activity.[7] A necessary part of this work was community discussion (the project included a total of forty-five research conversations with women on the Island who had attempted to access abortion services between 1979 and 2013), in which the community members shared their input and the research committee shared its findings. This approach had the effect of inspiring many members of the community to organize in protest of Prince Edward Island's regulations.

One of the first groups to emerge out of this project did so in 2011. The Prince Edward Island Reproductive Rights Organization (PRRO) formed with the goal of "inform[ing] PEI residents of their reproductive rights resulting from 1988's Supreme Court ruling" (PRRO, n.d.).[8] The group, composed predominantly of young activists, aimed to "challenge the current legislation in PEI and make abortion accessible to Islanders, as the federal legislation states it should be" (ibid.). The PRRO was responsible for "the first reproductive rights rally in twenty years on Prince Edward Island," held on November 19, 2011. This rally, and the media that followed, pressured the government to include details of how women on the Island could access abortion in the province on its webpage for the first time (Brown, Ehrlich, and MacQuarrie, forthcoming).

The PRRO would later align with the Prince Edward Island Abortion Rights Network (ARN), a larger group composed of both "individuals and organizations working together to ensure that all women living in Prince Edward Island have access to publicly funded, accessible, safe abortion services in their own province," which began to take shape in 2010 (ARN 2015–16). Importantly, although the University of Prince Edward Island research group is also aligned with ARN, it views itself as a sister organization. MacQuarrie explained that, since research is a slow process that is "not always compatible with immediate actions," the project team was concerned about "silencing or quieting activism" and thought it was better to continue its advisory role while leaving space for activism. Although, she went on to point out, "it was the energy of the research that started to get a community organization in place."

The impact of ARN would prove substantial. Through the network's tireless activism, it was able to draw attention to Prince Edward Island's restrictive abortion regulation on a national level and pressure the government to change its policies. The network's informal structure also allowed it to expand and make the most of members with relevant specialties. MacQuarrie said that, in short order, ARN saw "lawyers come on, some physicians, political scholars, community citizens who'd been upset with how they'd been treated." She describes the process as "very egalitarian – power-sharing, lots of discussion, and grassroots work." A sizable amount of the group's efforts was dedicated to drawing public attention toward existing problems in the system, through consciousness raising, rallies, and engagement with the legislature. Indeed, it was so successful in providing a voice for those demanding improvements to abortion access in the province that abortion became a campaign issue in the 2015 provincial election.[9]

Leading up to his 2015 election, newly elected provincial Liberal leader Wade MacLauchlan promised to "reduce barriers" to abortions on the Island. True to form, after his victory, changes were made to the regulations governing abortion access, albeit outside the province. In June 2015, Prince Edward Island made arrangements with a hospital in Moncton, New

Brunswick, to provide abortion access to women from Prince Edward Island without the necessity of a referral. Speaking about this initiative, the premier announced: "Women will be able to directly access the service without a doctor's referral or medical office signature or going through the preliminary steps that have been required. This new arrangement will provide confidential, timely health care and ensure continuity of service." He further noted that the province "has an obligation to be in line with the Charter of Rights and Freedoms and the Canada Health Act" (CBC News 2015c).

This move signalled an improvement in services, but it fell short of the major change needed for the government to meet its Charter obligations. The premier's employment of rights language to justify his government's response to the case did demonstrate the continued resonance of rights for Canadians, particularly when one considers its use to justify polices to members of the legislature and public with deeply held anti-abortion views. It was not, however, substantiated with policies affirming these apparent rights, in either a negative or a positive sense of the word. The government also failed to offer any overt recognition of the links between abortion and women's equality, or suggestions for how it might realize these rights through policy over time.

In an effort to pressure the government into action, on January 5, 2016, a new group, Abortion Access Now PEI (AAN PEI), a sister organization of ARN, released a statement of its intent to file suit against the government.

> For over two decades, we have advocated for on-Island, safe, legal access to abortion. Unfortunately, it is clear to us that nothing short of a court order will prompt the government to comply with its obligations to PEI residents under the Charter of Rights and Freedoms," said Ann Wheatley, cochair of Abortion Access Now PEI. Every other province provides safe legal access to abortion within its jurisdictions. "Only PEI refuses to do so. It is time for our equality rights to matter. Prince Edward Island's discriminatory and unlawful abortion policy must end." Colleen MacQuarrie, cochair of Abortion Access Now PEI, concluded: "With our planned legal challenge, Abortion Access Now PEI will seek full and unrestricted access to on-Island, publicly funded abortion services for PEI women. (ARN 2016)

The notice of application sought a declaration that the existing abortion policy in the province was unconstitutional both for its inconsistencies with the Health Services Act and its violation of sections 15 ("Equality Rights"), 7 ("Life, liberty and security of person"), and 12 ("Right not to be subjected to any cruel and unusual treatment or punishment") of the Charter. The

Women's Legal Education and Action Fund (LEAF), which called on the government to "abide by the Charter of Rights and Freedoms and treat its citizens with the dignity afforded to citizenship of every other province" (LEAF 2016), supported this legal challenge. In it, LEAF made explicit reference to section 15 of the Charter, which protects the equality of Canadian citizens, listing "access to abortion (along with other elements of reproductive health care such as access to contraception, information and support for parenting) [as] critical for equality rights to be realized" (ibid.). As was true of provincial litigation addressing abortion in other jurisdictions, this case alleged a violation of women's citizenship rights through a violation of Charter rights, alongside claims that these regulations violated the Canada Health Act.

In response to this application, Prince Edward Island premier Wade MacLauchlan ceded the problems with the existing provincial polices on abortion, promising to address them. In a statement, MacLauchlan revealed that "the province likely wouldn't have been able to successfully defend itself against that suit" because "a provincial abortion rights policy – like the one P.E.I. has – is contrary to the Canadian Charter of Rights and Freedoms." He went on to say that his government will ask "Health PEI to plan for a new women's reproductive health centre [to be located in a hospital] that will offer a number of services, including medical and surgical abortions" (Fraser and Sinclair 2016). Health and wellness minister Rob Henderson then went on to say, "When the new women's reproductive health centre is in place," which could be as early as the end of 2016, "[the] government will cease the service funding agreement [with Halifax]," though the "Moncton service will remain in place for Island women who choose to use it" (ibid.).[10] This solution was met with a warm welcome from Prime Minister Trudeau, who said, "A woman's right to choose is fundamental in Canada" (Trudeau 2016).

Responses to this application from both levels of government are noteworthy. At the provincial level, the government has conceded that its regulations would likely be found in violation of the Charter and have moved to improve its policies rather than engage in a protracted and costly legal battle. This admission signals the continued utility of a rights framework to improve access to abortion. By acknowledging problems with its policies, the government is tacitly admitting that its stance on access, and the limited services on the Island, violate women's rights to equality and security. Unfortunately, failing to make these reasons explicit diminishes the significance of this action. If the province was to take a clear stance on women's equal citizenship, it may open the door for more challenges and policy changes in future, which the government may wish to avoid. By simply modifying existing abortion policies without engaging in a broader discussion, abortion is once again treated as a stand-alone issue, detached from larger equality claims.

Trudeau's response to the actions of the government of Prince Edward Island seem more in keeping with this broader debate but also stops short of acknowledging abortion as a right necessary for women's equality. Since the federal government's plans to address problems with abortion access across the country have not been made public, if such a plan is indeed in place, it is challenging to evaluate the implications of this statement. Does the federal government plan to recognize abortion as a matter of equality in policy, thereby forcing changes at the provincial level? Does it plan to take up the path of Martin's Liberal government by pursuing provinces for violations of the Canada Health Act when they fail to meet certain standards of abortion provision? The strategy remains opaque, though there have already been attempts to clarify this stance in the House.

The ongoing abortion rights activism on Prince Edward Island has also been a topic in the House of Commons. A pro-choice march protesting the province's lack of abortion services in Charlottetown in March 2016 led NDP MP Sheila Malcolmson to assert, "A commitment to women's rights must be more than talk and promises; it must mean concrete action" and to ask Health Minister Jane Philpott to guarantee access to abortion services for all women, regardless of their region of residence (CBC News 2016). In response, Philpott avoided using rights language, stating, "There should be access to all medically necessary services on the basis of need and not on the basis of ability to pay. I will continue to work with my colleagues to make sure access is available to all Canadians" (ibid.). Notably, Philpott had already agreed, following her appointment, that "our government will examine ways to better equalize access for all Canadian women" but has yet to provide details about what this process will entail and when results can be expected (ibid.).

This approach is, thus far, in keeping with the federal government's framing of abortion. Trudeau has been clear about his party's stance on abortion as a rights issue, saying: "I am perfectly comfortable with Canadians knowing that the Liberal Party is unequivocal in its defense of women's rights. We are the party of the Charter. We are the party that stands up for people's rights. We will continue to do so" (Zilio 2015). That said, although the government has embraced pro-choice language and vocalized a commitment to improving access through rights recognitions, the changes it envisions, and how it aims to bring them about, are not yet clear. Although it has embraced a language of Charter rights, what little action has been taken so far has been through the auspices of improving the delivery of health services, not a broader recognition of abortion as a matter of women's equality. Nonetheless, there is reason for optimism, even though securing lasting change is an ongoing process.

This reality has not escaped abortion rights advocates in Prince Edward Island or in the rest of Canada. In the aftermath of the announcement by Premier MacLauchlan, abortion rights activism on the Island has not dissipated. Activists stress that there is still important work to be done, particularly to improve access for women in rural areas of the province (Doucette 2016). Recognition of the shortcomings of the government's admission that the restrictions the province imposed on abortion violated women's equality rights are being received enthusiastically, but with the acknowledgment that improvements to access on the Island will not necessarily safeguard access for all women. In this way, activists continue to reflect insights from the reproductive justice movement. MacQuarrie, elaborating on ARNs meetings, was clear that its goals extended beyond abortion access, saying that the group's work is "about the ability to choose to have children as well as not; it's all about making sure women's lives are supported in ways that allow them to make choices." She also pointed out that the members of ARN are active in movements focusing on projects including poverty eradication and anti-racism, which they understood as deeply tied to abortion access. Although abortion remains a central focus for the group, it cannot be understood as separate from women's equality broadly conceived.

The Limits of Morgentaler

The situation in Prince Edward Island was decided out of court, but the threat of a court case was nonetheless instrumental in securing changes to the province's abortion policy – a fact that has not escaped activists in Canada. Hannah Gray, a member of Reproductive Justice New Brunswick (RJNB) discussing the organization's work, said, "We've tried lobbying, we've tried political action, we've tried speaking directly to them and it seems like one of the only options left is litigation." She went on to say that the group wishes to avoid litigation but, in reference to the situation in Prince Edward Island, "it's definitely clear that it's one of the only ways to make politicians move" (Doucette 2016).

In the decades after *R v. Morgentaler* (1988), the courts have played a substantial role in delineating the reach of the decision and the obligations of provinces and territories in upholding it. Although rulings in both provincial and federal courts have overwhelmingly favoured the pro-choice cause, the specifics of these rulings suggest a wariness of the courts to recognize a positive right to access. This caution is appropriate, as the allocation of resources necessitates the democratic legitimacy of elected officials. Unfortunately, the federal government has yet to rise to the task. The resulting standoff has left abortion rights in limbo. Absent any clear rights protections, access issues have been deemed the responsibility of the provinces, all of which have taken divergent approaches to regulating the procedure. Despite some provinces, such as New Brunswick and Prince Edward Island, having recently bowed to pressure from activists, even governments there have remained reluctant to act proactively to address their Charter responsibilities. The result is profoundly different levels of access both within and between provinces and territories.

In some cases, this variance in access has meant the de facto recriminalization of services; in others, a commitment to recognizing abortion access as a right necessary for women's equality. In a climate where, until very recently, the government had repeatedly vowed not to reopen the abortion debate, we were asked to believe that no news on abortion is, in effect, good news. In this way, silence and inaction have become stand-ins for affirmation of abortion rights, when this attitude actually represents the maintenance of a troubling status quo that treats abortion as taboo and inaction as the best we can hope for.

To say that *R. v. Morgentaler* (1988) was not the final battle of reproductive rights in Canada, as it is often touted, is not to diminish its significance. *Morgentaler*, and related court cases that followed, both federal and provincial, continue to validate Charter claims that uphold women's equality. Joanna Erdman (2014) affirms that

> *Morgentaler* stands for the principle that governments cannot hold out access rights to abortion that are illusory – access rights that guarantee no real access to services. *Morgentaler* stands for the principle that governments cannot hide behind arbitrary policies, those with unnecessary requirements – hospital-only, physician-referred – which have no connection to any legitimate objective such as, safety, cost, or access. Governments cannot delay and create barriers to reproductive health care without reason, without need, and without justification. These arbitrary rules are constitutionally offensive. This is the ruling of *Morgentaler.*

The logic of the *Morgentaler* decision seems to be that arbitrary regulations and uneven access threaten women's rights to life, liberty, and security of the person. Although the case in question was focused specifically on the realities of section 251 of the Criminal Code, in the years following the decision, it has become apparent that the failure of governments to recognize abortion as an equality right has produced inequalities in access comparable to those deemed unconstitutional in *Morgentaler*.

If women understand their desires for reproductive autonomy as (at worst) shameful or (at best) special rights, they will continue to see the female body as exceptional. The acceptance of abortion rights as citizenship rights is crucial before women can understand themselves as full citizens, deserving of equality. The ability of women to exercise their rights to reproductive control can be realized only when they truly believe themselves to be equal.

To this end, rights recognitions continue to provide a valuable platform to improve access to abortion care. The language of rights has resonance in Canada, as well as the power to pressure the state into action. It also creates a sense of legitimacy and permanence that plays an important role in the ability of women to internalize their value as Canadian citizens. With multiple avenues of rights recognition open, it is high time for Canadians not only to fight for their rights but also to start feeling that their governments ought to be doing the same.

Appendix A: Abortion and the Canada Health Act

A 2003 Canadian Abortion Rights Action League report, duplicated in Palley (2006, 575), outlines the specific ways in which the principles of the Canada Health Act have been violated by the provinces in their regulation of abortion. Although many of these claims are now outdated after changes in provincial policies, they nonetheless help illustrate how this act applies in the case of abortion.

Portability is violated when provinces place abortion, along with cosmetic surgery, on the excluded list for reciprocal billing of other provinces.

Accessibility is breached when provinces such as Prince Edward Island refuse to provide any abortion services, forcing women to travel to the mainland to receive care.

Comprehensiveness is dishonoured by the four provinces of Nova Scotia, New Brunswick, Quebec, and Manitoba when they refuse to pay for a medically necessary procedure performed in a freestanding clinic rather than a hospital.

Public administration is disregarded when, as a result of hospital mergers between Catholic and secular hospitals, the publicly funded Catholic-run institutions eliminate all reproductive health care services for women, including contraception and abortion.

Finally, the principle of *universality* is clearly meaningless when it comes to abortion because the availability of hospital services can vary from 0 percent to 35 percent, depending on where a woman lives.

Appendix B: Abortion Access by Province

Health Canada does not have a publicly accessible list of clinics and hospitals that provide abortion services. This lack of information is a significant barrier faced by anyone who needs to access an abortion. Numerous organizations, including the Abortion Rights Coalition of Canada and Action Canada for Sexual Health and Rights, have attempted to offer information on the changing nature of access in the provinces and territories in order to guide individuals to their closest service points. However, with fluctuating numbers of hospitals resulting from amalgamations, closures, and openings, exact figures are hard to keep up-to-date. The tendency to miscount clinics that are situated in hospitals, which are sometimes counted as clinics and other times as hospitals, further complicates these numbers. Finally, the entrance of Mifegysmo onto the Canadian market could increase the total number of access points for services and require a rehashing of this information. As it stands, these tables reflect the most current information about abortion access in the three provinces discussed in Chapter 3.

Below is a reproduction of a table compiled by ARCC in 2016, which contains the most up-to-date information available on clinic services in Canada. Note the differences in the number of clinics listed for Quebec. This is not actually inconsistent with the above table. Quebec is unique in having private clinics as well as CLSCs and women's health centres. According to a joint 2010 report by Canadians for Choice (now part of Action Canada for Sexual and Reproductive Health) and the FQPN, Quebec has

Provinces	Hospitals	Clinics	Details
New Brunswick	3 of 28 (11%)	1	Abortion services provided at Clinic 554 are not covered under provincial medicare.
Ontario	39 of 194 (20%)	11	Ten of the eleven clinics are located in Ottawa or the Greater Toronto Area. Access is minimal in Northern Ontario.
Quebec	31 of 129 (24%)	36	Women are still responsible for some fees at private clinics.

Note: According to a joint 2005 year report by Canadians for Choice (now part of Action Canada for Sexual and Reproductive Health) and the FQPN, only twenty-one hospitals in Quebec perform abortions, ten fewer than identified by ARCC in 2013. The figure from the most recent ARCC study is included in this table in recognition of these changes.

Source: ARCC 2013, 2016; FQPN and CFC 2010, 39.

twenty-three CLSCs, four private clinics, and three women's health centres, and only the latter two were counted as clinics by the ARCC.

I have made one modification to the entry for Prince Edward Island, which is marked by an asterisk, in recognition of the recent changes to abortion access in the province announcement by the premier.

List of Abortion Clinics in Canada

The following pages contain a complete list of clinics across Canada, including hospitals with a dedicated abortion clinic or women's health clinic. Otherwise, hospitals are not listed unless they are the only facility(s) providing abortions in that province or territory. Gestational limits are indicated where known; these are surgical abortions unless specified otherwise. Note: Some private clinics may provide medical abortions; contact the Action Canada Access Line, next page.

Region	Clinic Name	City	Phone	Info/Website/Email
National pro-choice groups (info, referrals)	Action Canada for Sexual Health and Rights (Note: This group is a November 2014 merger of the former Action Canada for Population and Development, Canadians for Choice, and Canadian Federation for Sexual Health.)	Ottawa	Action Canada Access Line: 1-888-642-2725 Office: 613-241-4474	24-hour, Canada-wide, toll-free number that provides information on reproductive and sexual health and referrals on pregnancy options. info@sexualhealthandrights.ca http://www.sexualhealthandrights.ca/ Click on "Find a Service Provider" for a list of sexual health centres in your province. Norma Scarborough fund – an emergency fund to help with travel and accommodation expenses (call hotline).
	National Abortion Federation	Victoria	Canadian referrals: 1-877-257-0012 Financial assistance: 1-800-772-9100 Canadian office: 250-598-1858 US office: 1-800-772-9100	www.prochoice.org (US) canada@prochoice.org
	Fédération du Québec pour le planning des naissances	Montreal	514-866-3721	www.fqpn.qc.ca info@fqpn.qc.ca
	Abortion Rights Coalition of Canada	Vancouver	n/a	www.arcc-cdac.ca info@arcc-cdac.ca (This list: www.arcc-cdac.ca/list-abortion-clinics-canada.pdf)

(Continued)

Region	Clinic Name	City	Phone	Info/Website/Email
Alberta	Kensington Clinic	Calgary	403-283-9117	Up to 20 weeks www.kensingtonclinic.com
	Woman's Health Options Clinic	Edmonton	780-484-1124	Up to 19 weeks and 6 days http://womanshealthoptions.com info@whol.ca
	Pregnancy Options Line (hotline for all of British Columbia)	BC	1-888-875-3163 604-875-3163 (in Lower Mainland)	Services: Counselling, referrals, some hospital/clinic contact info, contraception referrals. You must leave a voicemail; will be returned within forty-eight hours during weekdays.
British Columbia	Women's Services Clinic, Kelowna General Hospital	Kelowna	250-980-1399	Hours: Monday and Tuesday: 8:30 a.m.–2:30 p.m.; Wednesday: 8 a.m.–12 p.m., most Thursdays.
	CARE Program, BC Women's Hospital & Health Centre	Vancouver	604-875-2022 1-888-300-3088 x2022 (hotline for all of British Columbia; referrals, etc.)	Up to 23 weeks and 6 days Book an appointment online: www.bcwomens.ca/care http://www.bcwomens.ca/our-services/gynecology/abortion-contraception
	Elizabeth Bagshaw Women's Clinic	Vancouver	604-736-7878 1-877-736-7171	Up to 16 weeks www.ebwc.ca info@ebwc.ca
	Everywoman's Health Centre	Vancouver	604-322-6692	www.everywomanshealthcentre.ca ewhc@everywomanshealthcentre.ca
	Willow Women's Clinic	Vancouver	604-709-5611	Medical abortions up to 7 weeks, surgical up to 10 weeks www.medicalabortion.ca willowwomensclinic@yahoo.ca
	Vancouver Island Women's Clinic	Victoria	250-480-7338	Up to 20 weeks www.viwomensclinic.ca

Manitoba	Health Sciences Centre, Women's Hospital	Winnipeg	204-787-1980	www.hsc.mb.ca
	Women's Health Clinic	Winnipeg	204-477-1887 1-866-947-1517 ext. 103	Up to 16 weeks www.womenshealthclinic.org whc@womenshealthclinic.org
New Brunswick	Note: Funded abortion services are currently only available at three hospitals in New Brunswick. Reproductive Justice New Brunswick hotline: 506-451-9060 How to Access an Abortion in New Brunswick: http://rjnb.org/how-to-access-abortion-new-brunswick/			
	Clinic 554	Fredericton	1-855-978-5434	Up to 16 weeks http://www.clinic554.ca/ Abortions are not funded. Cost is about $700 to $850, depending on gestational length.
	Bathurst Chaleur Regional Hospital	Bathurst	506-544-3000	Up to 13 weeks, 6 days. No doctor's referral required, but only Bathurst-area women are acccpted. www.chfn.ca/centres/bathurst-chaleur-regional-hospital
	Dr. Georges-L.-Dumont University Hospital Centre	Moncton	506-862-2770	Up to 13 weeks, 6 days. No doctor's referral required. info@vitalitenb.ca
	The Moncton Hospital	Moncton	Toll-free: 1-844-806-9205	Up to 13 weeks, 6 days. No doctor's referral required. PEI patients funded by the PEI government. Horizon@HorizonNB.ca http://en.horizonnb.ca/home/facilities-and-services/services/clinics/family-planning-clinic.aspx

(Continued)

Region	Clinic Name	City	Phone	Info/Website/Email
Newfoundland	Athena Health Centre (formerly Morgentaler Clinic)	St. John's	709-754-3572 1-800-755-2044	Up to 15 weeks. http://www.thrivecyn.ca/directory-of-services/health/athena-health-centre-formerly-the-morgentaler-clinic/ athenahealthcentre@bellaliant.com
Nova Scotia	Queen Elizabeth II Health Sciences Centre, Termination of Pregnancy Unit	Halifax	902-473-7072	Up to 15 weeks and 6 days PEI patients accepted with referral; funded by the PEI government.
Ontario	Brampton Women's Clinic	Brampton	905-789-7474	Up to 16 weeks (only partly funded) http://bramptonwc.com/ info@bramptonwc.com Appointment requests: http://www.bramptonwomensclinic.com/contact/
	Women's Clinic, Hamilton Health Sciences Hospital	Hamilton	905-389-5068	www.hamiltonhealthsciences.ca/body.cfm?ID=232
	Pregnancy Options Program/Abortion Clinic, London Health Science Centre	London	519-685-8204	Up to 22 weeks www.lhsc.on.ca/Patients_Families_Visitors/Womens_Health/tap.htm
	Freeport Health Centre, Grand River Hospital Freeport Health Centre, Grand River Hospital	Kitchener	519-749-4254	www.grhosp.on.ca (general)

Mississauga Women's Clinic	Mississauga	905-629-4516	Up to 15 weeks (only partly funded) www.mwclinic.com info@mwclinic.com
Morgentaler Clinic	Ottawa	613-567-8300 Appts: 613-567-3360	Up to 17 weeks www.morgentaler.ca/contact_ottawa.html
Bay Centre for Birth Control	Toronto	416-351-3700	Medical abortion up to 7 weeks; surgical up to 8 weeks Women's College Hospital: BCBC@wchospital.ca (Note: Appointments must be booked by phone, not email) All services: http://www.womenscollegehospital.ca/programs-and-services/bcbc/ Abortion care: http://www.womenshealthmatter.ca/health-centres/sexual-health/abortion/
Bloor West Village Women's Clinic	Toronto	416-849-4595 1-877-849-4595	www.bloorwestwomensclinic.com Contact form: http://www.bloorwestwomensclinic.com/contact/
Cabbagetown Women's Clinic	Toronto	416-323-0642 1-800-399-1592	Up to 22 weeks www.cabbagetownwomensclinic.com
Choice in Health Clinic	Toronto	416-975-9300 1-866-565-9300	Up to 15 weeks www.choiceinhealth.ca
Morgentaler Clinic	Toronto	416-932-0446 1-800-556-6835	Up to 19.5 weeks www.morgentaler.ca/contact.html mclinic@passport.ca
Scott Clinic	Toronto	416-962-5771	Up to 16 weeks http://scottclinic.ca
Women's Care Clinic	Toronto (North York)	416-256-4139	Up to 20 weeks (only partly funded) http://womenscareclinic.ca info@womenscareclinic.ca

(*Continued*)

Region	Clinic Name	City	Phone	Info/Website/Email
Prince Edward Island	No services, unless you can find a doctor willing to provide a medical abortion (with drugs). You will probably have to travel outside the province. Funded abortions are available in Moncton, New Brunswick, or Halifax, Nova Scotia. Clinic 554 in Fredericton accepts PEI patients, but abortions are not funded. * On March 31, 2016, PEI premier Wade MacLauchlan announced that his government intends to create an abortion clinic in a PEI hospital before the end of 2016. Once this clinic is in operation, no access will be available to PEI women in Halifax, but services in Moncton will still be available.			Information: http://peiacsw.wordpress.com/abortion-access-info-pei/ (Also see listings under New Brunswick and Nova Scotia.)
Quebec	Clinique des femmes de l'Outaouais	Hull	819-778-2055	www.cliniquedesfemmes.com
	Centre de Santé des Femmes	Montreal	514-270-6114	www.csfmontreal.qc.ca/servi.htm info@csfmontreal.qc.ca
	CLSC des Faubourgs	Montreal	514 527-2361	https://jeannemance.ciusss-centresudmtl.gouv.qc.ca/votre-csss/nos-points-de-service/clsc-et-clinique/clsc-des-faubourgs-sanguinet/.
	Clinique Médicale l'Alternative	Montreal	514-281-6476	www.cliniquedelalternative.com
	Clinique Morgentaler	Montreal	514-844-4844 1-888-401-4844	Up to 20 weeks www.morgentalermontreal.ca mclinique@gmail.com
	Clinique Médicale Femina	Montreal	514-843-7904	www.clinique-femina.com femina@clinique-femina.com

	Clinique de planification des naissances, Centre hospitalier universitaire de Québec	Quebec	418-525-4444	Up to 16 weeks www.chuq.qc.ca/fr/les_soins/autres_soins/clinique_planification_naissances.htm
Saskatchewan	Women's Health Centre, Regina General Hospital	Regina	306-766-0586 1-800-563-9923	Up to 16 weeks http://www.rqhealth.ca/programs/in_hospital_care/women_hlth_centre.shtml
	College Park Medical Clinic	Saskatoon	306-955-2600	Up to 12 weeks, both surgical (in hospital) and medical using methotrexate ($75 cost for drugs) http://collegeparkmedicalclinicsk.ca cpmc@sasktel.net
	Saskatoon City Hospital	Saskatoon	306-244-7989 (Sexual Health Centre referrals)	Up to 12 weeks Referrals available from Sexual Health Centre: http://sexualhealthcentresaskatoon.ca/preg/ab_stoon.php
	Saskatoon Community Clinic	Saskatoon	306-652-0300	Medical abortions using methotrexate, up to 7 weeks. No doctor's referral necessary. www.saskatooncommunityclinic.ca/ member.relations@communityclinic.sk.ca
Territories	NOW – Northern Options for Women (at Stanton Territorial Hospital)	Yellowknife, Northwest Territories	867-765-4018 Outside Yellowknife: 1-888-873-5710	Up to 16 weeks routinely Up to 20 weeks depending on provider availability www.northernoptionsforwomen.com
	Baffin Regional Hospital	Iqaluit, Nunavut	867-979-7352	
	Whitehorse General Hospital	Whitehorse, Yukon	867-393-8700	www.whitehorsehospital.ca

Source: ARCC 2016. For updates, see http://www.arcc-cdac.ca/list-abortion-clinics-canada.pdf.

Notes

Introduction

1 In thinking about the significance of the Charter, it is important to recognize that the inclusion of the rights it protects, which we as Canadians have come to think of as reflecting some of our most fundamental values, were by no means foregone conclusions. The addition of two separate sex equality guarantees in the Charter (sections 15 and 28), and a third in the Constitution Act (section 35(4)), were the direct product of a committed women's lobby (Baines 2015–16, 112).

2 I make reference to the concepts of reproductive autonomy, bodily autonomy, and autonomy more generally throughout this book. Each of these references is meant to allude to the need for individuals to make decisions about their bodies and lives independently and without coercion. Although *bodily autonomy* refers specifically to decisions made about one's physical person, and *reproductive autonomy* to all aspects of life relating to reproduction, I am effectively treating these terms as synonyms as they pertain to discussions about abortion access.

3 The first national action of the Canadian's women's movement was the Abortion Caravan, discussed in more detail on pages 34–35.

4 In this way, abortion access is a necessary – though insufficient – condition for the realization of women's equality.

5 Roseneil et al. (2013, 901) remind us that the range of criticisms I discuss in this section, from the public-private split to suggestions that women lack the rationality or perspective for full citizenship, "have been almost exclusively the critical terrain of feminist and queer scholars" and have therefore "largely remained marginal to 'citizenship studies.'"

6 For more on the significance of equal citizenship from a gendered perspective, see Ruth Lister's *Citizenship: Feminist Perspectives* (2003); Paul Kershaw's *Carefair:*

Rethinking the Responsibilities and Rights of Citizenship (2005); Jane Jenson and Alexandra Dobrowolsky's Shifting Representations of Citizenship: Canadian Politics of 'Women' and 'Children,' (2004); and Rosemary Nossiff's *Gendered Citizenship: Women, Equality, and Abortion Policy* (2007).

7   For more on the challenges to the implementation of citizenship, see Carole Pateman, The *Sexual Contract* (1988) and "The Patriarchal Welfare State" (1992); Ruth Lister (1997, 2010); Nira Yuval-Davis's, *Gender and Nation* (1997); and T.H. Marshall (2006).

8   Alison Jaggar (2005, 95) suggests that "perhaps the most direct feminist assault on traditional conceptions of citizenship is implicit in the slogan emblematic of Western second-wave feminism, 'The personal is political.'"

9   Throughout this book I refer to women's experiences of citizenship as they relate to reproduction. I do, however, want to recognize that not everyone who experiences unwanted pregnancies is a cisgendered woman. Individuals who identify as genderqueer and male also need access to services and may face additional barriers because they are not necessarily able to access what are often seen as women-only services. Many may already face barriers accessing health care in general. Nonetheless, analysis relating to abortion access across disciplines continues to exclusively reference women. Moreover, the history of the regulation of abortion in Canada is a deeply gendered one. Long-standing assumptions about the expected role of women in society, regardless of whether they can or chose to reproduce, continues to inform the regulation of abortion across the country. For these reasons, I continue to refer to women in this book, but I do so recognizing that the gendered assumptions upon which restrictions to abortion are based are themselves outdated and need to be challenged so that everyone, regardless of how they identify, can receive the care they need.

Chapter 1: The Anti-abortion, Pro-choice, and Reproductive Justice Movements

1   Some of the most notable examples of works on pro-choice and anti-abortion activism in Canada include Brodie, Gavigan, and Jenson 1992; Saurette and Gordon 2013, 2016; Stetson 1996; Tatalovich 1997; and Haussman 2005. The work on reproductive justice in Canada, however, is far less established (examples include Shaw 2013; Danforth, n.d.) so I rely more heavily on sources from the United States (such as L. Ross 2006; Chrisler 2012, 2013; and Briggs et al. 2013) to make claims about the movement.

2   In *Without Apology*, Shannon Stettner (2016) hypothesizes that the historical strength of socialist feminism in Canada, which was employed by many women involved in the Abortion Caravan as well as in the Ontario Coalition of Abortion Clinics, may be linked to a slower adoption of a reproductive justice framework in parts of Canada, since socialist feminists were already calling for a treatment of abortion care in line with many of the broader goals of reproductive justice.

3   The names given to activist groups working on abortion are themselves profoundly political. Groups opposing its mandate, for example, often refer to the pro-choice movement as the pro-abortion movement. In so doing, they seem to suggest that the group advocates abortions for all women, regardless of circumstance or desire. I therefore employ the term *pro-choice* because it most accurately depicts the goals of

the movement. Likewise, the group I refer to as the anti-abortion movement is more likely to call themselves the pro-life movement; members of the pro-choice movement also commonly use the term *anti-choice*. I have selected the term *anti-abortion* as most impartially depicting the group's stance. The *pro-life* designation is misleading, as it is not readily apparent to those outside the movement whose life is worth protecting, not to mention the reality that fetal life is not recognized in law or policy in Canada, let alone as somehow trumping a woman's right to life. The phrase *anti-choice*, which suggests that the group opposes women's agency, though accurate, has been misappropriated by these groups, which claim that women can exercise choice, but only when that choice is not to become pregnant in the first place. (This interpretation of choice is deeply troubling. This view leaves no room for discussions relating to sexual violence and also denies women's rights to live their lives on their own terms, including full sexual lives.)

4 The movement toward "woman-centred" language in the anti-abortion movement has also been documented in the United States and Australia (Cannold 2002).
5 *Borowski v. Canada (Minister of Justice)*, [1981] 2 S.C.R. 575, para 2.
6 One such controversy occurred leading up to the 2015 federal election, in which some Saskatoon postal workers refused to deliver postcards depicting a graphic image of an aborted fetus (Canadian Press 2015).
7 In stark contrast to this framing, the United Nations (2014, 1) has found that countries with restrictive abortion laws and policies have higher rates of both unsafe abortion and maternal mortality (1).
8 The composition and role of TACs are discussed further in Chapter 2. These committees, in operation between 1969 and 1988, were composed of at least three doctors who had the power to approve a woman's request for a legal abortion. Their uneven operation across Canada ultimately led the Supreme Court to rule that section 251 of the Criminal Code, which created them, was unconstitutional.
9 *Roe v. Wade*, [1973] 410 U.S. 113.
10 As I contend in the previous section, positive rights recognitions are also important for Canadian pro-choice activists. This portrayal of pro-choice activism relies heavily on the US model.
11 Concerns about the limitations of liberal rights as tools to promote change are not without merit. Traditional liberal rights frameworks stress that all citizens are inherently equal and ought to have the same opportunities; any differences in situation will therefore be the result of individual effort. Although the foundations of a system rooted in nondiscrimination may seem laudable in an idealized world, advocates of this viewpoint have often used the ideal of a level playing field to ignore systematized inequalities faced by individuals in the real world. If we ignore the different realities individuals face by virtue of factors, including their biology, ancestry, or social prejudice, and only consider individuals citizens where their experiences overlap, we end up in the ironic situation of dramatically reinforcing inequality under the umbrella of promoting it.

Supporters of such a framework might suggest that creating protections for individuals and groups means the promotion of equality of outcome over opportunity, yet these supporters often refuse to see existing inequalities as indicators of unequal opportunity structures, opting instead to see a lack of effort or poor decision making

as the sole culprits. These views are evident in assertions that a gender pay gap, for example, is not an issue because women simply chose lower-paying jobs (Lipman 2015).
12 Despite naming differences, pro-choice organizations have regularly come out in support of reproductive justice activism in public demonstrations. For example, the Abortion Rights Coalition of Canada (ARCC) and the Ontario Coalition for Abortion Clinics (OCAC) both participated in the Pan-Canadian Day of Action for Reproductive Justice: Equal Access Now! (https://ocac-choice.com). Likewise, the FQPN, whose tagline stresses the need for choice and the right to sexual and reproductive health, has posted literature on the reproductive justice movement (OCAC 2012; FQPN 2014a).
13 The only group consistently recognized by interviewees as conforming to a reproductive justice approach in Canada is the Native Youth Sexual Health Network. An organization that focuses on Indigenous youth in both Canada and the United States, it works on projects ranging from "reclaiming rites of passage" to the sex trade to environmental justice (NYSHN 2015). The lack of widespread mobilization of this or other movements led most interviewees to express: "We don't have a reproductive justice movement in Canada." Interview with FQPN representative, June 11, 2015.
14 This and the following quotation are from an interview with Sandeep Prasad, June 12, 2015. Action Canada for Sexual Health and Rights formed in 2014 with the merger of three existing organizations: Canadians for Choice, the Canadian Federation for Sexual Health, and Action Canada for Population and Development.
15 Interview with FQPN representative, June 11, 2015. The English translation of the group's name is the Quebec Federation for Planned Pregnancy.
16 Ibid.
17 Interview with Jessi Taylor, June 25, 2015.
18 A representative of the FQPN also noted that lack of racial diversity as a reason it could not become a full-fledged reproductive justice group. Interview with FQPN representative, June 11, 2015.
19 Although a right to health care may be seen as limited to Canadian citizens, many pro-choice groups in Canada continue to advocate for anyone in the country to have access to these services, and for the UN reproductive rights guarantees to be realized worldwide.
20 Jessica Danforth was born Jessica Shaw, and earlier work under her former name is cited in later chapters.
21 Certainly, the specific challenges minority groups in Canada face have not historically taken centre stage in reproductive rights advocacy. The forced sterilization of aboriginal and "mentally ill" women, the fallout of residential schools, and the funding and language barriers immigrants and refugees face, to name just a few issues, are often overlooked or treated as separate from discussions of reproductive rights.

Chapter 2: Federal Politics and the Supreme Court

1 Miriam Smith (2002, 29) agrees that the Charter has had an impact on politics in Canada, but she is careful to point out that these changes are not necessarily detrimental: "We might find that the 'judicialization' of Canadian politics has occurred more at a symbolic and ideological level than at an instrumental or policy level." She

goes on to suggest that "groups are [now] able to use rights claims to produce a symbolic and contentious politics that challenges the previously dominant 'codes' of Canadian society."

2 That said, the Trudeau government's openness about its pro-choice stance may lead to a more open discussion in the House, but only time will tell.

3 As a point of interest, 1869 was also the year the Catholic Church amended its views on abortion. In her historical study of abortion, Betsy Hartmann (1995, 259) writes: "Even the Catholic Church was relatively tolerant of early abortion – not until 1869 did Pope Pius IX declare all abortion to be murder."

4 Angus McLaren and Arlene McLaren (1997, 123) explain: "In the first decades of the century, birth control has been associated either with feminists calling for women to have the right to control their own bodies or with leftists striving for a democratization of contraception. As a result, the respectable middle classes, though they employed birth control, shied away from a public defence of a practice whose only vocal proponents were radicals."

5 Concerns about the classist and racist nature of reproductive policies have emerged alongside advances in assisted reproductive technologies that are often prohibitively expensive for most demographics.

6 Although there were many vocal advocates for contraception in Canada at the time, McLaren and McLaren focus on the roles played by some of the most influential: A.R. Kaufman (business owner), A.H. Tyrer (author, propagandist, and Protestant churchman), and Mrs. Mary C. Hawkins (community activist and founder of the Hamilton birth control clinic), all of whom endorsed eugenicist policies. For more on their specific roles in the birth control debate, see McLaren and McLaren, *The Bedroom and the State* (1997).

7 For more details concerning TACs, see Badgley (1977) and Brodie, Gavigan, and Jenson (1992).

8 Interview with Dr. Carolyn Bennett, February 10, 2011. She went on to say that the feeling among these physicians was that "a woman's decision had been medicalized, as though a tribunal could decide whether she was putting her life in danger."

9 Indeed, the United States would liberalize its abortion laws four years later in *Roe v. Wade* (1973).

10 In a 2003 *Globe and Mail* interview, Morgentaler explained that, although he could not save his own mother, who died during in Auschwitz, he realized he could save other mothers: "It was an unconscious thought. It became almost like a command. If I help women to have babies at a time when they can give love and affection, they will not grow up to be rapists or murders. They will not build concentration camps."

11 Morgentaler identified strongly as a humanist, an ethical stance that values human agency, critical thought, and empiricism over faith. In a 1985 interview with the *Canadian Medical Association Journal*, Morgentaler talks about the importance of the quality of life for the potential future child, saying, "I think the most important consideration is that the child should be born at a time when it can be provided with what is absolutely essential for its emotional and physical development," and going on to say that "it's ludicrous to talk about the rights of embryos when we have over-population and so much misery in the world" (Hengel 1985, 491).

12 *Morgentaler v. the Queen*, [1976] 1 S.C.R. 616 (hereafter cited as *Morgentaler* 1976) at 657.
13 *Morgentaler* 1976 at 657.
14 Interview with feminist legal scholar, June 8, 2011.
15 Later that same year, an arsonist attacked the Toronto clinic. The clinic was not irreparably damaged by this attack and reopened in 1984, but the women's bookstore housed in the same building was seriously damaged. The bookstore, which was something of a feminist institution in Toronto, did eventually reopen but has since officially closed its doors (NAF 2010; Pelrine 1983, 221).
16 In response, the province promised "not [to] seek to shut down the Toronto Clinic while the appeal was pending" (NAF 2010). In the meantime, with the appeal still pending, Dr. Scott opened a second Toronto clinic in 1986. The clinic was raided and new charges were laid against Scott, as well as against Morgentaler and their colleague Dr. Colodny, but the attorney general stayed the case in anticipation of the Supreme Court appeal. The charges were eventually dropped in 1987 before the preceding case made it to the Supreme Court.
17 *R. v. Morgentaler*, [1988] S.C.R. 30 at 32 (1988) (hereafter cited as *Morgentaler* 1988).
18 *Morgentaler* 1988 at 37.
19 Dr. Morgentaler was awarded the Order of Canada in 2008, Canada's highest civilian honour, for his "commitment to increased healthcare options for women, his determined efforts to influence Canadian public policy and his leadership in humanist and civil liberties organizations" (Governor General of Canada 2008, 10).
20 *Murphy v. Dodd*, [1989] O.J. 1587; *Diamond v. Hirsch*, [1989] M.C.Q.B. (unreported); *D.D. v. V.F.*, [2001] B.C.S.C. 1419; *Tremblay v. Daigle*, [1989] 2 S.C.R. 530.
21 *Tremblay v. Daigle*, [1989] 2 S.C.R. 530 at 531 (hereafter cited as *Tremblay*).
22 Ruth Lister (2003, 127) warns that "even though they [women] are as likely to encounter violence in the private as in the public sphere, women's fear of male violence constrains their freedom in the latter."
23 *Tremblay* at 571.
24 This and the preceding quotation are from *Tremblay* at 537.
25 Tremblay's known abusive behaviour was an issue Daigle raised in the case, but the issue was largely ignored in the legal deliberations. Many people no doubt felt some grim satisfaction when Tremblay was charged for numerous incidents of domestic abuse later in life (Radio-Canada 2012).
26 *Tremblay* at 555.
27 This case was heard only six years after marital rape was criminalized in Canada. The decision of the Court to ignore the implications of domestic violence in this case may therefore reflect lingering beliefs about the seriousness of violence against women. Indeed, in 1982, NDP MP Margaret Mitchell "was laughed at by MPs in the House of Commons when she demanded the government take action to stop domestic violence" (Alphonso and Farahbaksh 2009).
28 *Borowski v. Canada (Attorney General)*, [1989] 1 S.C.R. 342 at para. 49.
29 *Minister of Justice (Can.) v. Borowski*, [1981] 2 S.C.R. 575, 578.
30 Even though women MPs did not vote as a block against Bill C-43, their decision to block the Mitges amendment is nonetheless a significant moment in Canadian

political history. Brodie (1992, 88) points out that, at least in this one instance, "the nominal representation of women in the House of Commons did make a difference."
31 An Act to amend the Criminal Code (injuring or causing the death of an unborn child while committing an offence), House of Commons of Canada, Second Session, Thirty-Ninth Parliament, 56 Elizabeth II, 2007.
32 Michelle Robidoux, manager of the Ontario Coalition of Abortion Clinics, described Ruth as "a pro-choice senator who people relied on as a kind of an ally," suggesting that she meant these comments to be helpful and not as a threat, citing an insider's understanding of the politics surrounding the issue in the Conservative Party caucus. However, the idea that the best way to ensure protection of existing rights is through "the silencing of anybody who disagrees with the government" is a disturbing trend. Interview with Michelle Robidoux, March 30, 2011.
33 Interview with Abby Lippman, January 16, 2011.
34 Interview with Catherine Megill, June 12, 2011.
35 Interview with Michelle Robidoux, March 30, 2011.
36 Interview with FQPN representative, May 12, 2011.
37 Exactly how far this policy will extend, and whether it will cover existing approaches to access, as well as future votes, is not yet clear. Indeed, Trudeau came under fire for his support of PEI Liberal leader Wade MacLauchlan after MacLauchlan said in a provincial debate on women's issues that he favours the provincial status quo when it comes to abortion access (Maloney 2015). Since making this statement, MacLauchlan, now premier of Prince Edward Island, announced that the province would begin offering abortion services.
38 Up for Debate identifies as "an alliance of over 175 women's organizations and their allies from across Canada, representing more than 4 million people" working together to raise awareness about women's rights leading up to the 2015 federal election (Up for Debate 2015).
39 Once exception could be the mandate letter for the Minister of International Development and La Francophonie, which stresses the need to close "existing gaps in reproductive rights and health care for women" in Canada's maternal, newborn, and child health initiative, though this letter also fails to make explicit reference to abortion (Trudeau 2015a).

Chapter 3: Abortion in the Provinces

1 The one exception is the ruling in *Jane Doe et al. v. Manitoba* (2005), which found that provincial delays in access to funding violated section 15 of the Charter.
2 For more on the history of abortion access in New Brunswick, see Katrina R. Ackerman's "'Not in the Atlantic Provinces': The Abortion Debate in New Brunswick, 1980–1987," (2012).
3 The government's changes to the Medical Act could be read as showing a deeply felt, emotional opposition to abortion rights recognitions, or a desire to stifle rights discussion. However, Alison Brewer, the former leader of the New Brunswick NDP, suggested that this action was highly strategic and not necessarily demonstrative of anti-abortion views by Hatfield himself: "Hatfield had created a hole in the legislation you could drive a truck through. Hatfield was a smart man and a lawyer, and

he had recorded in *Hansard* that he was setting up a bill against the Morgentaler Clinic. You cannot set up a piece of legislation that is directed at one person, and Hatfield would have known that. But at the same time, he was a political animal and he was pandering to a certain portion of the electorate." Interview with Alison Brewer, January 30, 2011.

4 *Morgentaler v. New Brunswick (Attorney General)*, [1989] N.B.Q.B. No. 311 (hereafter cited as *Morgentaler* 1989).
5 Interestingly, when McKenna opposed the creation of an abortion clinic by Morgentaler, he was in the exceptional position of having an entirely Liberal legislature. The only other province ever to experience single-party dominance in a legislature was Prince Edward Island in 1935, when the Liberal Party won all thirty seats.
6 This and the preceding quotation are from *Morgentaler* 1989, para. 15 and para. 4 respectively.
7 Despite the court order, Morgentaler was never paid for the procedures (Hughes 2014).
8 New Brunswick, Legislative Assembly of New Brunswick Debates, May 5, 1989. This statement is actually incorrect, as New Brunswick considered abortion an excluded service on reciprocal billing agreements between the provinces at this time.
9 New Brunswick, Legislative Assembly of New Brunswick Debates, February 22, 1994.
10 Interview with Alison Brewer, January 30, 2011.
11 New Brunswick, Legislative Assembly of New Brunswick Debates, December 2, 1993.
12 New Brunswick, Legislative Assembly of New Brunswick Debates, February 22, 1994.
13 *Morgentaler v. New Brunswick*, [1994] N.B.Q.B. No. 302.
14 *Morgentaler v. New Brunswick*, [1994] N.B.Q.B. No. 302 at para. 42.
15 Judy Burwell, former director of the Fredericton Morgentaler Clinic, noted that the success of Morgentaler's Toronto clinic allowed him to subsidize clinics like those in Fredericton and St. John's, which serve smaller populations and are more difficult to maintain. Interview, January 24, 2011.
16 *Province of New Brunswick v. Morgentaler*, [2009], N.B.C.A. No. 26 (hereafter cited as *Morgentaler* 2009) at para. 1.
17 *Morgentaler* 2009 at para. 1 and para. 14.
18 *Morgentaler v. New Brunswick*, [2004] N.B.Q.B. No. 139 at para. 17. The Coalition for Life and Health was composed of eight groups: New Brunswick Right to Life Association, Roman Catholic Diocese of Saint John, Focus on the Family (Canada), REAL Women of Canada, Canadian Physicians for Life, Catholic Civil Rights League, Christian Legal Fellowship, and the Evangelical Fellowship of Canada.
19 *Morgentaler v. New Brunswick*, [2008] N.B.Q.B. No. 258 (hereafter cited as *Morgentaler* 2008).
20 *Morgentaler* 2008 at para. 19.
21 *Morgentaler* 2008 at para. 26.
22 *Morgentaler* 2009.
23 Interview with Dr. Jula Hughes, January 17, 2011.
24 *New Brunswick Labour and Employment Board, A.A. v. Province of New Brunswick (Department of Health)*, [2011] N.B.L.E.B. No. HR-005–10 (hereafter cited as *Labour Board* 2011).

25 *Labour Board* 2011 at para. 14.
26 *Labour Board* 2011 at para. 14.2 and para. 8.2.
27 *Labour Board* 2011 at para. 53
28 *Labour Board* 2011 at para. 56.
29 New Brunswick, Legislative Assembly of New Brunswick Debates, December 8, 2004.
30 Interview with Alison Brewer, January 30, 2011; interview with Rosella Melanson, January 10, 2011.
31 Dawn Fowler, Canadian director of the National Abortion Federation, stressed that no one group can take credit for the repeal of aspects of Regulation 84-20, explaining that "NAF had been working since 2006 in New Brunswick trying to persuade the government to change 84-20." Email exchange with Dawn Fowler, June 30, 2016.
32 The call for funding actually made two separate funding promises: one in case it was able to meet its $100,000 target, and one in the event that it did not. If RJNB was able to raise the necessary money, its aim was to lease the former clinic building and "further explore options to encourage family practitioners who support a person's right to full reproductive services, including the right to abortion." The group acknowledges that this was a band-aid solution but hoped it would help give New Brunswickers a "fighting chance to access their rights under the Charter of Rights and the Canada Health Act." If it was unable to meet its target, the money raised would be put toward "renewed efforts to overturn the Medical Services Payment Act" (RJNB 2014). Notably, when RJNB did meet its initial funding target, it decided to raise the target to $200,000, in the hopes of being able to purchase the equipment inside the clinic as well.
33 Changes to the policy took effect on January 1, 2015 (CBC News 2014c).
34 Since the hospital requires that an ultrasound be performed before a woman can access an abortion, patients must book two appointments at one of these facilities, and these appointments cannot always be scheduled on the same day. Since only cities in the province offer these services, this can pose a significant barrier in terms of travel, cost, and privacy. This is also a problem for women from Prince Edward Island attempting to access services (their government recently reached an arrangement with the Moncton hospital to allow PEI women to access its facilities) (CBC News 2015a).
35 Ontario, Legislative Assembly of Ontario Debates, February 8, 1988.
36 *Murphy v. Dodd*, [1989] O.J. No. 1587.
37 Ontario, Legislative Assembly of Ontario Debates, July 5, 1989.
38 Ontario, Legislative Assembly of Ontario Debates, July 24, 1989. The MPP mentioned in the text is Dalton McGuinty Sr. (in office 1987–90), father of former Ontario premier Dalton McGuinty Jr. McGuinty went on to say, "There is the view also that when Madam Justice Wilson referred to the unborn baby as 'potential life,' she put forth a statement of nonsense in the light of scientific evidence. The unborn baby is actual life – actual human life," foreshadowing a series of backbencher bills that would later attempt to recriminalize abortion (ON *Hansard*, July 24, 1989).
39 All Robidoux quotations in this passage are from an interview with Michelle Robidoux, March 30, 2011.
40 Copyright Queen's Printer for Ontario, 2011. Reproduced with permission.
41 Interview with Planned Parenthood Representative March 31, 2011.

42 *Association pour l'accès à l'avortement v. Procureur General du Québec*, [2006] Q.C.C.S. 4694.
43 This case did not rely on Charter grounds (either Canada's charter or the Quebec charter) when rendering its decision. For more on this case, see: Mel Cousins's, "Health Care and Human Rights after *Auton* and *Chaoulli*," (2009).
44 This and the following quotations in this passage are from an interview with FQPN representative, May 12, 2011.
45 The English translation for Centre de santé des femmes de Montréal is Women's Health Centre of Montreal.
46 Quebec, National Assembly of Quebec, May 19, 2010.
47 Interview with Conseil representative, June 13, 2011.
48 Interview with Quebec clinic representative, June 13, 2011.
49 Ibid.
50 Interview with Patrick Powers, February 14, 2011.
51 Interview with Conseil representative, June 13, 2011.
52 *R. v. Morgentaler*, [1993] 3 S.C.R. 463 at 463 (hereafter cited as *Morgentaler* 1993).
53 *Morgentaler* 1993 at 463–64.
54 *R. v. Morgentaler*, [1991] S.C.N.S. No. 02392.
55 *Morgentaler* 1993 at 481.
56 *Doe et al. v. Manitoba*, [2004] M.B.Q.B. 285 (hereafter cited as *Doe* 2004).
57 *Doe* 2004 at para. 37.
58 *Doe* 2004 at para. 39.
59 *Doe* 2004 at para. 90.
60 *Jane Doe et al. v. Manitoba*, [2005] M.B.C.A. 109 at para. 9.
61 The Manitoba government amended its insurance policies before a judgment was rendered to include clinic services but "maintained that it was under no legal obligation to do so" (Erdman 2007, 1098).

Chapter 4: Abortion as Health Care

1 See Maioni (2012) for details about the division of powers in the constitution at Confederation.
2 These criteria were very much a precursor to the Canada Health Act.
3 The 2004 Canada Health Transfer was the final culmination of various provincial and federal cost-sharing initiatives: the Canadian Assistance Plan (CAP) was introduced in 1966, and later split to encompass both the CAP and the new Established Programs Financing in 1977, which would cover health and postsecondary education services no longer covered under the CAP. These transfer payments would eventually merge and evolve into the Canada Health and Social Transfer in 1995 before entering their most recent iteration.
4 The reality that no decisive definition of *medical necessity* exists in Canada leaves this term and its potential implications open to interpretation. Although it is possible that future jurisprudence will help settle the question of if, and to what degree, abortion should be considered a medical necessity, its force today is largely influenced by the willingness of governments to act on the belief that access to abortion care is medically required. For more on the legal and moral implications of this framework, see "The Public Funding of Abortion in Canada" (Kaposy 2009).

5 The scope of power a provincial government has over its provincial college of physicians and surgeons varies dramatically and is largely dependent on the specifics of the act that created the college. In some cases, including Ontario, the act gives the minister of health direct purview over its activities, whereas in others, such as New Brunswick, the act offers few specifics about this relationship.
6 *Canada Health Act* 1984.
7 It is not clear, for instance, that the same could be said of other reproductive health concerns, such as infertility. Several provinces have taken steps to provide some funding for in-vitro fertilization in recent years, yet the cost of these procedures, in conjunction with their success rates, may mean it is not reasonable to consider them a necessary service, at least not in all cases.
8 Of course, not everyone with female reproductive organs identifies as female.
9 Kaposy's (2009, 307) larger goal is to advance a defence of public funding for abortion services as a matter of justice, saying, "A threat to an essential non-health dimension of well-being is no more justifiable from the moral perspective than a threat to health."
10 This practice is referred to as conscientious objection and is discussed in more detail on pages 120–22.
11 Macfarlane (2014) does argue that justifications offered for the failure to provide services, however, could support rights claims.
12 Importantly, stating that abortion requires unique rights protections because of its significance to women's equality, and the long-standing resistance to the procedure that means it is constantly threatened, does not mean that other procedures do not require similar protections. Although a deeper exploration of other socially stigmatized health care issues is beyond the scope of this book, my treatment of abortion as an exceptional issue in this context is not meant to preclude similar treatment of other issues.
13 According to the Pro-Choice Action Network, in 1995, then Liberal health minister Diane Marleau ordered provinces refusing to fund clinic abortions to pay the entirety of abortion-related fees at clinics lest their transfer payments be docked. Five years later, "not one of the delinquent provinces has yet to pay in full for a clinic abortion, and only Nova Scotia has had transfer payments withheld" (over $200,000 so far) (Arthur 2000).
14 Interview with Judy Burwell, January 24, 2011.
15 Email exchange with Dawn Fowler, March 25, 2016.
16 Many medical schools also hold seats for students from specific locations in Canada. Most medical schools reserve the majority of seats for applicants from their own province, with the exception of Ontario, and may have higher entrance standards for out-of-province applicants.
17 Most residency placements are carried out in hospitals rather than in private clinics. This reality provides additional motivation for insuring various facilities continue to perform the procedure. It is therefore important that abortions continue to be performed in hospitals, not only so that women have more access to points of service but also to ensure that future physicians are exposed to the procedure and able to perform it.

18 Medical students cannot conscientiously object to learning the procedure if their school teaches it but they are not required to practise their skills during residency. Interview with Ontario physician, April 1, 2011.
19 Interview with CMA representative February 10, 2011. A collection exploring the nuances of conscientious object in the journal *Bioethics* (28, 1) cites a statement made by the executive director of the CMA Office of Ethics, Jeff Blackmer, as an impetus for its research. According to Blackmer, "The most that a physician who conscientiously objects to abortion has to do for a woman who wants an abortion is to 'indicate alternative sources where she [the patient] might obtain a referral' (i.e., a referral for a referral) and even that is only necessary when the patient specifically requests a referral" (McLeod and Downie 2014, ii).
20 The National Abortion Federation offers guidelines for women in Canada who encounter physicians who conscientiously object to providing care: the document *Has Your Physician Refused to Provide a Referral for Abortion Care? A Patient's Guide to Action* details the current policy in Canada, while making recommendations for how it may be improved. It also suggests that many provincial colleges are beginning to look at the compatibility of their policies with human rights codes.
21 This power dynamic is reflected in past legislation regulating abortion in Canada. The 1939 legal precedent that protected physicians in the United Kingdom for performing abortions that they felt were necessary to save a woman's life is one such example, as was Trudeau's 1969 amendment to the code to give physicians greater discretion in the performance of abortions (Haussman 2002, 63, 66). These cases are discussed in context in Chapter 2.
22 Keeping these barriers in mind, Action Canada for Sexual Health and Rights (2015a, 2) has argued that governments have a responsibility "to ensure that the conscientious objection of health professionals does not form a barrier [to] accessing sexual and reproductive health services."
23 This new policy concerns conscientious objection broadly, and it is by no means limited to abortion.
24 This procedure has a success rate of around 99 percent (NAF 2015a).
25 These procedures vary by patient and are relatively rare, as the overwhelming majority of abortions in Canada are performed in the first trimester. For more information on these procedures, see the NAF's *Clinical Policy Guidelines*.
26 One of the necessary drugs, Mifepristone, was developed in France, where it became available in 1988; the French minister of health referred to it as "the moral property of women" (Erdman, Grenon, and Harrison-Wilson 2008, 1768). The efficacy of the drug led to its inclusion on the WHO Model List of Essential Medicines (Erdman, Grenon, and Harrison-Wilson 2008, 1767).
27 The NAF clinical guidelines do specify, "If a misoprostol-alone or methotrexate-misoprostol regimen is offered when mifepristone is available, full information on the differences between the chosen regimen and mifepristone-misoprostol regimens should be addressed with the patient and informed consent obtained" (NAF 2015b, 13–14).
28 According to a representative from the distributor, Celopharma Inc., the delay is due to a "change in manufacturing site" (Szklarski 2016).

29 When asked about the reason for the discrepancy in the timeline for the drug's efficacy in Canada versus other jurisdictions, a representative of the Canadian Pharmacists Association said that "Health Canada approved Mifegymiso based on the clinical trial data that the manufacturer provided to the regulator (i.e., there were three trials that demonstrated efficacy at forty-nine days gestation). While this differs from the indication in other jurisdictions, it is quite possible that the manufacturer may, at a later date, apply to Health Canada for an indication in line with other jurisdictions. (While Health Canada avails itself of international policy decisions when approving new drugs, the approval decision is primarily based on the review of clinical trial data provided by the manufacturer.)" Interview, October 15, 2015.

30 Discussing the drug with the CBC, Dr. Wendy Norman of the Society of Obstetricians and Gynaecologists of Canada noted, "You also need to buy, stock, store and maintain a stock – that is, recognize when something's about to be out of date and change it over. And this is outside the expertise of physicians. We don't have training in this, speaking as a family doctor myself" (Lunn 2016).

31 Canadian Pharmacists Association representative, email exchange with Rachael Johnstone, October 15, 2015.

32 Mifegymiso will cost around $270, and it is not yet clear whether provincial health plans will cover the cost of the drug (Prasad 2016).

33 CLSCs are community health centres run by the Quebec government (available only in Quebec).

34 Quebec changed its policies following the decision in *Association pour l'accès à l'avortement v. Procureur General du Québec* (2006). This change is outlined in Chapter 3.

35 Interview with Sandeep Prasad, June 12, 2015.

36 Judy Burwell, former director of the Fredericton Morgentaler Clinic, noted such problems in New Brunswick: "They used to do abortions in Saint John at the regional hospital, and they stopped because people were being harassed. Doctors who did it were being harassed, nurses were walking out, instruments would disappear, it was just awful." Interview, January 24, 2011.

37 In the report, Canadians for Choice gathered information in three ways: (1) through hospital questionnaires (to learn about hospital policy and the types of services available), (2) through organizations surveys (targeting groups that serve as resources and first points of contact for women seeking abortion services), and (3) using a telephone questionnaire targeting hospitals (in which an actor pretended to be ten weeks pregnant and seeking information about abortion services, to see whether the response from the hospital matched the statistics on access gathered through the questionnaires) (Shaw 2006, 8–12). The approach undertaken for this research meant that the caller was often interacting with administrative workers or nurses rather than with the physicians who would be providing the procedure. As such, this study reflects the responses of specific points of contact within hospitals rather than the attitudes of physicians who provide care.

38 Interview with Anne Marie Messier, June 17, 2011.

39 Despite these constraints, in 2001, the provincial government, led by the Parti Québécois, provided funding to meet the service demands (FQPN and CFC 2010, 29).

40 Interview with FQPN representative, May 12, 2011.
41 After the closure of the Fredericton Morgentaler Clinic, a Kickstarter campaign raised funds to reopen a clinic on the same spot that would not only handle reproductive health care, including abortion, but also provide a full range of health services, with a commitment to "feminist, trauma-informed, harm reduction, and anti-racist practices" (Clinic 554 2015a).
42 Interview with Quebec clinic representative, June 13, 2011.
43 Although it may have been a more calming environment for many patients, the New Brunswick clinic was open only limited hours. In its final years, the clinic was open only one day a week, but this schedule was actually motivated by an increase in patient intake. According to Burwell, when she began working at the clinic in 2000, it was open only every second week. The number of patients scheduled on each day had also increased. Burwell explained that there used to be thirteen to fourteen women a day in the waiting room, but it was not uncommon to have nearly twenty in later years. She suggested that the reason for this jump was related to increasing difficulties for women attempting to access hospital abortions. Interview with Judy Burwell, January 24, 2011.
44 Interview with Anne Marie Messier, June 17, 2011. Gestational age in sonograms is based on the length of the fetus, variance in equipment, and differences in fetal size, making this a less than precise measure.
45 In all of the shootings, the main suspect was James Kopp, an anti-abortion extremist who was also responsible for a New York shooting in 1998 (ARCC 2006b, 2). Bizarrely, Kopp, who was tried in a US court, attempted to employ a necessity defence in court, a defence similar to the one Morgentaler used to challenge section 251 of the Criminal Code before the enactment of the Charter (CBC News 2007).
46 NAF's numbers comprise statistics from Canada and the United States, and, since 2013, also Colombia.
47 Interview with Tracey Methven, March 30, 2011.
48 Interview with Alison Brewer, January 30, 2011.
49 Interview with Ontario physician, April 1, 2011.
50 Interview with Peggy Cooke, February 23, 2011.
51 According to Downie and Nassar, the injunction only remains in force in five cities: Toronto, London, Brantford, Kitchener, and North Bay (2007, 161).
52 Interview with Ontario social activist, February 24, 2011.
53 Interview with Michelle Robidoux, March 30, 2011. In the Fredericton case, the outcome has been different. Jessi Taylor of RJNB reported that since the former Morgentaler Clinic became a family health clinic that also provides abortion care, demonstrations in the parking lot have not been a problem. This is likely because the demonstrators do not know which people to target because it is not clear why patients are going into the practice. Interview with Jessi Taylor, June 25, 2015.
54 Interview with FQPN representative, May 12, 2011.
55 Interview with Quebec clinic representative, June 13, 2011.
56 Interview with Anne Marie Messier, June 17, 2011.
57 Interview with Abby Lippman, January 16, 2011. The Quebec clinic representative and Anne Marie Messier also noted this in interviews, June 13, 2011 and June 17, 2011, respectively.

58 Anne Marie Messier and the Quebec clinic representative I interviewed both noted this, June 17, 2011 and June 13, 2011 respectively.
59 A *Star* report found that "the oldest of the 17 found in the Greater Toronto Area has been registered as a charity since 1968 and they appear to have a well-established donor pool" (Smith 2010). It is notable that 1968 was the same year Morgentaler opened his first clinic in Montreal.
60 Interview with Dr. Carolyn Bennett, February 10, 2011.
61 Of course, transparency does not guarantee change, but it would force governments to be more accountable for their decisions about what services are provided and why.
62 Michelle Robidoux said that such a move has not led to a reduction in protesters in some Ontario clinics, though Jessi Taylor noted that demonstrations outside the clinic did not seem to be a problem after the abortion clinic became a family health clinic (that also happens to provide abortions). Interview with Michelle Robidoux, March 30, 2011; interview with Jessi Taylor, June 25, 2015.

Chapter 5: Social Movement Activism in the Provinces

1 Canadian Gallup polls also recorded this shift. Since the polls began to question whether abortion should be legal "under any circumstances, legal only under certain circumstances, or illegal in all circumstances" thirty-five years ago, major change is evident. An overall rise was evident, not only in those who felt that abortion was permissible, from 84.2 percent of respondents in 1975 to 91 percent in 2000, but a shift toward those deeming it permissible in all circumstances versus certain circumstances was also evident, from 23.2 percent of 84.2 percent in 1975, to 39.3 percent of 91 percent in 2000 (Gallup Canada 1975; Gallup Canada 2000).
2 These threats have not been limited to individuals working in or making use of the facilities. In many instances, physicians' homes have been targeted for harassment.
3 All Toron quotations in this section are from an interview with Alison Toron, January 11, 2011.
4 All Cooke quotations in this chapter are from an interview with Peggy Cooke, February 23, 2011.
5 Emails recently released by the *Globe and Mail* between Horizon Health CEO John McGarry and his employees reveal McGarry's surprise that a hospital in Saint John might be willing to provide abortions, commenting on the city's "very significant Irish Catholic community" (Grant 2015).
6 All Hughes quotations in this section are from an interview with Dr. Jula Hughes, January 17, 2011.
7 The cost of abortion in New Brunswick has since risen and is now between $700 and $850 (Clinic 554 2015b).
8 Interview with Rosella Melanson, January 10, 2011.
9 A family health centre, Clinic 554, has since opened on the site of the old Morgentaler Clinic. The clinic does offer abortion services, but the requirement in Regulation 84-20 necessitating that abortions be performed in hospitals is still in place, so women must pay out of pocket to access these services.
10 In a recent statement, New Brunswick health minister Victor Boudreau said that the government are "monitoring the current program to see if more access is required" (Hazlewood 2016).

11 Interview with Judy Burwell, January 24, 2011.
12 Interview with Ontario social activist, February 24, 2011.
13 All Robidoux quotations in this section are from an interview with Michelle Robidoux, March 30, 2011.
14 Interview with Tracey Methven, March 30, 2011.
15 The commitment from men and women of all ages to the realization of women's rights to abortion access, as recounted by Robidoux, is demonstrative of the fact that abortion is not simply a young person's issue.
16 Interview with Agathe Gramet-Kedzior, September 18, 2011. After this interview was conducted, Canadians for Choice merged with the Canadian Federation for Sexual Health and Action Canada for Population and Development to form Action Canada for Sexual Health and Rights.
17 Interview with representative of Planned Parenthood Toronto, March 31, 2011.
18 Interview with representative of a government-affiliated organization created to promote women's health in Ontario, March 30, 2011.
19 Interview with Tracey Methven, March 30, 2011.
20 All Megill quotations in this section are from an interview with Catherine Megill, June 12, 2011.
21 Interview with Patrick Powers, February 14, 2011.
22 Interview with a representative of the FQPN, May 12, 2011.
23 Interview with Abby Lippman, January 16, 2011.
24 Interview with Anne Marie Messier, June 17, 2011.

Chapter 6: Never Going Back

1 Even though changes to Prince Edward Island's policies have occurred around the same time as the election of Trudeau's Liberal government, it is not necessarily true that the evolution in the province's abortion policies are solely a result of this event.
2 For a more extensive history of abortion in Prince Edward Island, see Katrina Ackerman's, "In Defence of Reason: Religion, Science, and the Prince Edward Island Anti-Abortion Movement, 1968–1988," (2014).
3 A more in-depth discussion of the reasons no hospital abortions were performed in Prince Edward Island after 1982 can be found in "Subverting the Constitution" (Brown, Ehrlich, and MacQuarrie, forthcoming).
4 *Morgentaler v. Prince Edward Island (Government of)*, [1994] G.S.C. No. 12726 (hereafter cited as *Morgentaler* 1994).
5 *Morgentaler* 1994, at para. 78.
6 The agency was dissolved in 1996 following the election of Conservative Premier Pat Binns.
7 Unless otherwise noted, all MacQuarrie quotations in this section are from an interview with Colleen MacQuarrie, June 5, 2015.
8 According to Colleen MacQuarrie, the PRRO was composed of young feminist activists who coexisted with ARN for a while before aligning with ARN, in large part because many of the core members of this group left the province for work and school-related reasons. Interview with Colleen MacQuarrie, June 5, 2015.

9   Abortion was also an issue at the federal level for PEI representatives. Indeed, Becka Viau, Charlottetown's federal Green Party MP candidate, is responsible for launching "The Sovereign Uterus," a blog "dedicated to publishing personal stories about abortion access and after care on Prince Edward Island" (Sovereign Uterus 2015). "Personal testimony," the blog states, "is integral to raising awareness, shattering stigma and breaking the silence around abortion on PEI." Viau was also responsible for starting "a petition calling for local abortion access and better communication around abortion services" (ARN 2015).

10 Following the premier's announcement, LEAF released a statement enthusiastically declaring, "Today is a good day for equality rights in PEI!" and commending the work of activists on the island:

> LEAF and AAN PEI are proud to have played a role in bringing about this historic change. This outcome would not have been possible without the tremendous efforts of the activists in PEI who have tirelessly advocated for abortion access in the province over the last three decades, as well as the brave women who have come forward to share their personal stories. Their extraordinary commitment and resolve have brought about this sea change in government policy. We are deeply honoured to work with them. (LEAF and AAN PEI 2016)

References

Abraham, Margaret, and Esther Ngan-ling Chow. 2011. "Rethinking Citizenship in Focus." In *Contours of Citizenship: Women, Diversity and Practices of Citizenship*, edited by Laura Maratou-Alipranti, Esther Ngan-ling Chow, Evangelia Tastsoglous, and Margaret Abraham, 1–22. Burlington, VT: Ashgate.

Ackelsberg, Martha. 2005. "Women's Community Activism and the Rejections of 'Politics': Some Dilemmas of Popular Democratic Movements." In *Women and Citizenship*, edited by Marilyn Friedman, 67–90. Oxford: Oxford University Press. http://dx.doi.org/10.1093/0195175344.003.0005.

Ackerman, Katrina. 2012. "'Not in the Atlantic Provinces': The Abortion Debate in New Brunswick, 1980–1987." *Acadiensis* 41 (1): 75–101.

–. 2014. "In Defence of Reason: Religion, Science, and the Prince Edward Island Anti-Abortion Movement, 1968–1988." *Canadian Bulletin of Medical History* 31 (2): 117–38.

ACPD (Action Canada for Population and Development). N.d. "About Us." Accessed July 3, 2015. http://www.sexualhealthandrights.ca/about-us/.

Action Canada (Action Canada for Sexual Health & Rights). 2015a. "Conscientious Objection." N.d. Accessed August 25, 2015. http://www.sexualhealthandrights.ca/wp-content/uploads/2015/07/Domestic-5_CO.pdf.

–. 2015b. "Election 2015: Sexual Health and Rights Recap." October 8. Accessed February 21, 2016. http://www.sexualhealthandrights.ca/election-2015-shr-recap/.

–. 2015c. "RU-486: What You Need to Know about the Recently Approved Abortion Pill." July 30. Accessed February 21, 2016. http://www.sexualhealthandrights.ca/ru-486-what-you-need-to-know-about-the-recently-approved-abortion-pill/.

Akin, David. 2016. "Trudeau OKs Canadian Dollars for Foreign Abortion Services." *Toronto Sun*, May 10. http://www.torontosun.com/2016/05/10/trudeau-oks-canadian-dollars-for-foreign-abortion-services.

Alphonso, Caroline, and Marjan Farahbaksh. 2009. "Canadian Law Only Changed 26 Year Ago." *Globe and Mail*, April 1. Accessed April 20, 2017. http://www.theglobeandmail.com/news/world/canadian-law-only-changed-26-years-ago/article1150644/.
ARCC (Abortion Rights Coalition of Canada). 2005. "Training of Abortion Providers/Medical Students for Choice." Last updated October. http://www.arcc-cdac.ca/postionpapers/06-Training-Abortion-Providers-MSFC.PDF.
–. 2006a. "A Listing of Anti-choice MPs." Last updated June 23. http://www.arcc-cdac.ca/action/conservative-danger.html.
–. 2006b. "Anti-choice Violence and Harassment." Last updated September. http://www.arcc-cdac.ca/postionpapers/73-Anti-choice-Violence-Harassment.pdf.
–. 2007. "Clinic Funding – Overview of Political Situation." Last updated August. http://www.arcc-cdac.ca/postionpapers/03-Clinic-Funding-Overview.PDF.
–. 2008. "Talking Points Against the 'Unborn Victims of Crime Act.'" Last updated May 6. http://www.arcc-cdac.ca/action/unborn-victims-act.htm.
–. 2013. "The Morgentaler Decision: A 25th Anniversary Celebration." Accessed February 27, 2016. http://www.morgentaler25years.ca/the-struggle-for-abortion-rights/access-by-province/.
–. 2012. "Anti-choice Private Members Bills and Motions Introduced in Canada Since 1987." Accessed August 26, 2015. http://www.arcc-cdac.ca/presentations/anti-bills.html.
–. 2015a. "Abortion Rights Coalition of Canada." Accessed February 27, 2016. http://www.arcc-cdac.ca/mission.html.
–. 2015b. "About Us." Accessed August 23, 2015. http://www.arcc-cdac.ca/about.html.
–. 2016. "List of Abortion Clinics in Canada." Accessed February 27, 2016. http://www.arcc-cdac.ca/list-abortion-clinics-canada.pdf.
Armstrong, Pat, and Hugh Armstrong. 2001. "Women, Privatization and Health Care Reform: The Ontario Case." In *Exposing Privatization: Women and Health Care Reform in Canada*, edited by Pat Armstrong, Carol Bernier Amaratunga, Jocelyn Bernier, Kay Jocelyne Willson, Karen Grant, and Ann Pederson, 163–215. Toronto: Broadview Press.
ARN (Abortion Rights Network PEI). 2015. "The Sovereign Uterus Blog Shares Stories from Islanders Accessing Abortion." June 7. Accessed April 7, 2016. http://www.abortionrightspei.com/content/page/front_news/article/32
–. 2015–16. "About Abortion Rights Network Prince Edward Island." Accessed April 7, 2016. http://www.abortionrightspei.com/content/page/front_about.
–. 2016. "Abortion Access Now PEI Challenges PEI's Abortion Policy." Accessed September 1, 2016. http://www.abortionrightspei.com/content/page/front_news/article/43.
Arthur, Joyce. 1999. "Abortion in Canada: History, Law, and Access." Pro-Choice Action Network. http://www.prochoiceactionnetwork-canada.org/articles/canada.shtml.
–. 2000. "Five basic Principles Not Met." Pro-Choice Action Network. Accessed August 20, 2015. www.prochoiceactionnetwork-canada.org/articles/healthact.shtml.
Arts4Choice. 2015. "Arts4Choice." Accessed August 3, 2015. http://www.arts4choice.com.

References

Asal, Victor, Mitchell Brown, and Renee Gibson Figueroa. 2008. "Structure, Empowerment and the Liberalization of Cross-National Abortion Rights." *Politics and Gender* 4 (2): 265–84. http://dx.doi.org/10.1017/S1743923X08000184.

Association of Faculties of Medicine of Canada. 2008. "Committee on Accreditation of Canadian Medical Schools (CACMS)." https://www.afmc.ca/accreditation/committee-accreditation-canadian-medical-schools-cacms.

Badgley, Robin F. 1977. *The Committee on the Operation of the Abortion Law*. Ottawa: Minister of Supply and Services.

Baines, Beverley. 2015–16. "Constitutionalizing Women's Equality Rights: There Is Always Room for Improvement." *Atlantis* 37.2(1): 112–19.

Bakan, Abigail, and Dava Stasiulis. 2005. *Negotiating Citizenship: Migrant Women in Canada and the Global System*. Toronto: University of Toronto Press.

Bauch, Hubert. 1977. "Vote on Abortion Disturbs Executive." *Montreal Gazette*, May 30. Accessed August 4, 2015. https://news.google.com/newspapers?nid=1946&dat=19770530&id=wh4uAAAAIBAJ&sjid=laEFAAAAIBAJ&pg=2419,3280919&hl=en.

Bennett, Carolyn. 2008. "The Politics of Abortion: The Work of a Politician." In *Of What Difference? Reflection on the Judgment and Abortion in Canada Today*, 57–62. Toronto: University of Toronto: Faculty of Law. https://5aa1b2xfmfh2e2mk03kk8rsx-wpengine.netdna-ssl.com/wp-content/uploads/ofwhatdifference.pdf.

Blackmer, Jeff. 2007. "Clarification of the CMA's Position Concerning Induced Abortion." *Canadian Medical Association Journal* 176 (9): 1310. http://dx.doi.org/10.1503/cmaj.1070035.

Blackwell, Tom. 2013. "Fewer Rural Doctors Willing to Perform Abortions as Health Workers Face Increased Hostility in Small Towns, Study Suggests." *National Post*, July 24. Accessed October 2, 2015. http://news.nationalpost.com/news/canada/fewer-rural-doctors-willing-to-perform-abortions-as-health-workers-face-increased-hostility-in-small-towns-study-suggests.

Bourgeois, Sonya. 2014. "Our Bodies Are Our Own: Connecting Abortion and Social Policy." *Canadian Review of Social Policy* 70: 22–33.

Briggs, Laura, Faye Ginsburg, Elena R. Gutiérrez, Rosalind Petchesky, Rayna Rapp, Andrea Smith, and Chikako Takeshita. 2013. "Roundtable: Reproductive Technologies and Reproductive Justice." *Frontiers* 34 (3): 102–25. http://dx.doi.org/10.5250/fronjwomestud.34.3.0102.

Brodie, Janine. 1992. "Choice and No Choice in the House." In *The Politics of Abortion*, edited by Janine Brodie, Shelley Gavigan, and Jane Jenson, 57–116. Toronto: Oxford University Press.

Brodie, Janine, Shelley Gavigan, and Jane Jenson, eds. 1992. *The Politics of Abortion*. Toronto: Oxford University Press.

Brown, Alister, and Bill Sullivan. 2005. "Abortion in Canada." *Cambridge Quarterly of Healthcare Ethics* 14 (3): 287–91.

Brown, Lori, Shoshanna Ehrlich, and Colleen MacQuarrie. 2017. "Subverting the Constitution: Anti-abortion Policies and Activism in the United States and Canada." In *Abortion: History, Politics, and Reproductive Justice after Morgentaler*, edited by Shannon Stettner, Kristin Burnett, and Travis Hay. Vancouver: UBC Press.

Brown, Wendy. 1995. *Identities, Politics, and Rights*. Ann Arbor: University of Michigan Press.

Bryden, Joan. 2014. "Justin Trudeau Clarifies That Anti-abortion Liberal Incumbents Would Be Forced to Vote Pro-choice." *National Post*, June 18. Accessed February 21, 2016. http://news.nationalpost.com/news/canada/canadian-politics/justin-trudeau-clarifies-that-anti-abortion-liberal-incumbents-would-be-forced-to-vote-pro-choice.

Campaign Life Coalition. 2015. "About Us." Accessed August 16, 2015. https://www.campaignlifecoalition.com/index.php?p=About_Us.

Canadian Pharmacists Association. 2015. "CPhA Statement on Health Canada Approval of Mifegymiso." July 30. Accessed October 30, 2015. http://www.pharmacists.ca/advocacy/advocacy-activities/cpha-statement-on-health-canada-approval-of-Mifegymiso/.

Canadian Press. 1977. "Executive Opposition Ignored: PQ Favour Abortion Reform." *Ottawa Citizen*. May 30.

—. 2014. "Trudeau: Not Up to Male MPs to Take Away Women's Abortion Rights." *Huffington Post*, November 8. http://www.huffingtonpost.ca/2014/06/11/justin-trudeau-abortion-male-mps-women_n_5485007.html.

—. 2015. "Saskatoon Postal Workers Told to Deliver Graphic Anti-abortion Flyer Targeting Trudeau: CUPW." *Huffington Post*, August 5. http://www.huffingtonpost.ca/2015/08/05/saskatoon-posties-told-to-deliver-anti-abortion-flyers-that-target-trudeau-cupw_n_7941552.html.

Cannold, Leslie. 2002. "Understanding and Responding to Anti-choice Woman-Centred Strategies." *Reproductive Health Matters* 10 (19): 171–19. http://dx.doi.org/10.1016/S0968-8080(02)00011-3.

CBC News. 2007. "Abortion Sniper Asks for Mercy in Federal Trial." January 9. Accessed August 10, 2015. http://www.cbc.ca/news/world/abortion-sniper-asks-for-mercy-in-federal-trial-1.650857.

—. 2009. "Abortions Shouldn't Fall under Bill 34: Quebec Doctors." August 18. Accessed August 9, 2015. http://www.cbc.ca/news/canada/montreal/abortions-shouldn-t-fall-under-bill-34-quebec-doctors-1.818464.

—. 2010a. "Cardinal's Abortion Remarks Anger Politicians." May 17. Accessed August 3, 2015. http://www.cbc.ca/news/canada/montreal/cardinal-s-abortion-remarks-anger-politicians-1.890873.

—. 2010b. "No Abortion in Canada's G8 Maternal Health Plan." April 26. http://www.cbc.ca/news/politics/no-abortion-in-canada-s-g8-maternal-health-plan-1.877257.

—. 2011. "Tories Defunding Planned Parenthood, MP Says." April 20. Accessed August 4, 2015. http://www.cbc.ca/news/politics/tories-defunding-planned-parenthood-mp-says-1.979677.

—. 2013a. "Doctor Loses Legal Fight over Abortion Policy." May 17. Accessed August 3, 2015. http://www.cbc.ca/news/canada/new-brunswick/doctor-loses-legal-fight-over-abortion-policy-1.1372763.

—. 2013b. "P.E.I. Abortion Policy Needs Clarity, Says Group." January 28. Accessed June 9, 2015. http://www.cbc.ca/news/canada/prince-edward-island/p-e-i-abortion-policy-needs-clarity-says-group-1.1413174

—. 2014a. "Liberals Shift Policy on Abortion Rights." April 28. http://www.cbc.ca/news/canada/new-brunswick/liberals-shift-policy-on-abortion-rights-1.2623956.

—. 2014b. "Morgentaler Clinics in Fredericton Performs Last Abortions before

References

Closure." July 18. Accessed August 5, 2015. http://www.cbc.ca/news/canada/new-brunswick/morgentaler-clinic-in-fredericton-performs-last-abortions-before-closure-1.2710909.

—. 2014c. "New Brunswick Abortion Restriction Lifted by Premier Brian Gallant." November 27. Accessed August 5, 2015. http://www.cbc.ca/news/canada/new-brunswick/new-brunswick-abortion-restriction-lifted-by-premier-brian-gallant-1.2850474.

—. 2014d. "Anti-abortion Candidates Need Not Apply in 2015, Justin Trudeau Says." May 7. Accessed August 5, 2015.

—. 2015a. "Abortions Access Made Easier for P.E.I. Women." June 2. Accessed August 9, 2015. http://www.cbc.ca/news/canada/prince-edward-island/abortion-access-made-easier-for-p-e-i-women-1.3096669.

—. 2015b. "Reproductive Justice New Brunswick Lauds New Abortion Clinic." January 17. Accessed August 5, 2015. http://www.cbc.ca/news/canada/new-brunswick/reproductive-justice-new-brunswick-lauds-new-abortion-clinic-1.2916547.

—. 2015c. "Abortion Access Made Easier for P.E.I. Women." June 2. http://www.cbc.ca/news/canada/prince-edward-island/abortion-access-made-easier-for-p-e-i-women-1.3096669.

—. 2016. "P.E.I. Abortion Access Questioned in House." March 9. http://www.cbc.ca/news/canada/prince-edward-island/abortion-rights-access-pei-1.3483046.

Chase, Steven. 2013. "Tory Backbencher Upset about Being 'Muzzled' Abandons Abortion Motion." *Globe and Mail*, April 17. Accessed July 31. http://www.theglobeandmail.com/news/politics/tory-backbencher-upset-about-being-muzzled-abandons-abortion-motion/article11342715/.

Chrisler, Joan C., ed. 2012. *Reproductive Justice: A Global Concern*. Santa Barbara: Praeger.

Chrisler, Joan C. 2013. "Introduction: A Global Approach to Reproductive Justice—Psychosocial and Legal Aspects and Implications." *William and Mary Journal of Women and the Law* 20 (1): 1–24.

—. 2014. "A Reproductive Justice Approach to Women's Health." *Analyses of Social Issues and Public Policy* 14 (1): 205–9. http://dx.doi.org/10.1111/asap.12056.

CIHI (Canadian Institute for Health Information). 2007. *Reciprocal Billing Report, Canada, 2004–2005*. Ottawa: CIHI.

—. 2013. "Induced Abortions Reported in Canada in 2013." Accessed August 25, 2015. https://www.cihi.ca/sites/default/files/document/induced_abortion_can_2013_en_web.xlsx.

Clark, Campbell. 2010. "Birth Control Won't Be in G8 Plan to Protection Mothers, Tories Say." *Globe and Mail*, March 17. Last updated August 23, 2012. http://www.theglobeandmail.com/news/politics/birth-control-wont-be-in-g8-plan-to-protect-mothers-tories-say/article4312323/.

Clinic 554. 2015a. "Our Care." Accessed August 25, 2015. http://www.clinic554.ca/care.html.

—. 2015b. "Reproductive Health" Accessed August 10, 2015. http://www.clinic554.ca/reproductivehealth.html.

CMA (Canadian Medical Association). 1988. *CMA Policy: Induced Abortion*. Ottawa: CMA.

–. 2012. "Provincial and Territorial Divisions of the CMA." http://archive.is/huBP.
College of Physicians and Surgeons of New Brunswick. 2005. "General Information." http://www.cpsnb.org/english/who.html.
Collier, Roger. 2012. "Medically Necessary: Who Should Decide?" *Canadian Medical Association Journal* 184 (16): 1770–71. http://dx.doi.org/10.1503/cmaj.109-4307.
Cook, Rebecca J., and Bernard M. Dickens. 2014. "Reducing Stigma in Reproductive Health." *International Journal of Gynaecology and Obstetrics* 125 (1): 89–92. http://dx.doi.org/10.1016/j.ijgo.2014.01.002.
Cook, Rebecca J., Bernard M. Dickens, and Mahmoud F. Fathalla. 2003. *Reproductive Health and Human Rights: Integrating Medicine, Ethics, and Law*. New York: Oxford University Press. http://dx.doi.org/10.1093/acprof:oso/9780199241323.001.0001.
Cousins, Mel. 2009. "Health Care and Human Rights after *Auton* and *Chaoulli*." *McGill Law Journal* 54 (4): 717–38.
Danforth, Jessica. N.d. "Reproductive Justice – for Real, for Me, for You, for Now." Native Youth Sexual Health Network. Accessed August 23, 2015. http://www.nativeyouthsexualhealth.com/reproductivejustice.pdf.
David, Victoria Jane. 2006. "Induced Abortion Guidelines." *Journal of Obstetrics and Gynaecology Canada* 184: 1014–27.
Delacourt, Susan. 2010a. "Aid Groups Advised to 'Shut the F--- Up' on Abortion." *Toronto Star*, May 3. Accessed August 4, 2015. https://www.thestar.com/news/canada/2010/05/03/aid_groups_advised_to_shut_the_f_up_on_abortion.html.
–. 2010b. "Tory MP introduces 'coerced abortion' bill." *The Star*, April 15. Accessed April 20, 2017. https://www.thestar.com/news/canada/2010/04/15/tory_mp_introduces_coerced_abortion_bill_1.html.
Department of Finance. 2014. "History of Health and Social Transfers." Government of Canada, Department of Finance. Last modified December 15. https://www.fin.gc.ca/fedprov/his-eng.asp.
Desmarais, Louise. 1999. *Mémoires d'une bataille inachevée: la lutte pour l'avortement au Quebec, 1970–1992*. Montreal: Editions Traut d'Union.
Dickens, Bernard M. 1976. "The Morgentaler Case: Criminal Process and Abortion Law." *Osgoode Hall Law Journal* 14 (2): 229–74.
Do, Trinh Theresa. 2014. "Harper Won't Fund Abortion Globally Because It's 'Extremely Divisive.'" CBC News, May 29. http://www.cbc.ca/news/politics/harper-won-t-fund-abortion-globally-because-it-s-extremely-divisive-1.2658828.
Dobrowolsky, Alexandra, and Jane Jenson. 2004. "Shifting Representations of Citizenship: Canadian Politics of 'Women' and 'Children'." *Social Politics* 11 (2): 158–80.
Doucette, Keith. 2016. "Abortion Rights Groups Say Access Still a National Problem Despite PEI Win" *Globe and Mail*, April 8. http://www.theglobeandmail.com/news/national/abortion-rights-groups-say-access-still-a-national-problem-despite-pei-win/article29576410/.
Downie, Jocelyn, and Carla Nassar. 2007. "Barriers to Access to Abortion through a Legal Lens." *Health Law Journal* 15: 143–73.
Dunn, Sheila, and Rebecca Cook. 2014. "Medical Abortion in Canada: Behind the Times." *Canadian Medical Association Journal* 186 (1): 13–14. http://dx.doi.org/10.1503/cmaj.131320.

References

Dunsmuir, Mollie. 1998. "Abortion: Constitutional and Legal Developments." In *Current Issue Review* 89–10E. Ottawa: Library of Parliament. http://www.publications.gc.ca/Collection-R/LoPBdP/CIR/8910-e.htm.

Echo (Echo: Improving Women's Health in Ontario). 2011. *Recommendations to Improve Abortion Services in Ontario: Reports from the Expert Panel*. Toronto: Echo.

Eckholm, Erik. 2013. "Case Explores Rights of Fetus Versus Mother." *New York Times*, October 23. Accessed August 25, 2015. http://www.nytimes.com/2013/10/24/us/case-explores-rights-of-fetus-versus-mother.html?_r=0.

Eggertson, Laura. 2005. "Dosanjh to Act on Canada Health Act Violations." *Canadian Medical Association Journal* 172 (7): 862. http://dx.doi.org/10.1503/cmaj.050243.

Environics Institute. 2010. *Focus Canada 2010: Public Opinion Research on the Record Serving the Public Interest*. Toronto: Environics Institute.

Erdman, Joanna. 2007. "In the Back Alleys of Health Care: Abortion, Equality and Community in Canada." *Emory Law Journal* 56: 1093–155.

—. 2014. "Improve Access to Abortion." Impact Ethics. May 30. Accessed August 10, 2015. https://impactethics.ca/2014/05/30/improve-access-to-abortion/.

Erdman, Joanna, Amy Grenon, and Leigh Harrison-Wilson. 2008. "Medication Abortion in Canada: A Right-to-Health Perspective." *American Journal of Public Health* 98 (10): 1764–69. http://dx.doi.org/10.2105/AJPH.2008.134684.

Farney, James. 2009. "The Personal Is Not Political: The Progressive Conservative Response to Social Issues." *American Review of Canadian Studies* 39 (3): 242–52. http://dx.doi.org/10.1080/02722010903146076.

Ferguson, Sue. 1999. "Building on the Strengths of the Socialist Feminist Tradition." *Critical Sociology* 25 (1): 1–15. http://dx.doi.org/10.1177/08969205990250010201.

FMSQ (Fédération des médecins spécialistes du Québec). 2009. "Individual Hearings on Bill 34: The FMSQ Strongly Criticizes the Minister's Approach." Accessed July 5, 2015. https://www.fmsq.org/e/centredepresse/communiques/coms/20090527.html.

FQPN (Fédération du Québec pour le planning des naissances). 2014a. "Comprendre la justice reproductive." Accessed August 23, 2015. http://www.fqpn.qc.ca/actualites/comprendre-la-justice-reproductive/.

—. 2014b. *Reproductive Justice, or Applying a Social Justice Lens to Sexual, Reproductive and Maternal Health and Rights*. Montreal: FQPN.

FQPN and CFC (Fédération du Québec pour le planning des naissances and Canadians for Choice). 2010. *Focus on Abortion Services in Quebec*. Ottawa: FQPN and CFC.

Fraser, Sara, and Jesara Sinclair. 2016. "Abortion Services Coming to P.E.I., Province Announces." CBC News, March 31. http://www.cbc.ca/news/canada/prince-edward-island/pei-abortion-reproductive-rights-1.3514334.

Friedman, Marilyn. 2005. "Introduction." In *Women and Citizenship*, edited by Marilyn Friedman, 3–12. Oxford: Oxford University Press. http://dx.doi.org/10.1093/0195175344.003.0001.

Galloway, Gloria. 2012. "Tory MP Presses for Ban on Sex-Selective Abortion Motion." *Globe and Mail*, December 5. Accessed July 31, 2015. http://www.theglobeandmail.com/news/politics/tory-mp-presses-for-ban-on-sex-selective-abortion-motion/article6002606/.

Gallup Canada. 1975. "Variable q10a: Approve of Legal Abortions." Canadian Gallup Poll (July) #378. Odesi. Accessed April 3, 2012.

–. 2000. "Variable Abort: Abortion Legal under Circumstances." Canadian Gallup Poll (November) #378. Odesi. Accessed April 3, 2012.
Gavigan, Shelley. 1992. "Beyond Morgentaler: The Legal Regulation of Reproduction." In *The Politics of Abortion*, edited by Janine Brodie, Shelley Gavigan, and Jane Jenson, 117–46. Toronto: Oxford University Press.
Glauser, Wendy. 2014. "Controversy over Doctor's Right to Say 'No.'" *Canadian Medical Association Journal* 183 (13): E483–84.
Gleeson, Kate. 2011. "The Strange Case of the Invisible Woman." In *Gender, Sexualities and Law*, edited by Anna Grear, Rachel Anne Fenton, and Kim Stevenson, 215–26. New York: Routledge.
Goodyear, Sheena. 2015. "RU-486: What You Need to Know about the Recently Approved Abortion Pill." CBC News, July 30. Accessed August 9, 2015. http://www.cbc.ca/news/canada/ru-486-what-you-need-to-know-about-the-recently-approved-abortion-pill-1.3173657.
Government of New Brunswick. 1984. *New Brunswick Regulation 84-20 under the Medical Services Payment Act*. Fredericton: Government of New Brunswick.
Governor General of Canada. 2008. "Governor General Announces New Appointments to the Order of Canada." http://www.gg.ca/document.aspx?id=12828.
Grant, Kelly. 2014a. "Health Canada Decision on Abortion Pill Set for Mid-January." *Globe and Mail*, January 13. Accessed December 26, 2014. http://www.theglobeandmail.com/life/health-and-fitness/health/health-canada-decision-on-abortion-pill-set-for-mid-january/article22183863/.
–. 2014b. "Decision on Whether to Approve Abortion Pill for Canadians Delayed Again." *Globe and Mail*, December 23. Accessed July 5, 2015. http://www.theglobeandmail.com/life/health-and-fitness/health/health-canada-decision-on-abortion-pill-set-for-mid-january/article22183863/.
–. 2015. "New Brunswick Fell Just Shy of Fulfilling Commitment to Expand Abortion Access, Documents Reveal." *Globe and Mail*, May 21. Last updated May 22, 2015. Accessed August 26, 2015. http://www.theglobeandmail.com/news/national/why-nbs-english-hospitals-limited-new-abortion-services-to-moncton/article24554165/.
Gray, Charlotte. 1988. "Capital Accounts: The Politics of Abortion." *Canadian Medical Association Journal* 139 (4): 327–28.
Greschner, Donna. 1990. "Abortion and Democracy for Women: A Critique of *Tremblay v. Daigle*." *McGill Law Journal* 35 (3): 633–69.
Griffee, Susannah. 2011. "Crisis Pregnancy Center Bill May Face Court Challenge." NBC New York, March 2. Accessed August 25, 2015. http://www.nbcnewyork.com/news/local/Bill-to--117257763.html.
Guttmacher Institute. 2015. "International Abortion: Legality and Safety." Accessed August 4, 2015. https://www.guttmacher.org/international/abortion/legality-and-safety.
Hartmann, Betsy. 1995. *Reproductive Rights and Wrongs: The Global Politics of Population Control*. Cambridge: South End Press.
Haussman, Melissa. 2002. "Of Rights and Power: Canada's Federal Abortion Policy, 1969–1991." In *Abortion Politics, Women's Movements, and the Democratic State: A Comparative Study of State Feminism*, edited by Dorothy McBride Stetson, 63–86. New York: Oxford University Press.
–. 2005. "Canada: Limited Access Despite Public Health Care." In *Abortion Politics*

References

in North America, edited by Melissa Haussman, 75–104. Boulder: Lynne Rienner.
Hazlewood, Julianne. 2016. "P.E.I. Abortion Decision Fuels Access Concerns in New Brunswick." CBC News, April 1. http://www.cbc.ca/beta/news/canada/new-brunswick/abortion-access-new-brunswick-pei-1.3515841.
Health Canada. 2007. "Canada Health Act Annual Report 2006–2007." Ottawa: Ministry of Health.
—. 2010. "Canada's Health Care System (Medicare)." http://www.hc-sc.gc.ca/hcs-sss/medi-assur/index-eng.php.
—. 2012. "Canada's Health Care System." October 9. Accessed August 9, 2015. http://healthycanadians.gc.ca/health-system-systeme-sante/system-systeme/about-apropos-eng.php.
—. 2013. *Canada's Health Act: Annual Report, 2012–2013*. http://www.hc-sc.gc.ca/hcs-sss/alt_formats/pdf/pubs/cha-ics/2013-cha-lcs-ar-ra-eng.pdf
—. 2016. "Mifegymiso: Myths vs. Facts." Last updated October 13, 2016. http://www.hc-sc.gc.ca/dhp-mps/prodpharma/activit/fs-fi/mifegymiso-fs-fi-eng.php.
—. 2017. "Drugs and Health Products: Mifegymiso." Last updated January 1, 2017. http://www.hc-sc.gc.ca/dhp-mps/prodpharma/sbd-smd/drug-med/sbd-smd-2016-mifegymiso-160063-eng.php.
Hengel, Rick L. 1985. "An Interview with Dr. Henry Morgentaler." *Canadian Medical Association Journal* 133 (5): 490–95.
Herman, Didi. 1994. "The Christian Right and the Politics of Morality in Canada." *Parliamentary Affairs* 47 (2): 268–79.
Hirschl, Ran. 2004. *Towards Juristocracy: The Origins and Consequences of the New Constitutionalism*. Cambridge, MA: Harvard University Press.
Hoffman, John. 2004. *Citizenship beyond the State*. London: Sage.
Hughes, Jula. 2014. "The Closure of the Morgentaler Clinic and the Rule of Law in New Brunswick." Institute for Feminist Legal Studies at Osgoode, April 16. Accessed August 5, 2015. http://ifls.osgoode.yorku.ca/nbabortion/.
Jaggar, Alison. 2005. "Arenas of Citizenship: Civil Society, the State, and the Global Order." In *Women and Citizenship*, edited by Marilyn Friedman, 91–110. Oxford: Oxford University Press. http://dx.doi.org/10.1093/0195175344.003.0006.
Jenson, Jane. 1992. "Getting to Morgentaler: From One Representation to Another." In *The Politics of Abortion*, edited by Janine Brodie, Shelley Gavigan, and Jane Jenson, 15–56. Toronto: Oxford University Press.
Kaposy, Chris. 2009. "The Public Funding of Abortion in Canada: Going beyond the Concept of Medical Necessity." *Medicine, Health Care, and Philosophy* 12 (3): 301–11. http://dx.doi.org/10.1007/s11019-008-9164-9.
—. 2010. "Improving Abortion Access in Canada." *Health Care Analysis* 18 (1): 17–34. http://dx.doi.org/10.1007/s10728-008-0101-0.
Kaposy, Chris, and Jocelyn Downie. 2008. "Judicial Reasoning about Pregnancy and Choice." *Health Law Journal* 16: 281–304.
Kennedy, Mark. 2012. "New Poll Shows Most Canadians Support Abortion – with Some Restrictions." *National Post*, July 4. Accessed August 5, 2015. http://news.nationalpost.com/news/canada/new-poll-shows-most-canadians-support-abortion-with-some-restrictions.
Keown, John. 1988. *Abortion Doctors and the Law: Some Aspects of the Legal Regulation of Abortion in England from 1803 to 1982*. Cambridge: Cambridge University Press. http://dx.doi.org/10.1017/CBO9780511563683.

Kershaw, Paul. 2005. *Carefair: Rethinking the Responsibilities and Rights of Citizenship*. Vancouver: UBC Press.

Kirkey, Sharon. 2015. "Doctors Who Refuse to Provide Services on Moral Grounds Could Face Discipline under New Ontario Policy." *National Post*, March 6. Accessed July 20, 2015. http://news.nationalpost.com/news/canada/doctors-who-refuse-to-provide-services-on-moral-grounds-could-face-discipline-under-new-ontario-policy.

—. 2016. "Home Abortion Pill about to Hit Market in Canada, but Has Already Garnered Criticism." *National Post*, April 19. http://news.nationalpost.com/news/canada/0420-na-abortion.

Koyama, Atsuko, and Robin Williams. 2005. "Abortion in Medical School Curricula." *McGill Journal of Medicine* 8 (2): 157–60.

LEAF (Women's Legal Education and Action Fund). 2016. "LEAF Proudly Supports Abortion Access Now PEI's Legal Challenge to Prince Edward Island's Discriminatory Abortion Policy." January 15. Accessed March 21, 2016. http://www.leaf.ca/leaf-proudly-supports-abortion-access-now-peis-legal-challenge-to-prince-edward-islands-discriminatory-abortion-policy/.

LEAF and AAN PEI (Women's Legal Education and Action Fund and Abortion Access Now PEI). 2016. "LEAF and AANPEI Welcome Announcement That PEI Government Will End Its Discriminatory Abortion Policy." March 31. http://us10.campaign-archive1.com/?u=948eb06d0d00537fe844b6e9c&id=777b1cb14b&e=59b9ab5931.

LeBlanc, Daniel. 2014. "Trudeau Now Says All Liberals MPs Must Vote Pro-choice." *Globe and Mail*, June 18. Accessed February 21, 2016. http://www.theglobeandmail.com/news/politics/trudeau-says-all-liberals-mp-will-have-to-vote-pro-choice/article19218815/.

Lipman, Joanne. 2015. "Let's Expose the Gender Pay Gap." *New York Times*, August 13. http://www.nytimes.com/2015/08/13/opinion/.

Lister, Ruth. 1997. *Citizenship: Feminist Perspectives*. Basingstoke, UK: Macmillan. http://dx.doi.org/10.1007/978-1-349-26209-0.

—. 2003. *Citizenship: Feminist Perspectives*. 2nd ed. Hampshire, NY: Palgrave Macmillan.

—. 2007. "Inclusive Citizenship: Realizing the Potential." *Citizenship Studies* 11 (1): 49–61. http://dx.doi.org/10.1080/13621020601099856.

—. 2010 "Citizenship and Community." In *Understand Theories and Concepts in Social Policy*, 195–222. Bristol: Polity Press.

Luna, Zakiya. 2011. "'The Phrase of the Day': Examining Contexts and Co-optation of Reproductive Justice Activism in the Women's Movement." *Critical Aspects of Gender in Conflict Resolution, Peacebuilding, and Social Movements*, edited by Anna Christine Snyder and Stephanie Phetsamay Stobbe, 219–46. Winnipeg: Emerald.

Luna, Zakiya, and Kristin Luker. 2013. "Reproductive Justice." *Annual Review of Law and Social Science* 9 (1): 327–52. http://dx.doi.org/10.1146/annurev-lawsocsci-102612-134037.

Lunn, Susan. 2016. "Abortion Pill Can Now Legally Be Prescribed in Canada, but Is Still Unavailable." CBC News, July 6. http://www.cbc.ca/news/politics/ru-486-abortion-pill-canada-1.3665865.

Luxton, Meg. 2006. "Feminist Political Economy in Canada and the Politics of Social Reproduction." In *Social Reproduction: Feminist Political Economy Challenges*

Neo-Liberalism, edited by Kate Bezanson and Meg Luxton, 11–44. Montreal: McGill-Queen's University Press.

Macfarlane, Emmett. 2013. *Governing from the Bench: The Supreme Court of Canada and the Judicial Role*. Vancouver: UBC Press.

—. 2014. "The Dilemma of Positive Rights: Access to Health Care and the *Canadian Charter of Rights and Freedoms*." *Journal of Canadian Studies* 48 (3): 49–78.

MacKenzie, Chris. 2005. *Pro-Family Politics and Fringe Parties in Canada*. Vancouver: UBC Press.

MacQuarrie, Colleen, Jo-Ann MacDonald, and Cathrine Chambers. 2014. *Trials and Trails of Access Abortion in PEI: Reporting on the Impact of PEI's Abortion Policies on Women*. http://projects.upei.ca/cmacquarrie/files/2014/01/trials_and_trails_final.pdf.

Maioni, Antonia. 2010. "Citizenship and Health Care in Canada." *International Journal of Canadian Studies* 42: 225–42. http://dx.doi.org/10.7202/1002179ar.

—. 2012. "Health Care." In *Canadian Federalism*, 3rd ed., edited by Herman Bakvis and Grace Skogstad, 165–82. Don Mills, ON: Oxford University Press.

Maloney, Ryan. 2015. "Justin Trudeau's Abortion Stance Conflicts with Support of P.E.I. Liberals: NDP." *Huffington Post*, April 16. Accessed February 21, 2016. http://www.huffingtonpost.ca/2015/04/16/trudeau-abortion-pei-liberals-ndp-wade-maclauchlan_n_7078458.html.

Mans, Lori K. 2003–4. "Liability for the Death of a Fetus: Fetal Rights or Women's Rights?" *University of Florida Journal of Law and Public Policy* 15: 295–312.

Marshall, T.H. 2006. "Citizenship and Social Class." In *The Welfare State Reader*, 2nd ed., edited by Christopher Pierson and Francis Castles, 3–51. Cambridge: Polity Press.

Martin, Sandra. 2013. "Abortion Rights Crusader Henry Morgentaler, Revered and Hated, Dead at 90." *Globe and Mail*, May 29. Accessed July 31, 2015. http://www.theglobeandmail.com/news/national/abortion-rights-crusader-henry-morgentaler-revered-and-hated-dead-at-90/article12221564/?page=all.

Matthews, Scott. 2005. "The Political Foundations of Support for Same-Sex Marriage in Canada." *Canadian Journal of Political Science* 38 (4): 841–66. http://dx.doi.org/10.1017/S0008423905040485.

Mayeda, Andrew, and Althia Raj. 2011. "Harper Vows Not to Reopen Abortion Debate as Prime Minister." *National Post*, April 21. Accessed August 25, 2015. http://news.nationalpost.com/news/canada/canadian-politics/harper-vows-not-to-reopen-abortion-debate-as-prime-minister.

McLachlin, Beverley. 2001. "Courts, Legislatures and Executives in the Post-Charter Era." In *Judicial Power and Canadian Democracy*, edited by Peter H. Russell and Paul Howe, 63–72. Montreal: McGill-Queen's University Press.

McLaren, Angus, and Arlene Tigar McLaren. 1997. *The Bedroom and the State: The Changes Practices and Politics of Contraception and Abortion in Canada, 1880–1997*, 2nd ed. Toronto: Oxford University Press.

McLeod, Carolyn, and Jocelyn Downie. 2014. "Let Conscience Be Their Guide? Conscientious Refusals in Health Care." *Bioethics* 28 (1): ii–iv. http://dx.doi.org/10.1111/bioe.12075.

Mickleburgh, Rod. 2014. "Garson Romalis Risked His Life to Perform Abortions." *Globe and Mail*, February 21. http://www.theglobeandmail.com/news/british-columbia/

garson-romalis-risked-his-life-to-perform-abortions/article17052093/?page=all. Accessed July 25, 2015.

Montreal Gazette. 1976. "Face Facts, Levesque Says: Update Abortion View, MDs Told." May 14.

Morton, Frederick L. 1992. *Morgentaler v. Borowski: Abortion, the Charter, and the Courts.* Toronto: McClelland and Stewart.

Morton, Frederick L., and Rainer Knopff. 2000. *The Charter Revolution and the Court Party.* Toronto: University of Toronto Press.

Moulton, Donalee. 2003. "New Brunswick Assailed over "Sexist" Abortion Laws." *Canadian Medical Association Journal* 169 (7): 700.

NAF (National Abortion Federation). 2010. "History of Abortion in Canada." Accessed January 10, 2011. https://www.prochoice.org/canada/history.html.

–. 2013. "NAF Canada Ad in the *Globe and Mail*." January 28. http://www.nafcanada.org/ad-globe-mail.html.

–. 2015a. "Abortion." Accessed June 9, 2016. https://prochoice.org/think-youre-pregnant/im-pregnant-what-are-my-options/abortion/.

–. 2015b. *2015 Clinical Policy Guidelines.* Washington, DC: National Abortion Federation.

–. 2015c. *2015 Violence and Disruption Statistics.* Washington, DC: National Abortion Federation.

–. N.d. "Access to Abortion in Canada." http://www.nafcanada.org/access-abortion-ca.html.

New Brunswick Human Rights Commission. 2014. *2013–2014 Annual Report.* Fredericton: Human Rights Commission of New Brunswick. http://www2.gnb.ca/content/gnb/biling/hrc-cdp.html.

Nossiff, Rosemary. 2007. "Gendered Citizenship: Women, Equality, and Abor-tion Policy." *New Political Science* 29 (1): 61–76. http://dx.doi.org/10.1080/07393140601170818.

NYSHN (Native Youth Sexual Health Network). 2015. "Areas of Work." Accessed August 3, 2015. http://www.nativeyouthsexualhealth.com/areasofwork.html.

OCAC (Ontario Coalition for Abortion Clinics). 2012. "October 20th Day of Action! Reproductive Justice for All!" October 18. https://ocac-choice.com/tag/reproductive-justice/.

–. 2015. "About OCAC." Accessed August 23, 2015. https://ocac-choice.com/about/.

Office of the Prime Minister. 2011. "New Maternal, Newborn and Children Health Initiatives." January 26. http://news.gc.ca/web/article-en.do?m=/index&nid=585959.

Overby, Marvin, Raymond Tatalovich, and Donley Studlar. 1998. "Party and Free Votes in Canada: Abortion in the House of Commons." *Party Politics* 4 (3): 381–92. http://dx.doi.org/10.1177/1354068898004003006.

Palley, Howard A. 2006. "Canadian Abortion Policy: National Policy and the Impact of Federalism and Political Implementation on Access Services." *Publius* 36 (4): 565–86. http://dx.doi.org/10.1093/publius/pjl002.

Paperny, Anna. 2016. "Abortion Pill: Canadian Prescribers to Get Training for Mifegymsio This Month." Global News, April 5. http://globalnews.ca/news/2619664/abortion-pill-canadian-prescribers-to-get-training-for-Mifegymiso-this-month/.

Parliament of Canada, Standing Senate Committee on Social Affairs, Science and Technology. 2002. "Part III: The Health Care Guarantee." In *The Health of*

Canadians – The Final Role. Ottawa: Standing Senate Committee on Social Affairs, Science and Technology. http://www.parl.gc.ca/Content/SEN/Committee/372/soci/rep/repoct02vol6-e.htm.

Pateman, Carole. 1988. *The Sexual Contract.* Cambridge: Polity Press.

–. 1992. "The Patriarchal Welfare State." In *The Welfare State Reader*, 2nd ed., edited by Christopher Pierson and Francis Castles, 134–52. Cambridge: Polity Press.

Payton, Laura. 2011. "Planned Parenthood's Canadian Funding Renewed." CBC News, September 22. Accessed August 3, 2015. http://www.cbc.ca/news/politics/planned-parenthood-s-canadian-funding-renewed-1.981977.

–. 2014. "Tom Mulcair Warns Rona Ambrose against Politics in RU-486 Application." CBC News, January 28. Accessed August 25, 2015. http://www.cbc.ca/m/touch/politics/story/1.2514611.

Pelrine, Eleanor. 1975. *Morgentaler: The Doctor Who Couldn't Turn Away.* Scarborough, ON: New American Library.

–. 1983. *Morgentaler: The Doctor Who Couldn't Turn Away.* 2nd ed. Halifax: Goodread Bibliographies.

Petchesky, Rosalind Pollack. 2008. "Beyond 'A Woman's Right to Choose': Feminist Ideas about Reproductive Rights." In *The Reproductive Rights Reader: Law, Medicine, and the Construction of Motherhood*, edited by Nancy Ehrenreich, 106–10. New York: NYU Press.

Picard, Andre. 2009. "We Need Fewer Barriers to Abortion, Not More." *Globe and Mail*, August 13. Last updated September 6, 2012. Accessed August 25, 2015. http://www.theglobeandmail.com/life/health-and-fitness/we-need-fewer-barriers-to-abortion-not-more/article789306/.

–. 2016. "Abortion Pill's Sexist Regulations Deny Women True Reproductive Choice." *Globe and Mail*, May 3. http://www.theglobeandmail.com/opinion/abortion-pills-sexist-regulations-deny-women-true-reproductive-choice/article29826789/.

Pierson, Ruth Roach. 1993. "The Politics of the Body." In *Strong Voices.* Vol. 1 of *Canadian Women's Issues*, edited by Ruth Roach Pierson, Marjorie Griffin Cohen, Paula Bourne, and Philinda Masters. Toronto: James Lorimer.

Prasad, Sandeep. 2016. "How One Drug Could Change Abortion Access in Canada." *Huffington Post*, November 1. http://www.huffingtonpost.ca/sandeep-prasad/abortion-access-in-canada_b_8955348.html.

Price, Kimala. 2010. "What Is Reproductive Justice? How Women of Color Activists Are Redefining the Pro-choice Paradigm." *Meridians* (Indiana University Press) 10 (2): 42–65. http://dx.doi.org/10.2979/meridians.2010.10.2.42.

Pro-Choice Action Network. 1999. "Abortion in Canada." Accessed August 17, 2015. http://www.prochoiceactionnetwork-canada.org/articles/canada.shtml.

PRRO (PEI Reproductive Rights Organization). N.d. "About PRRO." Accessed April 9, 2016. http://prro.lostwarren.com/abou/.

Radio-Canada. 2012."Jean-Guy Tremblay arrêté pour violence conjugale." April 10. Accessed August 3, 2015. http://ici.radio-canada.ca/nouvelle/556949/quebec-arrestation-tremblay-jguy.

REAL Women of Canada. 2015. "About Us." Accessed August 16, 2015. http://www.realwomenofcanada.ca/about-us/.

Rebick, Judy. 2005. *Ten Thousand Roses: The Makings of a Feminist Revolution.* Toronto: Penguin Canada.

Reid, Michelle Siobhan. 2013. "Access by Province." Abortion Rights Coalition of Canada. Accessed August 4, 2015. http://www.morgentaler25years.ca/the-struggle-for-abortion-rights/access-by-province/.

Richardson, Don. 2011. "N.B. Stands Firm on Abortion Policy." *Daily Gleaner*, January 30.

Richer, Karine. 2008. *Abortion in Canada: Twenty Years after R. v. Morgentaler*. Ottawa: Library of Parliament.

RJNB (Reproductive Justice New Brunswick). 2014. "Help Us Ensure Access to Safe Abortion in N.B." FundRazr. Accessed June 9, 2016. https://fundrazr.com/campaigns/aoCmf.

Rodgers, Sanda, and Jocelyn Downie. 2006. "Abortion: Ensuring Access." *Canadian Medical Association Journal* 175 (1): 9. http://dx.doi.org/10.1503/cmaj.060548.

Roseneil, Sasha, Isabel Crowhurst, Ana Cristina Santos, and Mariya Stoilova. 2013. "Reproduction and Citizenship/Reproducing Citizens: Editorial Introduction." *Citizenship Studies* 17 (8): 901–11. http://dx.doi.org/10.1080/13621025.2013.851067.

Ross, Loretta. 2006. "Understanding Reproductive Justice: Transforming the Pro-choice Movement." *Off Our Backs* 36 (4): 14–19.

Ross, Ryan. 2013. "Province Reviewing Funding for Medical School Seats." *Montreal Guardian*, April 18. Accessed July 20, 2015. http://www.theguardian.pe.ca/News/Local/2013-04-18/article-3222488/Province-reviewing-funding-for-medical-school-seats/1.

Russell, Peter H. 2004. *Constitutional Odyssey: Can Canadians Become a Sovereign People?* Toronto: University of Toronto Press.

Saurette, Paul, and Kelly Gordon. 2013. "Arguing Abortion: The New Anti-abortion Discourse in Canada." *Canadian Journal of Political Science* 46 (1): 157–85. http://dx.doi.org/10.1017/S0008423913000176.

—. 2016. *The Changing Voice of the Anti-abortion Movement: The Rise of "Pro-woman" Rhetoric in Canada and the United States*. Toronto: University of Toronto Press.

Schwartzman, Lisa. 2002. "Feminist Analyses of Oppression and the Discourse of 'Rights': A Response to Wendy Brown." *Social Theory and Practice* 28 (3): 465–80. http://dx.doi.org/10.5840/soctheorpract200228319.

Sethna, Christabelle, and Marion Doull. 2013. "Spatial Disparities and Travel to Freestanding Abortion Clinics in Canada." *Women's Studies International Forum* 38: 52–62. http://dx.doi.org/10.1016/j.wsif.2013.02.001.

Shaffer, Martha. 1993–94. "Foetal Rights and the Regulation of Abortion." *McGill Law Journal* 39: 58–100.

Shaw, Jessica. 2006. *Reality Check: A Close Look at Accessing Abortion Services in Canadian Hospitals*. Ottawa: Canadians for Choice.

—. 2013. "Full-Spectrum Reproductive Justice: The Affinity of Abortion Rights and Birth Activism." *Studies in Social Justice* 7 (1): 143–59.

Smith, Connell. 2015. "Horizon Health to Offer Abortion Services Only in Moncton Hospital." CBC News, February 24. Accessed August 5, 2015. http://www.cbc.ca/news/canada/new-brunswick/horizon-health-to-offer-abortion-services-only-in-moncton-hospital-1.2970019.

Smith, Joanna. 2010. "Deception Used in Counselling against Women." *Toronto Star*, August 7. Accessed August 25, 2015. https://www.thestar.com/news/canada/2010/08/07/deception_used_in_counselling_women_against_abortion.html.

Smith, Miriam. 2002. "Ghosts of the Judicial Committee of the Privy Council: Group Politics and Charter Litigation in Canadian Political Science." *Canadian Journal of Political Science* 35 (1): 3–29. http://dx.doi.org/10.1017/S000842390277813X.

—. 2005. "Social Movements and Judicial Empowerment: Courts, Public Policy, and Lesbian and Gay Organizing in Canada." *Politics and Society* 33 (2): 327–53. http://dx.doi.org/10.1177/0032329205275193.

Solinger, Rickie. 2013. *Reproductive Politics: What Everyone Needs to Know*. New York: Oxford University Press.

Sovereign Uterus. 2015. "The Sovereign Uterus." Accessed August 3, 2015. https://thesovereignuterus.wordpress.com/.

Stabile, Carol. 1998. "Shooting the Mother: Fetal Photography and the Politics of Disappearance." In *The Visible Woman: Imaging Technologies, Gender, and Science*, edited by Paula A. Treichler, Lisa Cartwright, and Constance Penley, 171–97. New York: NYU Press.

Statistics Canada. 2005. "Induced Abortion Statistics." Statistics Canada. http://www.statcan.gc.ca/pub/82-223-x/82-223-x2008000-eng.htm.

Stettner, Shannon. 2016. *Without Apology: Writings on Abortion in Canada*. Edmonton: Athabasca University Press.

Stetson, Dorothy McBride. 1996. "Feminist Perspective on Abortion and Reproductive Technologies." *Abortion Politics: Public Policy in Cross-Cultural Perspective*, edited by Marianne Githens and Dorothy McBride Stetson, 211–24. New York: Routledge.

Steuter, Erin. 2004. "He Who Pays the Piper Calls the Tune: Investigation of a Canadian Media Monopoly." *Web Journal of Mass Communication Research* 7 (4): 1–45.

Szklarski, Cassandra. 2016. "Canadian debut of abortion pill Mifegymiso delayed to January." *Globe and Mail*, November 28. http://www.theglobeandmail.com/news/national/canadian-debut-of-abortion-pill-mifegymiso-delayed-to-january/article33070260/.

Tatalovich, Raymond. 1997. *The Politics of Abortion in the United States and Canada: A Comparative Study*. Armonk, NY: M.E. Sharpe.

TC Media. 2014. "P.E.I. Abortion Policy to Hold Line Despite Trudeau's Stance, Says Ghiz." *Journal Pioneer* 9 (May). Accessed 10 May, 2014. http://www.journalpioneer.com/News/Local/2014-05-09/article-3718076/P.E.I.-abortion-policy-to-hold-line-despite-Trudeaus-stance,-says-Ghiz/1.

Thomson-Philbrook, Julia. 2014. "Doctor Knows Best: The Illusion of Reproductive Freedom in Canada." In *Fertile Ground: Exploring Reproduction in Canada*, edited by Stephanie Paterson, Francesca Scala, and Marlene Sokolon, 230–54. Montreal: McGill-Queen's University Press.

Tromp, Stanley. 2013. "Mulroney-Era Documents Reveal Detailed Debate of Canada's Abortion Laws." *Globe and Mail*, November 17. Accessed August 3, 2015. http://www.theglobeandmail.com/news/national/mulroney-era-documents-reveal-detailed-debate-of-canadas-abortion-laws/article15476897/?page=all.

Trudeau, Justin. 2015a. "Minister of International Development and La Francophonie." Accessed January 21, 2017. http://pm.gc.ca/eng/minister-international-development-and-la-francophonie-mandate-letter.

—. 2015b. "Minister of Status of Women Mandate Letter." Accessed February 21, 2016. http://pm.gc.ca/eng/minister-status-women-mandate-letter.

–. 2016. Twitter post. March 31, 11:03 a.m. https://twitter.com/justintrudeau/status/715600442328268800.
Turner, Bryan. 2008. "Citizenship, Reproduction and the State: International Marriage and Human Rights." *Citizenship Studies* 12 (1): 45–54. http://dx.doi.org/10.1080/13621020701794166.
United Nations. 1995. "Platform for Action" United Nations Fourth World Conference on Women. Accessed June 15, 2016. http://www.un.org/womenwatch/daw/beijing/platform/health.htm.
United Nations, Department of Economic and Social Affairs, Population Division. 2014. *Abortion Policies and Reproductive Health around the World*. United Nations publication.
Up for Debate. *2015*. "Up for Debate: Who We Are." Accessed February 21, 2016. http://upfordebate.ca/who-we-are.
Vickers, Jill. 2010. "A Two-Way Street: Federalism and Women's Politics in Canada and the United States." *Publius* 40 (3): 412–35. http://dx.doi.org/10.1093/publius/pjq006.
White, Linda A. 2014. "Federalism and Equality Rights Implementation in Canada." *Publius* 44 (1): 157–82. http://dx.doi.org/10.1093/publius/pjt019.
WHO (World Health Organization). 2003. "WHO Definition of Health." Accessed September 1, 2016. http://www.who.int/about/definition/en/print.html.
–. 2012a. "Maternal Health." http://www.who.int/topics/maternal_health/en/.
–. 2012b. *Safe Abortion: Technical and Policy Guidance for Health Systems*. 2nd ed.
Yuval-Davis, Nira. 1997. *Gender and Nation*. London: Sage.
Zilio, Michelle. 2015. "Trudeau Defends Abortion Position after Graphic Flyers Target Liberal Leader." CTV News, May 13. http://www.ctvnews.ca/politics/trudeau-defends-abortion-position-after-graphic-flyers-target-liberal-leader-1.2371906.

Index

abortion: back-alley, 113, 150–51, 156; clinical guidelines, 123–24; Criminal Law Amendment Act (1969), 36, 56–59, 61, 69, 97; decriminalization, 28, 36–37, 45, 49, 79, 148, 156, 158; de facto legalization 60, 98; delisting 94; "on demand," 35, 56; first trimester 62, 99, 123–24, 190n25; gendered implications, 78, 113; gestational limits, 63, 70, 122, 127, 169–75, 192n44; "harms women," 29, 31–33, 123–24, 151; medicalization of 4, 92; as murder, 17, 69, 95, 149, 183n3; public perception, 9, 28, 33, 47, 52, 63, 141, 152; referrals, 111, 120–22, 136, 190n19; self-induced, 156; sex-selective, 74; as "socially undesirable conduct," 158; therapeutic abortion committees (TACs), 34, 56, 62, 84, 97. *See also* surgical abortion; Mifegymiso; violence

abortion access: complications in implementation, 6–8; facilities (*see* hospitals; clinics; and centres locaux des services communautaires [CLSCs]); patchwork of services, 38, 105, 136, 156; rural, 92, 119, 126–27, 129, 130, 146, 154, 164; travel, 92, 123. *See also* bubble zones; conscientious objection; protestors

Abortion Access Now PEI (AAN PEI), 161

Abortion Caravan, 34–35,

Abortion Rights Coalition of Canada (ARCC), 35, 38, 45–46, 72, 148, 167

Abortion Rights Network (ARN), 160–61, 164

Ackelsberg, Martha, 18

Action Canada for Population and Development (ACPD), 46

Action Canada for Sexual Health and Rights, 38, 43, 129, 151, 167–68

Alberta, 170

Ambrose, Rona, 125

anti-abortion: fetal rights, 26, 29–33, 61, 64–65, 68–74, 79; "gendercide," 74; history, 28–33; "pro-family," 29; "pro-woman" discourse, 29–32, 71–72; protestors, 131–34, 142–46,

151; "value change," 33; violence, 130–33, 136, 144–45, 151. *See also* backbencher bills; crisis pregnancy centres
association pour l'accès à l'avortement, 98
Association pour l'accès à l'avortement v. Procureur General du Québec, 98–99
autonomy: anti-abortion movement, 32; legal precedent, 53, 62, 66–68, 79, 103; necessary for citizenship, 17, 19, 166; political recognition of, 93, 100, 155; reproductive/bodily, 14–15, 34, 66, 76, 79, 103, 139

backbencher bills, 29–30, 32–33, 96, 142
Badgley Report, 60, 104
  Badgley, Robin, 60
Basford, Ronald, 59
Bédard, Marc-André, 97
Bennett, Carolyn, 56–57, 137–38
Bill C-43, 70–71
birth control, 18, 55, 122, 135, 183n4
Blackmer, Jeff, 190n19
Bloc Québécois, 72
Borowski, Joe, 30, 68–69
Borowski v. Canada, 64, 68–69
Bourgeois, Sonya, 29–30
Breitkreuz, Garry, 72–74
Brewer, Alison, 85–86, 90, 132, 185n3
Brodie, Janine, 15, 63–64, 141
Brown, Lori, 158
Brown, Wendy, 41
Bruinooge, Rod, 73
bubble zones, 123, 136, 138, 145, 151
Burwell, Judy, 116, 131, 148

Campaign Life Coalition, 29
Campbell, Kim, 70
Canada Abortion Rights Action League (CARAL), 34–35, 60–61, 150, 177
Canada Health Act: compliance with 78, 91, 109, 111–16, 149, 161; Dispute Avoidance and Resolution (DAR), 116–17; funding, 5, 11, 114; preamble, 112; principles, 108, 111–12, 115, 139; violations of, 5, 87, 90, 109, 162–63. *See also* medical necessity
Canada Health Transfer (CHT), 108, 115–16, 188n3
Canada Social Transfer, 108
Canadian Assistance Plan (CAP), 108
Canadian Bill of Rights, 58
Canadian Medical Association (CMA): abortion policy, 88, 120–22; code of ethics, 121; organization, 118; rights and responsibilities of physicians, 118, 120
Canadian Pharmacists Association (CPhA), 126
Canadians for Choice (CFC), 35, 129–30, 134, 151, 167–68
Cannold, Leslie, 31–32
Cannon, Lawrence, 75
Centre de santé des femmes de Montréal (CSFM), 99, 130–31, 154
centres locaux des services communautaires (CLSCs), 128, 130
Charter of Rights and Freedoms: abortion as a Charter right, 77–78; criticisms, 13; drafting, 61; enactment, 11, 23, 26, 30, 36, 47; impact, 11–12, 23, 26, 36, 47, 50, 53; party of the, 163–64; positive rights, 102, 105; responsibility to uphold, 53–54, 83, 105, 157, 161–62, 165; rights recognitions, 12–14; scrutiny, 51–52, 71; section 2 ("conscience"), 103–4; section 7 ("security of the person"), 3, 36, 57, 87, 103–5, 161; section 12 ("cruel and unusual treatment"), 161; section 15 ("equality"), 6, 14, 87, 103–4, 161–62, 165; signatories, 82; transformative power, 51–52
child birth: right to control birthing options, 40; risks, 54, 113

children: childcare, 108, 150; decision to have, 46; desire to raise a child in a safe environment, 66; health, 75; option to have, 49, 113, 164; responsibility for, 41; right to have, 27, 40; timing and spacing of, 39, 46
choice. See pro-choice
Chrisler, Joan, 39
citizenship: and abortion rights, 4, 15–21, 26, 33, 92, 127–28, 162; as contested concept, 15; and health care, 107, 114; inclusive narrative, 16–17; women's equal, 4, 24, 92, 127–28, 162
Clement, Tony, 116–17
Clinic 554, 91
clinic(s): bubble zones, 123, 136, 138, 145, 151; Centre de santé des femmes de Montréal (CSFM), 99, 130–31, 154; Clinic 554, 91; closure, 44, 86, 90–92, 130, 143, 147–48; feminist approach, 131; guidelines, 100, 123–24; medical abortion, 122–23; Morgentaler, 35, 44, 57–58, 103, 131, 143–47; no need for, 90; protestors, 86, 123, 131–35, 138, 143–46, 151; raids, 35, 57, 60–61; reciprocal billing, 117–18; reliance on, 95, 128, 130–31; standards, 100; surgical abortion, 123; temporary injunction, 133–34, 145; violence, 130–33, 136, 144, 151
Co-operative Commonwealth Federation, 107
Coalition for Life and Health, 87
College of Physicians and Surgeons: New Brunswick, 86, 121; Ontario, 121; Quebec, 100, 121; responsibilities, 118, 189n5
Committee on the Accreditation of Canadian Medical Schools (CACMS), 119
conception: belief that life begins at, 17, 32, 70, 158; date, 131
Confederation, 54, 107

conscientious objection, 120–22, 129, 139
Conseil du statut de la femme, 100
Conservative Party: anti-abortion MPs, 64, 72–75, 86; anti-abortion sentiment, 77, 96; government, 74–75, 98, 116–17. See also Harper, Stephen; Lord, Bernard; Mulroney, Brian
contraception. See birth control
Cooke, Peggy, 132–33, 143, 146–47, 151–52
courts: judicial empowerment, 26; Morgentaler amendment, 59; "of public opinion," 141; refusal to convict Morgentaler, 36, 58–61, 97
Criminal Code: Bill C–43, 52, 70–71; definition of human being, 32–33, 73; laws adopted from Britain, 54–55; restrictions on contraception, 55; section 251, 36, 56–59, 61, 69, 97
Criminal Law Amendment Act (1969), 36, 56–59, 61, 69, 97
crisis pregnancy centres: description of, 134; funding for, 134; legislation regulating, 135; Mother & Child Welcome House, 144

Daigle, Chantal, 65–67
decriminalization of abortion: impact on governments; 148, 158; impact on litigation, 36; impact on social movement activism, 28, 37, 45, 49; impetus for; 55, 80
defence of necessity, 36, 55, 58–59. See also R. v. Bourne
demonstrators. See protestors
Dickson, Brian, 62
Dietsch, Michael Murray, 93
Dispute Avoidance Resolution (DAR), 116–17
doctors. See physicians
Dodd, Barbara, 93
Doe et al. v. Manitoba, 102–4

Dosanjh, Ujjal, 116
Douglas, Tommy, 107
Downie, Jocelyn, 67
drugs. See Mifegymiso; morning-after pill; Plan B; RU-486

Echo (Echo: Improving Women's Health in Ontario), 95
Ehrlich, Shoshanna, 158
Epp, Ken, 72, 74
Erdman, Joanna, 104, 114, 165
equality rights. See Charter of Rights and Freedoms

facilities: nursing stations, 138; women's health centres, 162. *See also* clinic(s); centres locaux des services communautaires (CLSCs); crisis pregnancy centres; hospital(s)
family: medicine/doctor, 56–57, 21, 136–37, 139; nuclear, 29; planning, 55, 75, 78, 91, 129; "threats to the," 29; traditional, 29, 49, 153. *See also* "pro-family" movement
father's rights, 56, 65, 79
federal government. *See* backbencher bills; Criminal Code; Harper, Stephen; Mulroney, Brian; Trudeau, Justin
federalism: division of powers, 7, 80, 107, 116; and healthcare, 115–18; "open federalism," 78, 109
Fédération des médecins spécialistes du Québec (FMSQ), 100
Fédération du Québec pour le planning des naissances (FQPN), 38, 43, 77, 99, 130, 134, 153
feminism: second-wave, 20, 34, 180*n*8; socialist, 180*n*2; women's movement, 15, 26, 61
feminist(s): activism, 34–38, 60–61, 79, 82, 98, 150; approach to abortion care, 131; of colour, 38; views on abortion, 12, 19–20, 31, 34–49, 111, 154; views on citizenship, 16, 18–20; young, 44

Ferguson, Sue, 19
fetal rights: 26, 29–33, 61, 64–65, 68–74, 79
Fowler, Dawn, 117–18

G8 summit, 75, 77–78, 99, 153
Gallant, Brian, 91
Garnett, Paulette, 89
Gavigan, Shelley, 15, 36, 66, 111, 114
gender: expectations; 20; roles, 55; social significance, 15, 78, 89, 113–15, 139; stereotypes, 20; voting according to, 64, 70
gestational limits, 63–64, 70, 122, 127
Ghiz, Robert, 159
Gordon, Kelly, 29–30
Gray, Hannah, 164
Green, Brad, 87
Green Party of Canada, 72
Greschner, Donna, 67

Hajdu, Patty, 78
Hall, Barbara, 121–22
Harper, Stephen: abortion access abroad, 75–78; government, 74–78, 95–96, 101, 109, 116; "reopening the abortion debate," 52, 74–75, 101
Harris, Mike, 94–95, 130
Hatfield, Richard, 83–86, 185*n*3
Haussman, Melissa, 38
health: citizenship right, 107, 114; definition, 75, 108, 111–13; determinants of, 112; essential care, 94; federal transfer payments, 107–8, 115–16; maternal, 76; "maternal, newborn, and child," 75, 77–78, 99; origins of public health care, 107–9; principal social good, 107; transparency, 108, 110, 137–40. *See also* Canada Health Act
Health Canada, 7, 10, 124–27
Health Services Act, 161
Henderson, Rob, 162

Hoffman, John, 16
Hospital and Health Services Commission, 158
hospital(s): abortion restricted to, 56, 83–85, 90–91, 97, 103, 157–62, 165; amalgamations, 128–29; barriers to access, 129–31, 135; clinics replacing, 95, 128; expansion, 137; funding, 91, 94, 98–99, 108, 115–16, 128, 130–31, 151, 158; harassment, 191*n*36; religious hospitals, 128–29; services, 129–30; safety, 132; therapeutic abortion committees (TACs), 56, 58–59, 97; trustee boards, 129; wait times, 98; QEII, 159
House of Commons: "abortion debate," 52, 71, 73, 165; backbencher bills, 29–30, 32–33, 96, 142; Bill C–43, 52, 70–71; women MPs voting as a block, 64
Hughes, Jula, 88–90, 145–46
human rights: claims, 88–90, 129; reproductive rights as, 39, 41, 46; women's, 39–40
Human Rights Act, 99
Human Rights Commission: New Brunswick, 88–89; Ontario, 122

injunctions: against pregnant women, 65–67, 93; against "procuring a miscarriage," 56; against protestors around clinics, 133–34, 145
International Conference on Population and Development (1994) (ICPD), 38–39
International Covenant on Economic, Social and Cultural Rights, 114

Jamieson, Stuart, 90
Jenkins, David, 158
Jenkins, George, 86
Jenson, Jane, 15, 56
Johnston, Richard Frank, 93
judicialization, 5, 182*n*1

jury refusal to convict Morgentaler, 58–61, 150

Kaposy, Chris, 67, 111–13
Keown, John, 54
Kruger, Ellen, 60–61

Labour and Employment Board. *See* New Brunswick Human Rights Commission
Lamer, Antonio, 62, 107–8
Lang, Otto, 59
Laskin, Bora, 69
LEAF. *See* Women's Legal Education and Action Fund (LEAF)
Lévesque, René, 97
Liberal Party. *See* Gallant, Brian; Ghiz, Robert; MacLauchlan, Wade; Martin, Paul; Trudeau, Justin
Lippman, Abby, 76, 154
Lister, Ruth, 16, 18
Lockyer, James, 85
Lord, Bernard, 116
Lord Ellenborough's Act (1803), 54–55
Luker, Kristin, 42
Luna, Zakiya, 42, 47

Macfarlane, Emmett, 51, 62, 102, 105
MacKenzie, Chris, 28
MacLauchlan, Wade, 160, 162, 164
MacQuarrie, Colleen, 158–61, 164
Maioni, Antonia, 107–8
Malcolmson, Sheila, 163
Manitoba: abortion access in, 171; clinic, 60–61, 103–4; *Doe et al. v. Manitoba* (2004), 102–4; Health Services Insurance Act, 104; Manitoba Regulation 46/93, 104; *Winnipeg Child and Family Services (Northwest Area) v. D.F.G.*, 67, 73
Manitoba Regulation 46/93, 104. *See also* Manitoba
Martin, Keith, 72–73
Martin, Paul, 109, 163
maternal health, 76

Matthews, Scott, 47
McClelland, Carman, 93
McGuinty, Dalton, 93
McKenna, Frank: "fight of his life," 85; government, 84–86; Regulation 84-20, 85–86, 88, 91, 148; unofficial abortion policy, 85
McLachlin, Beverley, 11
medical abortion. *See* Mifegymiso
Medical Care Act, 107
medical necessity, 36, 55, 108–9, 111–15
medical school: curriculum, 6–8, 119–20; McGill, 154; subsidization, 119
Medical Students for Choice, 119–20
medicalization, 4, 92
medicare, 84–85, 117, 156, 158
Meerburg, Leslie, 125
Megill, Catherine, 76, 153–54
Melanson, Rosella, 90, 147
Messier, Anne Marie, 130–31, 138, 154
methodology, 7–11
Methven, Tracey, 132, 149–50, 152
Mifegymiso: approval process, 125; description, 124–25; restrictions, 126–27, 138. *See also* RU-486
Ministry of Health and Long-Term Care
miscarriage: procuring, 56; similarity to medical abortion, 124
Morgentaler, Henry: arrest, 58; clinics, 35, 44, 57–58, 103, 131, 143–47; communications with New Brunswick government, 83, 87; death, 88; early life, 57; imprisonment, 59; jury's refusal to convict, 36, 58–61, 97; medical license, 84, 86; Order of Canada, 184*n*19; public interest standing, 87–88.
Morgentaler v. Prince Edward Island (Minister of Health and Social Services), 158
morning-after pill, 154
Mother & Child Welcome House, 144. *See also* crisis pregnancy centres

Mulcair, Thomas, 77, 125
Mulroney, Brian: Bill C–43, 52, 70–71; government, 51–52, 63–64, 69, 71, 142; new parliamentary process, 63
Murphy, Gregory, 93
Murphy v Dodd, 93
Muskoka Initiative, 75, 77–78, 99

National Abortion Federation (NAF), 38, 46, 117–18, 123–24, 127, 132
Native Youth Sexual Health Network (NYSHN), 42, 182*n*13
New Brunswick: abortion in, 83–92; Coalition for Life and Health, 87; College of Physicians and Surgeons, 86, 121; Hatfield amendment, 83–86, 185*n*3; Human Rights Act, 99; Medical Act, 83, 85, 185*n*3; Medical Services Payment Act, 85–86; Regulation 84–20, 85–86, 88, 91, 148. *See also* Gallant, Brian; Hatfield, Richard; Lord, Bernard; McKenna, Frank; Mulroney, Brian
New Brunswick Advisory Council on the Status of Women, 90, 147
New Brunswick Human Rights Commission, 88–89
New Brunswick v. Morgentaler, 86
New Brunswick Right to Life, 144
New Democratic Party (NDP): federal, 60, 72, 77, 93, 100, 125, 163; New Brunswick, 85; Saskatchewan, 68
Newfoundland, 172
Norman, Wendy, 127
Northwest Territories, 175
Nossiff, Rosemary, 17
Nova Scotia: abortion access in, 172; Medical Services Act, 103; *R. v. Morgentaler* (1993), 102–3
Nunavut, 175

Offences Against the Person Act (1869), 55
Ontario: abortion in, 92–96; Ministry of Health and Long-Term Care, 95. *See also* McGuinty, Dalton

Ontario Coalition of Abortion Clinics (OCAC), 94, 133, 149–50
Ontario Human Rights Commission, 122
Ouellet, Marc, 77

Palley, Howard, 129
Palmer, Dorothy, 55
Parti Québécois, 60, 97–98
patriarchy, 153
pay equity, 49
Penner, Roland, 60–61
Petchesky, Rosalind Pollack, 41
Philpott, Jane, 163
physicians: harassment/violence against, 6, 9, 119, 131–32, 136, 142, 145; imprisonment of, 56, 59; safeguarding their domain, 54; training, 6–8, 95–96, 119–20, 126. *See also* College of Physicians and Surgeons; conscientious objection
Pierson, Ruth Roach, 34–35
Plan B, 154
Planned Parenthood: International, 76; Montreal, 153; Toronto, 95, 151
policy: population control, 39; void, 4, 65, 142
Powers, Patrick, 101, 153
Prasad, Sandeep, 43, 129
pregnancy: "constitutionally irrational," 32; incarceration, 67; removal of agency, 32; unplanned, 32, 144, 150; unwanted, 21, 32, 48, 56–57, 66, 113, 136, 146, 149–50, 152; violence against pregnant women, 74
Price, Kimala, 42
Prince Edward Island (PEI): Abortion Rights Network (ARN), 160–61, 164; community-based study, 159–60; Health and Community Services Agency, 159; Health Services Act, 161; Health Services Payment Act, 159; history of access, 158–64; Hospital and Health Services Commission, 158; medical advisory committee, 158; Reproductive Rights Organization (PRRO), 159–60; Resolution 17, 158. *See also* Ghiz, Robert; *Morgentaler v. Prince Edward Island (Minister of Health and Social Services)*; MacLauchlan, Wade
Prince Edward Island Reproductive Rights Organization (PRRO), 159–60
privacy. *See also Roe v. Wade*
pro-choice: history, 34–38; links with reproductive justice, 43–49; protests, 34, 67, 91, 159–60, 163; scrutiny of framework, 36–37
"pro-family" movement, 29. *See also* anti-abortion
pro-life. *See* anti-abortion
pro-life caucus, 71–74, 77
protestors: anti-abortion, 86, 123, 131–35, 138, 143–46, 151; pro-choice, 34, 67, 91, 159–60, 163
providers. *See* physicians
provincial regulations. *See* Manitoba Regulation 46/93; Regulation 84–20; Resolution 17
PRRO. *See* Prince Edward Island Reproductive Rights Organization (PRRO)

Quebec: abortion in, 96–102; Bill 34, 100; clinics, 57, 60, 84, 97–100, 128, 131, 134, 136; de-facto legalization of abortion, 97; feminism, 82, 97–98, 153; motion on abortion as a right, 99–100; National Assembly, 96–97, 99–100. *See also Association pour l'accès à l'avortement v. Procureur General du Québec*; Lévesque, René
Quebec Charter, 65–66
Quebec Ministry of Health and Social Services, 99

Quebec National Assembly, 96–100
Quiet Revolution, 58, 153

R. v. Bourne, 55–56, 59
R. v. Morgentaler (1988): decision, 62–63; "final battle for reproductive rights," 36, 53, 142, 165; principles affirmed by, 165; validation of state interest in pregnancy, 53, 62
R. v. Morgentaler (1993), 102–3
REAL Women of Canada, 29
Rebick, Judy, 35
reciprocal billing, 117–18
Regulation 84-20, 85–86, 88, 91, 148. *See also* New Brunswick
religion: Catholic, 58, 128–29, 145, 153, 183*n*3; Islamic, 149; Jewish, 149; Protestant, 145, 153.
reproductive justice (RJ): appropriation of reproductive justice rhetoric, 40, 42–43, 46; history, 38–42; links with pro-choice, 43–49; links with social justice 12, 42–43, 152, 157; SisterSong, 39–40, 46
Reproductive Justice New Brunswick (RJNB), 42, 44, 90–92, 148, 164
Resolution 17, 158. *See also* Prince Edward Island (PEI)
rights: to children, 27, 40, 46; criticisms of, 13–14, 40–41; father's, 65, 79; fetal, 26, 30–33, 61, 64–65, 69–74, 79 (*see also* Borowski, Joe); gendered, 20, 31, 78; holistic understanding of, 28, 56; human, 39–41, 46, 88–90, 129; individual, 12–14, 18, 26–28, 41–42, 50; legitimacy, 4, 12, 23, 26, 47, 166; liberal, 26, 41; negative, 6, 27, 37, 40, 42, 46, 52, 102–3, 105, 157; "nominal universalism," 41; to parent, 27, 40; positive, 6, 20–21, 40, 42, 46, 50, 68, 98, 102–5, 111, 165; power to shift public opinion, 14; social acceptance, 114, 141. *See also* Charter of Rights and Freedoms

Robichaud, Elvy, 116
Robidoux, Michelle, 77, 94, 96, 133, 149–51
Roe v. Wade, 35, 42, 49, 62
Romalis, Garson, 132
Ross, Loretta, 39–40, 45
RU–486, 38, 124, 149. *See also* Mifegymiso
Ruth, Nancy, 75

Saskatchewan, 30, 68, 76, 107, 175
Saurette, Paul, 29–30
Schwartzman, Lisa, 41
Scott, Robert, 60–62
self-determination. *See* autonomy
Senate: defeat of Bill C–43, 52–53, 70–71, 142
sex education, 29, 48
Sexual Health Network of Quebec, 101
Sharma, Supriya, 127
SisterSong, 39–40, 46
Smith, Miriam, 26
Smoling, Leslie, 60–62
social justice, 27, 33–34, 48, 98. *See also* reproductive justice (RJ)
social movements. *See* anti-abortion; pro-choice; reproductive justice (RJ)
Society of Obstetricians and Gynaecologists of Canada, 118, 127
Solinger, Rickie, 35, 37
Soudas, Dimitri, 76
Sovereign Uterus, 196*n*9
Stabile, Carol, 31
state interest in the fetus, 62
Stetson, Dorothy McBride, 31
stigma: avoidance by governments, 6; and classification of abortion as health, 96, 109; implications for abortion access, 95, 114, 138, 140, 151–52; other procedures facing, 112–13; physicians, 132, 136; and its purpose for anti-abortion, 15; status quo, 165; stigma and interviewees, 9–10
Supreme Court: Charter interpretation, 23; denied leave to appeal, 86–87;

judicial reasoning supporting positive rights, 105
surgical abortion: on PEI, 83, 158, 162; the procedure, 122–25; use of, 7, 24

Taylor, Brent, 86
Taylor, Jessi, 44
therapeutic abortion committees (TACs), 56–57, 59, 62, 84
Toron, Alison, 143–46
Toronto Public Health, 132, 149–50
Tremblay, Jean-Guy, 65–66, 184*n*25
Tremblay v. Daigle, 14, 30, 53, 64–69, 71
Trost, Brad, 75–76
Trudeau, Justin: enforcement of Canada Health Act, 109; government, 77–79, 101; pro-choice platform, 72, 77–79, 101, 159, 162–63
Trudeau, Pierre Elliott. *See* Criminal Law Amendment Act (1969)
Turner, Bryan, 19–20

Union Nationale, 98
United Nations: definition of reproductive rights, 39; origins of reproductive justice, 38–40; Platform for Action, 17; rates of unsafe abortion, 75, 181*n*7
United States: fetal endangerment laws, 73–74; funding for Canadian anti-abortion, 134; Hyde amendment, 45; legal precedent, 61–64; legislation regulating crisis pregnancy centres, 135; *Roe v. Wade*, 35, 42, 49, 62; social activism, 25, 27, 35, 37–42, 45–49
Up for Debate, 77

Vickers, Jill, 97–98
violence: against clinic staff, 145, 151; against physicians, 6, 9, 119, 131–32, 136, 142; against pregnant women, 31, 40, 74, 130, 137, 143, 145; protestors, 144; targeting clinics, 131–33, 136, 142, 145, 151

Warawa, Mark, 74
Wheatley, Ann, 161
White, Linda, 7–8, 80, 115–16
Wilson, Bertha, 15, 62
Winnipeg Child and Family Services (Northwest Area) v. D.F.G., 67, 73
women: of colour, 38–40, 45; commiseration with Daigle, 67; gender roles, 113, 115, 155; Indigenous, 40, 42, 48; marginalized, 40–42; MPs voting as a block, 64
Women's Legal Education and Action Fund (LEAF), 162
Woodworth, Stephen, 32–33, 73, 125
World Health Organization (WHO): definition of maternal health, 75; definition of reproductive rights, 39; Mifegymiso recommendations, 127

Yukon, 175